COLLECTIVISM IN THE CHURCHES

COLLECTIVISM IN

THE CHURCHES

A DOCUMENTED ACCOUNT OF THE POLITICAL
ACTIVITIES OF THE FEDERAL, NATIONAL,
AND WORLD COUNCILS OF CHURCHES

BY
EDGAR C. BUNDY

THE CHURCH LEAGUE OF AMERICA

WHEATON, ILLINOIS   1961

DISTRIBUTED BY DEVIN-ADAIR COMPANY, NEW YORK 10, N. Y.

Library of Congress catalog card number: 57-13355

Manufactured in the United States of America

Fourth Printing, August 1961

21396

DEDICATION

To the thousands of faithful Protestant pastors who have sacrificed buildings, prestige, and pensions rather than bow to the orders of the Social Gospel hierarchy.

To the thousands of people who followed their example and support them.

FOREWORD

THIS BOOK is written by a Protestant. It is written about the Protestant churches. As a Protestant, the author has a right to protest. This right is inherent in Protestant beliefs.

When the distinguished author and lecturer John T. Flynn revealed certain collectivistic trends in Protestant churches in his famous chapter 10 of *The Road Ahead,* he immediately brought down the wrath of left-wing Protestant leaders and liberals upon his journalistic head. Mr. Flynn's revelations were merely taken from the official pronouncements of The Federal Council of the Churches of Christ in America, with page and paragraph cited, but this did not prevent those who were being exposed from attacking Mr. Flynn on the ground that he was a member of the Roman Catholic Church and therefore was incompetent to discuss what was going on in the Protestant world. If this kind of logic is correct, then the man who attempts to murder his wife in the front yard and is discovered by a policeman who rushes in to stop him is justified in telling the policeman to refrain, as he is not a member of the family.

The standard technique used today and down through the ages is not to answer the documentation but to attack the one who does the revealing. In this way they hope to silence him or so to discredit him that the public will not look into the documentation.

The writer of the Gospel of St. John revealed this technique nineteen centuries ago. It is recorded in his 8th chapter that, when the religious leaders of that day would not accept the claims of Jesus Christ as being the Son of God, they launched a fourfold personal smear against Him. In verse 13 they called Him a liar. In verse 19 they questioned His paternity. In verse 41 they insinuated that He was an illegitimate child. In verses 48 and 52 they went as low as any human being could go: they accused Him (the Son of God) of being possessed with the devil.

As the "recognized" religious leaders of the day, heads of a vast ecclesiastical system, they had powerful means of disseminating their propaganda. But He was not "recognized." He was an intruder in their ecumenicity. He took their members away from them—and the receipts in the treasury dropped as a result. They were tied up with the political system of the day and had powerful backing, for they could deliver the "church" vote. He only had a group of "dissenters," "splinter groups," "rabble-rousers," "separatists," and just plain poor folks who worshiped with Him in the fields and on the street corners instead of in the darkness of the temples. He was a force disrupting communal unity. He was a "fundamentalist" who was always quoting Scripture instead of citing their "recognized" professors of theology and social-action chairmen.

The truth is that Jesus Christ was not interested in lobbying before Pilate, Agrippa, or Caesar's government for betterment of social, economic, or political conditions. His Gospel was the Gospel of personal salvation, and to the Herodians he said: "Render therefore unto Caesar the things which are Caesar's; and unto God the things that are God's" (Matt. 22:21).

Jesus left his followers no legacy in the form of material comforts and a high standard of living. He left them only a cross and an eventual crown, to be obtained through persecution and martyrdom. His charge to them was to preach the Gospel and to make disciples who would follow in his train, regardless of the cost.

How things have changed! The changes are set forth in the pages that follow. "Incredible!" said an outstanding Christian layman after he had read the manuscript. "Maybe church folks should start reading the Bible and find out what Christianity really is!"

Maybe they should.

EDGAR C. BUNDY

CONTENTS

COLLECTIVISM IN THE CHURCHES

1 THE FEDERAL COUNCIL
IS ORGANIZED

Formation in 1908. Five preliminary steps. Harry F. Ward's part. Theodore Roosevelt declines invitation. Council attacks Congo conditions. Y.M.C.A. brought into Council. Methodist Bishop Hendrix first president. Early political involvements.

THE FEDERAL COUNCIL OF CHURCHES was officially formed during the week of December 2–8, 1908. Five preliminary steps, however, had earlier been taken, and these are recorded in the authoritative book *Origin and History of the Federal Council of the Churches of Christ in America*[1] by Elias B. Sanford, who was the honorary secretary of the Council from its beginning.

The first step consisted of a series of conferences on the development of state and local federations. These took place from 1890 to 1899. The second step was the organization of The National Federation of Churches in 1901 in Philadelphia. The third step was a Washington, D.C., conference held in 1902. The fourth step was the appointment of a Committee on Correspondence and the planning of federation work that was to be carried on in New England, New York, and the Middle West. The final preliminary step was the Inter-

[1] S. S. Scranton Co., Hartford, Conn., 1916.

Church Conference on Federation held in New York, November 15–21, 1905.

We shall deal briefly with each step. According to Dr. Sanford, the Rev. Harry F. Ward "came over from Chicago to help us launch The National Federation of Churches in 1900." Dr. Ward had formerly been pastor of a church doing settlement work in the Chicago stockyards, then became a teacher in the Boston University School of Theology.[2] (Later we will examine Dr. Ward's activities in detail.)

Dr. Sanford records that in the fall of 1894, during a meeting at Union Theological Seminary, the Rev. J. Winthrop Hageman called for the appointment of a committee "to consider the practicability of organizing a Federate Council of the Churches in New York City."[3]

As the next step, the newly established New York City Federation passed, on February 12, 1900, a resolution calling for the formation of a national federation of churches.[4] A national committee of twenty-five was appointed, and a letter urging federation was prepared and signed by the committee, and sent out to pastors of leading churches throughout the United States. The majority of the men signing this letter were recognized liberals in the field of religion.

While the plan for a national council was brewing, The Federation of Churches and Christian Workers for the State of New York was organized in Syracuse, November 13 and 14, 1900,[5] and soon it began to set up local federations of churches in cities throughout the state.

By the time the conference for the formation of The National Federation of Churches was held in Philadelphia, February 5 and 6, 1901, a number of federated groups had been

2 *Origin and History of the Federal Council of the Churches of Christ in America.*
3 *Ibid.,* p. 108.
4 *Ibid.,* p. 110.
5 *Ibid.,* p. 129.

formed over the country, following the pattern set in New York City. Among the cities were Hartford and New Haven, Connecticut; Jersey City, New Jersey; Syracuse, New York; Pittsburgh and Philadelphia, Pennsylvania; Cleveland, Ohio; and Chicago. All the city federations, and a number of denominational organizations or Bible societies, sent representatives to the Philadelphia meeting.

The second annual conference of The National Federation of Churches was held in Washington, D.C., February 4 and 5, 1902. Dr. Sanford, while he was making preliminary arrangements, called upon President Theodore Roosevelt at the White House with a group of ministers. He invited the President to address the conference but Roosevelt declined. Dr. Sanford, however, had set a precedent, followed ever since by Council leaders, of seeking to line up politicians on the Council's side.

After the Washington conference was concluded, a Committee on Correspondence was initiated, and arrangements were made for another conference in 1905. From February 1902 until November 15, 1905, this Committee on Correspondence, with Dr. Sanford as its secretary, traveled throughout the United States, visiting ministers, church federations, and theological seminaries and propagandizing for the contemplated New York City meeting of the Inter-Church Conference on Federation. An invitation was extended to President Roosevelt to address the opening session, but he again declined. (In spite of these first rebuffs by the President, church unionists have always pressed to have political leaders present at their conferences to lend an air of respectability and power. Neither Jesus Christ nor the Apostles ever called upon the temporal rulers of their day to address their conferences, nor did they ever call upon governments to advance the cause of the church. But times have changed.)

When the Inter-Church Conference on Federation met in

New York City in 1905, a formal proposal was made for the formation of a Federal Council of Churches, to take place in 1908. Dr. Sanford says:

> When the Inter-Church Conference on Federation adjourned, not only were the Protestant forces of the United States officially united as never before, but a definite program of action, in matters of common interest, had been placed in the hands of the committee authorized to carry forward the work made necessary by the adoption of the plan of federation, report to be made to the Federal Council of 1908.[6]

It may be concluded from this historian's account that the organization of the Federal Council in 1908 was merely a matter of form and ceremony; actually, the Council had been organized in New York in 1905 under the name of the Inter-Church Conference on Federation.

As if prophetic of the Federal, National, and World Councils' later expeditions into the field of international affairs, Dr. Sanford reveals[7] that the first major problem to be dealt with by this newly formed federation was "the pitiable condition of affairs in the Congo State [Africa]." As secretary, he wasted no time. He got in touch with the Secretary of State of the United States, the Hon. Elihu Root, and conveyed to him the sentiment of the church federation on conditions in that area. He traveled through the eastern half of the country, speaking on the Congo situation. On September 25, 1906, he wrote to President Theodore Roosevelt a long letter about King Leopold's cruel treatment of the residents of the Congo and on the intolerable race situation in the South of this country. The Inter-Church Conference then propagandized Congress with a pamphlet on the same situation.

6 *Ibid.*, p. 225.
7 *Ibid.*, Chapter 14, "Christian Unity in Action."

The next "major problem" that occupied Dr. Sanford's time was the "race track gambling campaign" in New York City. The "immigration problem" also was taken up, by the executive committee of the Inter-Church Federation. The Y.M.C.A. and Y.W.C.A. were next brought into the orbit of this Church Federation; they have been closely identified with the Federal-National and World Councils ever since.

The plan of federation adopted at the New York conference in 1905 actually became in 1908 the constitution of The Federal Council of the Churches of Christ in America. According to Dr. Sanford, constituent bodies which were represented in the conference of 1905 ratified and adopted the plan of federation in their highest national conventions.

It was decided at the 1908 meeting of The Federal Council of Churches that the honor of its first presidency should go to the Methodist denomination, because it had the largest membership. Bishop E. R. Hendrix of Kansas City, Missouri, was elected. The Federal Council authorized New York City as its headquarters. Also it recommended that offices be set up in four strategic centers of population.

Among the recommendations and resolutions passed by the first meeting of The Federal Council of Churches appear the following: close cooperation with the Religious Education Association and the National Educational Association to provide religious instruction in the secular schools of the country; creation of an International Court of Arbitral Justice as proposed by the Second Hague Conference "and hopes that the government of the United States will promote its establishment at the earliest possible day"; opposition to an increase of armaments; an appeal to the government of the United States to enter into treaties of arbitration with other states "without unnecessary delay."

At the closing session of the conference, Dr. Samuel J. Niccolls of St. Louis spoke about "the summery atmosphere of

Brotherly Love we here enjoy" and expressed great pleasure that the "bigotry and intense denominationalism" which formerly held the churches apart had now disappeared. Dr. Niccolls said:

> The song of the bird is in the trees, and the flowers are blooming; the frozen drift is slowly yielding to the genial spirit in the air—its crystals are being dissolved until they join in little rivulets, the laughing brook in the valley that goes on to join the river. Soon where it lay, the grass will be green and the violets and the anemones bloom. So bigotry is being dissolved.[8]

We will note later how this "brotherly love" and "genial spirit" *disappeared whenever Congressional committees, and Christians of other bodies that would not participate in the Socialistic and pacifist programs of The Federal Council of Churches, began to expose the subversive leaders of the Council who were undermining the church and the government of the United States as well.* These leaders used the powerful machinery of The Federal Council of Churches to brand other Christians with such unbrotherly words as "bigots," "vigilantes," "hatemongers," "apostles of discord," "dissenters," "splinter groups," "ministers of hate," and "Fascists."

Now let us see how this Federal Council grew in size, in scope, and in its power to disrupt the Protestant world.

8 *Ibid.,* p. 203.

2   THE NETWORK IS PLANNED: CITY, STATE, FEDERAL, WORLD COUNCILS

Plans laid for city and state councils. Wisconsin Federation. Policies filtered from top echelon of Federal Council to state and city echelons. Rabbis as associate members. St. Louis Federation, an offshoot of Federal Council. Ohio Pastors Convention. Washington Committee set up for lobbying. Home missions. Comity agreement. Quadrennial meeting. World Council proposed. World Missionary Conference, 1910. Ecumenical movement initiated. India and the "Social Gospel." Materialistic collectivism replaces Christian doctrine.

In his book *Christian Unity at Work*,[1] the Rev. Charles S. Macfarland, who was the first secretary of The Federal Council of Churches, writes on federal unity in state and city.

He outlines fully the over-all plan for the formation of state and city councils, that is, a federation of churches. The book includes the work of various contributors, of whom one, the Rev. Edward D. Eaton, discusses the work of a *state* federation. On page 1 of his report he says: "The Wisconsin Federation of Churches may be regarded as a typical state federation. It was organized in 1898, as the Wisconsin Federation of Reforms, as a result of the conviction, on the part of a number of Christian workers, that a state organization would enable them to bring to bear upon public sentiment and state legislation a more effective influence for social up-

1 Federal Council of Churches, 1913.

9

lift." The church was now to become *a lobbying group before the state legislature.*

In 1902 this group was renamed The Wisconsin Federation of Churches and Christian Workers. Mr. Eaton says that the state federation seemed to be of the greatest importance in enabling Christian bodies and their leaders to become better acquainted. It discouraged the waste caused by "rivalry and duplication in Christian service." He suggests, too, that the church federations make their influence felt on large organizations and in small communities.

Meanwhile, The Federal Council of Churches, in its own official biennial reports and in the works of its historians and secretaries, demonstrates that it has *a direct tie-in with the state and local councils of churches and that policies which are adopted at the top Federal Council level are filtered down to the lowest echelon of command.*[2] Mr. Eaton confirms it: "The work of the Federal Council can be but inadequately achieved unless the states are all thoroughly organized for interdenominational Christian cooperation."[3]

The Rev. Walter Laidlaw, secretary of The New York Federation of Churches, records the fact, in *Christian Unity at Work,* that the New York Federation was founded in 1901. He says: "We have in our federation a clerical conference in which clergy of 41 denominations are united, with rabbis as associate members." The New York Federation appears to be concerned mostly with the immigration problem and the persecution of Jews in Russia.

The Rev. Laidlaw states: "At another meeting addressed by Mr. Roosevelt, a Jewish Rabbi led 900 clergymen in the Lord's prayer." The local federation of churches, then, was not strictly a Protestant group at all but was reaching out and encompassing leaders of other religions. The Federal Council

2 See Appendix 1.
3 *Christian Unity at Work,* p. 113.

of Churches, according to its own records and biennial reports, is not wholly a Protestant or a Christian organization. It has accepted grants of money from non-Christian groups over a long period of years.

The Rev. Claire E. Ames of The Church Federation of St. Louis says, in his contribution to *Christian Unity at Work:*

> The problem of the relationship of the state and local federations to the Federal Council needs solution. The Federal Council stimulates the formation of state and city federations, and is a friendly adviser after their formation. A closer relationship is needed. . . . It is not too much to say that the cause of federations will be furthered or retarded as much by their success or failure, as by the actions and utterances of the Federal Council. At present, little supervision or comparative study of the many forms of federation is made. Direct and close relationship with the central office of the Federal Council, and through that office a relationship between the state and local federations, is imperative in the interest of the whole cause.[4]

"The Church Federation of St. Louis," he says, "was organized January 12, 1909, at the initiative of the delegates to the first meeting of the Federal Council and reorganized in February of this year." [5]

This is proof that one local church federation was organized as a result of delegates having attended the organization meeting of The Federal Council of Churches in 1908. We can conclude, then, from the evidence presented in the book by the secretary of The Federal Council of Churches, the Rev. Charles S. Macfarland, that *the state and local councils of*

4 *Ibid.,* p. 125.
5 *Ibid.,* p. 126.

churches are an organic part of the Federal Council of Churches system.

One form which the state council concept was to assume is the state pastor's convention, an excellent illustration of how The Federal-National Council of Churches operates on every level. The Columbus *Citizen*[6] carries the story of a January 1951 meeting of the Ohio Pastor's Convention, which meets annually in Columbus:

> A series of resolutions aimed at applying the principles of Christianity to everyday living concluded the Ohio Pastor's Convention Thursday.
>
> Among resolutions passed by the delegates at the four-day meeting at Memorial Hall were those which:
>
> Urged support of the United Nations, The National Council of Churches, fair employment practices legislation, weekday religious education, the Christian rural overseas program (CROP), and the displaced persons program.
>
> Commended the labor movement for interest in "wider fields of human endeavor than mere wages and hours," and urging the pastors to take active interest in labor-management relations.
>
> "Registered concern over the growing militarization of our country," called upon colleges and universities to resist the temptation to give control of their educational processes and policies for "the tempting mess of dollar policies which the military so enticingly holds out." Opposed universal military training and the lowering of the draft age to 18.

The Ohio Pastor's Convention is one of the largest meetings of Federal-National Councilites in any state, although it

6 Feb. 2, 1951.

by no means represents all the pastors in the state of Ohio. Thousands of pastors do not belong to the Ohio Pastor's Convention, to The Ohio Council of Churches, or to the National and World Councils. The Convention represents itself, however, as speaking for the pastors of Ohio. Its annual speakers are the leading lights of the National and World Councils of Churches, such as Bishop G. Bromley Oxnam, Dr. E. Stanley Jones, and Dr. John A. Mackay. The program of the Pastor's Convention is the program of the Federal-National Council. The Ohio Pastor's Convention is merely a state instrument for passing on the propaganda of the National Council to those local churches in Ohio which are affiliated with the National and World Councils. At their meeting on January 31, 1951, the Convention approved a resolution for strong civil rights legislation and urged revision of the United Nations charter to eliminate Nationalist China as a permanent member of the Security Council and replace her by an elective member.

These are not matters of Christian doctrine formulated for the salvation of the souls of individual church members in Ohio; they are matters of national and international politics upon which the Councils have taken a stand. To obtain grassroots support for their political stands, the Councils make use of the Ohio Pastor's Convention as a propaganda medium.

Whenever The National Council of Churches wants to have a crowd in a particular community for one of its propagandists, it sends the publicity material down the line through channels and secures the cooperation of all the local churches in the community whose denominations are in the Council of Churches. The local churches publicize the coming of the National Council speaker in their church bulletins and urge their people from the pulpits to attend. The National Councilite usually gets an excellent turnout. But individual pastors who are trying to bring Christian truth to their people can scarcely get a baker's dozen out for a protest meeting.

Dr. Elias B. Sanford reveals in his *Origin and History of the Federal Council* that in 1910 a meeting of leaders of those churches in Washington and its vicinity which were officially related to The Federal Council of Churches was called.

> This group of notable and lovable leaders, without a dissenting voice, bore testimony from personal knowledge, to the need of united action in meeting the responsibility of Christianity at the capital of the nation. Action was taken at this meeting creating what is known as the Washington Committee.

From then on, the records of The Federal-National Council of Churches show that strong lobbying and intervention in legislative affairs were conducted by this Washington action group, representing the Federal Council.

Another activity which The Federal Council of Churches assumed was home missions. The chairman of the committee on Home Missions was the Rev. Lemuel C. Barnes. His report, submitted to the Council meeting in 1912, stated that one of the recommendations made to the various mission boards which worked in cooperation with the Federal Council's committee was to "arrange to allot the entirely unoccupied fields [that is, within the United States] among the various bodies, so that each shall feel a special responsibility for a given field." [7] This was the comity agreement and was designed to eliminate "overlapping." A strong plea for a comity agreement was made by Bishop Francis J. McConnell, who urged that territories in cities, towns, and foreign countries be marked off for the several denominations. He said: "If we could get to some kind of an agreement, for the sake of illus-

[7] *Origin and History*, p. 516.

tration, say, in the Western part of our country, in the Home Missionary territory concerning the territory in which the different denominations are to work, and live absolutely by that agreement, it would tend to a greater effectiveness of the work of the Kingdom of God as a whole and tend to increasing the effectiveness of the separate denominations." [8]

As a result of this agreement, which has been in effect for many years, The Federal Council of Churches has attempted to dictate through its various city councils just where and when a particular denomination should be allowed to build a church. The Council does not like "competition" between churches. It does not, of course, take into consideration the fact that various churches believe and teach different things; it does not regard differences as being of any consequence, for the Federal Council does not, as we shall see in chapter 3, go "into the details of doctrine." The Federal Council has never been interested in the great doctrines of the Christian faith. It says that any denomination that comes into fellowship with it can interpret the divinity of Christ in any manner it sees fit and never be questioned.

This commission also recommended to The Federal Council of Churches "the formation of a *state Federal Council,* this being already effective in some states." Here, again, we can see the development of the *state councils of churches,* which, with the county and local councils, and in addition to the denominations affiliated with The Federal Council of Churches, would give the Federal Council a strong hold over Protestant church life in the United States. We shall see how successful they were, even to the point of excluding from radio stations, from public auditoriums, and from access to the press dissenting Protestant groups that would not go along with the Federal Council's "Social Gospel."

In the Introduction to his book *Christian Unity at Work*

[8] *Christian Unity at Work,* p. 28.

Dr. Macfarland says, writing of the Quadrennial Meeting held in Chicago in 1912, that the intent of the volume is

> to indicate the growth and trend of Federal Unity as it has taken shape and assumed vital reality during the past four years and to forecast the future work of unifying the religious forces of the nation and the world, as it is likely to progress under the present constitution of the council.

Dr. Macfarland indicates here that The Federal Council of Churches was not content with organizing in the United States but would soon seek to organize or unify the religious forces throughout the world. Already, in 1912, the idea of a World Council of Churches appears.

As an early step in the direction of a World Council, a World Missionary Conference was called in Edinburgh, Scotland, in 1910. This was the culmination of preliminary conferences held in New York, London, and Liverpool from 1854 through 1900. The sixth world conference had been convened in New York, being in session from April 21 to May 1, 1900. Significantly, this conference was called "The Ecumenical Missionary Conference." The word "ecumenical" (and "ecumenicity") has been used frequently by the promoters of the Federal, National, and World Councils of Churches. The average church member, however, has no idea of what "ecumenical" means. It means "pertaining to the entire inhabited world or belonging to the Christian church as a whole, or universal."

Many modern-day leaders of the ecumenical movement maintain that the concept of The World Council of Churches was first formulated at the Edinburgh conference in 1910. This is not true. According to the official historians of The Federal Council of Churches, a plan for an ecumenical movement was drawn up in The Ecumenical Missionary Conference in New York, in 1900.

At the close of the Edinburgh conference of ten years later, a continuation committee was set up which appointed John R. Mott as the chairman. Present-day leaders of The World Council of Churches designate Mr. Mott as the father of the ecumenical movement, which he was not.

Many of the largest missionary societies in the United States and throughout the world did not wish to be represented by The Federal Council of the Churches of Christ in America, and they never became a part of that organization. These missionary societies felt that the business of the church was to take the Gospel to whatever field the individual society might decide was a needy one. They wanted no part in the comity agreements of the Federal Council.

In his report on the Committee on Foreign Missions, the Rev. James L. Barton said that the concept of a federal council was introduced in India by American missionaries in 1911, and that the purpose was to bring the various Christian groups together to form a United Church.

A National Federal Council was to be set up, consisting of representatives chosen by the provincial councils.

Evidently this early work of the Federal Council representatives in India has borne fruit; *India is wholly in the camp of The World Council of Churches today and is seeking to exclude any missionaries belonging to groups which will not join up with The World Council of Churches or come out to the field under Council auspices.* Records show that many independent evangelical missionaries have been refused return visas to India, once they have left, because they did not concur in the World Council of Churches' "Social Gospel" program. A great number of these independent missionaries were pioneers in India; they were strong believers in teaching Christian doctrine. However, many modern missionaries, working under the auspices of the World Council, are on record as denying the great doctrines of the Christian faith. They have become social reformers and followers of the pacifism or non-violent-resistance movement of the late Mohandas K. Gandhi. Some, on their return to the United States, have openly declared that, although they went to India to carry the Gospel to the heathen, the heathen turned the tables and converted *them*. Today, India is largely friendly to the Communists and is hostile toward the United States, despite all the missionary endeavor carried on there.

The Committee on Foreign Missions of The Federal Council of Churches has urged that "union" publications and "union" theological schools be established overseas by the various denominations. This would tend to eliminate individuality of denomination and of interpretation of Christian doctrine. The publications and the graduates of the union colleges would conform to a single pattern.

The objective of the ecumenical movement appears to be to eliminate all differences in theology—even to eliminate theology itself—and eventually to form "one church for one world." When we discover that many leaders of this movement are men who deny the doctrines of historical Christianity and have supplanted them with socialism and communism, the plan is seen to be a collectivistic one.

3 HOW MATERIALISTIC COLLECTIVISM REPLACED CHRISTIAN FAITH

"Hague Conference" of the churches. "The mind of Christ." Council moves in on education, journalism, business. Cooperation replaces free enterprise. Bishop McConnell urges "new social climate." "Union" versus "unity." Dean Mathews denies the Faith and takes over from Caesar. "Details of doctrine" excluded. The "Social Gospel" replaces the Gospel of Christ. Chicago divinity school. Marxism conquers the liberals. The churchgoers ignored.

THE QUADRENNIAL MEETING of the Federal Council in 1912 was the first since its founding. In his opening address before the Council the president, Bishop E. R. Hendrix, made this remark:

> The Federal Council of the Churches is the great Hague Conference of the churches, which justifies its existence, not by doing the work of the churches, but by inspiring and directing, as well as unifying that work to avoid overlapping and waste. It is an inspiration even more than an organization, and so best represents the mind of Christ whose very Kingdom was "without observation." [1]

Here Bishop Hendrix makes The Federal Council of Churches representative of "the mind of Christ." Therefore,

1 *Christian Unity at Work*, p. 22.

19

according to this claim, anyone questioning the decisions of The Federal Council of Churches and its various and sundry commissions would actually be questioning "the mind of Christ." Indeed, under the guise of religion many things can be put over; people shrink from criticizing any action purporting to be of a religious nature. We shall see, then, as we proceed, how various Federal Council leaders were able to espouse the cause of communism and to consort with top leaders and policymakers of the Communist Party under the sanction of "the mind of Christ."

Bishop William M. Bell, in an address before the Federal Council, told the delegates that its influence must be felt in education and journalism, that "adequate touch and leadership" must be given to business. "One of these days," he says, "we are to have an American business life sanctified and purified. It is no Utopian dream. It will be business, not for colossal, individual realization, but business for human ministry and the elevation of all mankind." [2] We shall see later how the official pronouncements of The Federal Council of Churches have been anything but favorable to free enterprise. Federal Council leaders have sought time and time again to have the "profit motive" replaced with the "cooperative spirit."

Bishop Francis J. McConnell told the Quadrennial Meeting that the work of the Federated Movement of the Churches was bringing a very remarkable intellectual gain. The bishop sees truth not as something contained in doctrines or in creeds but in so-called "true living." This is the same Bishop McConnell whose prolific Communist-front record is discussed and recorded in eighty-four pages of United States government reports.

The bishop says that it is the duty of The Federal Council of Churches to produce a "new social climate," to arouse public opinion. He says: "We have not any social atmosphere of

2 *Ibid.,* p. 28.

the right kind; we have much of the wrong kind." He says that the only way to arouse public opinion and bring in a new social climate is to have a union of the churches. "That is the power of this Federal Council in what is known as social service and it has been a tremendous power."

He states further that there is no sense in having a number of churches open on Sunday night with just a handful in each church. He suggests that all the denominations come together in a united effort in one church on a Sunday night.

We have seen this carried out in our lifetime. The bishop and his followers seem not to know that one reason why there were handfuls in some churches on Sunday night was that the people were not getting any spiritual food and saw no sense in going; while, on the other hand, many of the independent Evangelical churches, such as the Moody Memorial Church in Chicago, were packed on a Sunday evening with four or five thousand people. Under the Federal Council plan, many Council churches are content today to come together, not for a Sunday or Wednesday evening service any more, since most Council churches are not even open on those nights, but for a Sunday morning service, because many of them, individually, cannot draw a handful of people. If one were to look into the historic confessions of faith, catechisms, or creeds of these denominations which come together, one would find doctrinal beliefs which would forbid them to come together in such a manner. But when these churches were so thoroughly captured by the liberals, who led them into the fellowship of The Federal Council of Churches, doctrine was no longer of any concern. The idea of getting together, regardless of belief, was the primary thing.

The Federal Council of Churches, its successor, The National Council of Churches, and The World Council of Churches have all sought to use a portion of St. John's Gospel, chapter 17, verse 21, lifted out of context, as a justification for organic union. These liberal church leaders have always confused the word "union" with the word "unity." The passage of Scripture reads as follows: "That they all may be one; as Thou, Father, art in Me, and I in Thee, that they also may be one in Us: that the world may believe that Thou hast sent Me." Taken in its context, this verse is from the prayer of Christ to His heavenly Father, back to whom He is soon going, following His Crucifixion.

Here He pleads for a spiritual unity for His disciples, not for an organic union of people who differ on the things He taught. Many people in the pews have swallowed the plea of the Council of Churches without realizing that it has been lifted out of its context in St. John's Gospel and has been reinterpreted by liberal church leaders to mean a union of physical churches here on earth instead of the spiritual unity that Christ called for in His Body, the true Church made up of Christian believers throughout the entire world.

Dean Shailer Mathews has made this Gospel passage a mere *pretext* for supporting the material work of The Federal Council of Churches. He then has the audacity to say about this portion of Scripture: "It is the prayer of a defeated soul who has fought the fight with the forces of the world about it and has been beaten." [3] This is blasphemy, to say the least. There is no hint of defeat in the entire prayer. This was the same triumphant Christ who, in the 10th chapter of St. John, seven chapters earlier, had said (17th and 18th verses): "Therefore doth my Father love me, because I lay down my life, that I might take it again. *No man taketh it from me, but I lay it down of myself. I have power to lay it down, and I have power to take it again.* This commandment have I received of my Father."

Dean Mathews, in his address before the Council, doesn't say that the Council must face the fundamental issue of how

3 *Ibid.*, p. 31.

to take the saving Gospel of Christ to a world lost in sin. Rather he says that the fundamental issue is the world, with its "selfishness, its commercialism, its harshness, its industrial injustice, its cheapening of young men's manhood—a terrible, often a hideous enemy." He then proceeds to criticize the Council of Nicaea for seeking unity through theological definition—in other words, through a clear statement of doctrinal beliefs.

That Dean Mathews of the University of Chicago divinity school should have been elected the new president of The Federal Council of Churches to succeed Bishop Hendrix is significant. Looking over the record of the Federal Council and its successor, the National Council, down through the years, one will find the startling fact that *men have been elevated to the highest position in the Council not because of their defense of the Gospel but because they were recognized modernists or liberals and were noted for their denials of historic doctrines of the Christian faith.* These Social Gospelers have never been interested in true theology or in defending the major premises of historic Christianity. Their concern has been to use the church as an instrument for social strife. We will see this, in chapter 9, in testimony given before a Congressional committee by former top leaders of the Communist Party who worked with many of these self-styled liberals within the framework of the Party.

In retiring as president of the Council, Bishop Hendrix had the effrontery to say, in his speech, that the Federal Council has "only been registering the history that God has been making, even more largely than in the earlier Councils of the Church at Nicaea and Constantinople."

Before we resume the history of the 1912 Quadrennial Meeting of the Council of Churches, let us look at the requirements for membership in The Federal Council of Churches as declared in the official publication *Furthering Christian Unity*.[4]

4 See p. 2.

We read: "All churches which share the basic faith in Jesus Christ as Divine Lord and Saviour, are eligible to membership." There is no quarrel so far; but the very next sentence makes this declaration meaningless: ". . . into the details of doctrine the Council does not enter, its function being practical rather than theoretical." How one interprets the phrase "Jesus Christ as Divine Lord and Saviour" makes no difference to The Federal Council of Churches. The Council leaders have stated over and over that they will not ask a definition of this phrase from any of their constituent bodies. You believe anything you want, so long as you accept this phrase, and you can become a Church Council member.

The Council relegates all doctrine to the realm of theory when it says that the function of the Council is "practical rather than theoretical." What is a theory? *The Winston Simplified Dictionary* defines it as "a speculative view or opinion, not necessarily founded on fact." For nearly two thousand years the great theologians of the Christian Church, its scholars, teachers, preachers, and evangelists have taught that the Christian faith is founded on certain factual doctrines contained in the New Testament. The Federal Council leadership seems to think that doctrine belongs in the realm of theory, or unproved opinion.

When the leaders of the Federal Council threw doctrine out the window, socialism came in and took over the churches.

In a history book being used in our secular high schools today, entitled *History of the American Way*,[5] the following appears under a subhead, "The Churches Play Their Part in a Reform Age" (emphasis added):

> When the historian looks at the church during these years, what does he find? *More important than anything else he finds a willingness to spend less time and energy*
>
> 5 Faulkner, Kepner, and Merrill, Harper & Bros., New York, 1950.

in thinking and preaching about the life to come, and more on trying to do something about conditions in this world. Church leaders were less occupied with debating the details of their different beliefs and more with fighting the evils around them. Seminaries where clergymen were trained also gave less attention to some of the old studies and more to sociology (the science of society).

In actual practice what did this mean? First of all, churches began to act together as never before. In 1908, for example, most of the Protestant churches joined in organizing the Federal Council of The Churches of Christ in America. The purpose of this was to make it possible to work together on certain matters. Many ministers and church bodies began to take a definite stand on many reforms and more actively enter such movements. We find, for example, many clergymen actively supporting the labor movement. The large churches in the cities, Catholic, Jewish, and Protestant, now concerned themselves with much more than simply religious education. There were church centers for social activities, athletics, and many other purposes. The church supported social workers as well as the city governments. This was what the young and enthusiastic clergymen called the "social gospel." It did much to change the American church and something to change America.[6]

The emphasis, then, was taken off the teaching and preaching of Christian doctrine and put on the Social Gospel, by which the material conditions of the world would be changed. It can be seen from this that the church was opening its doors wide for the entrance of the teachings of Karl Marx and his successors; for Marx was a materialist at heart and believed in changing the economic conditions of the world in order to

[6] *History of the American Way,* p. 573.

bring in a better world society. He was honest about it. He didn't believe in God, the supernatural, or the need for help from another world. Marx believed that if the people would follow his teachings, heaven would be made on earth; Utopia, or the Garden of Eden, would be a fact. A prime difference between Karl Marx and the modernist leadership of The Federal Council of Churches is that Marx did not play the hypocrite. He made no bones about what he believed and was trying to accomplish. The modernist church leader, however, uses biblical words and phrases to cover up his espousal of the Socialistic Gospel promulgated by Marx and his successors.

Christ's Great Commission was to go into all the world and preach the Gospel; and the Apostle Paul, the first great systematic theologian of the Christian Church, gave us the definition of the Gospel in I Corinthians, chapter 15, verses 1 through 23. According to St. Paul, the Gospel tells: "How that Christ died for our sins, according to the scriptures; and that he was buried, and that he arose again the third day according to the scriptures." The argument for the resurrection of the dead follows, and in verse 23 the statement that Christ is coming back again.

The modernist leaders of The Federal Council of Churches *have reversed the Great Commission.* Instead of going into all the world preaching the Gospel, *they have opened the church doors to the "world"—and the "world" has taken over the church.* That is why a secular historian can write that church centers were established "for social activities, athletics, and many other purposes." Among these other purposes, we may say, was the establishing of platforms for members of the Communist and Socialist parties to speak from.

Now back to the 1912 Quadrennial Meeting of The Federal Council of Churches. Bishop Hendrix turned over the presidency of The Federal Council of Churches to Dr. Shailer Mathews. What kind of theologian was Dr. Mathews? He was at one time the head of the University of Chicago divinity school, presumably a Northern Baptist Convention institution, which brought in the Disciples of Christ, Congregationalists, and Unitarians to form a Federated Theological Seminary. Dr. Mathews, a noted modernist in his day, delighted his theological students by ridiculing biblical teachings and accepted Christian doctrine. On the so-called Baptist faculty of the University he tolerated those men who supposedly were Baptists but actually were pastors of Unitarian churches, namely, Professor G. B. Foster, Professor Haydon, and Professor Merrifield.

One of the studies jointly produced by the divinity faculty while Dr. Mathews was there was the *Guide to the Study of Christian Religion*. The late Dr. Ernest Gordon, editor of the *Sunday School Times* and founder of the Gordon School of Theology in Boston, Massachusetts, has this to say concerning the study:

> One is struck with the lack of Christian insight and display; at times, too, with the writers' hostility to the obvious. These men have no perceptible love for Christ. Their whole interest in Him seems to be in the problems which He starts or may be made to start. Sometimes their theorizings are sheerly frivolous. Dean Mathews speaks about the "bourgeois social mind" as controlling the Christian interpretation of the past generation.[7]

In a Religious Education Association address published in 1910, Dean Mathews told his fellow educationists:

> The theology of democracy has yet to be written. Whereas, Calvinists spoke of God's election of man, the demo-

7 Quoted from *The Leaven of the Sadducees*, Ernest Gordon, Moody Bible Institute, Chicago, 1926, p 176.

crat speaks of man's election of God. The democratic spirit of the age is demanding that the church abandon sovereignty as the controlling concept of its theology and leaven itself with democracy.[8]

In other words, the concept of the Sovereignty of God is to be abolished in favor of a more democratic concept in which man will decide whether God shall be sovereign or not. Some of the pronouncements of Dean Mathews's faculty members against the Christian religion moved one Chicago daily newspaper to write (emphasis added):

> We are struck also with the hypocrisy and treachery of these attacks on Christianity. This is a free country and a free age and men can say what they choose about religion but this is not what we arraign these divinity professors for. *Is there no place in which to assail Christianity but a divinity school? Is there no one to write infidel books except the professors of Christian theology? Is the theological seminary an appropriate place for a general massacre of Christian doctrines?* We are not championing either Christianity or infidelity, but only condemning infidels masquerading as men of God and Christian teachers.[9]

Is it any wonder that in recent years the University of Chicago has been investigated by State and Federal government committees because of Communist activity on the campus and the espousal of Communist causes by professors on the faculty?

In his recent book, *Collectivism on the Campus*,[10] Professor E. Merrill Root relates that one divinity student, Robert Andelson, who could no longer stomach what was going on in

8 R.E. 1910, p. 84.
9 Quoted by Horsch in his book *Modern Religious Liberalism*, p. 276.
10 Devin-Adair Company, New York, 1955.

the University of Chicago divinity school, charged that Communist propaganda was emanating from the campus without any restrictions by the school authorities. The groundwork for this kind of activity had been laid by theologians many years before the Communist Party was organized in the United States.

It is noteworthy that the dean of this divinity school, Dr. Shailer Mathews, should have become the second president of The Federal Council of Churches. A more recent head of the same divinity school, *Dean Bernard M. Loomer, petitioned the President of the United States, Dwight D. Eisenhower, for a commutation of the death sentence for the two convicted atom spies, Julius and Ethel Rosenberg. The same dean had refused to give Robert Andelson his degree because he dared to criticize the Communist activity on the campus of the university.*

Mr. Manning Johnson, a former top official of the Communist Party in the United States, trained in the Lenin School of Political Warfare in Moscow, testified before a Congressional committee in 1953 as to the manner in which Marxism and modernism (liberalism) in religion go hand in hand:

Mr. JOHNSON. I would like to present to the committee an article published in the *Protestant*, April–May 1942. The author of the article is David Easton, and it is an article in which he follows the Communist Party line on religion by attempting to show in this article that Marxism and democracy and a liberal religious faith are one.

"SPIRITUALITY AND MARX
(By David Easton)

"The relation of Marxism to religion will never be understood if we stop with the slogan, 'Religion is the opiate of the people.' We should remember that Marx's sallies were primarily against those forms of religion which belittle man and discount his ideal aims. His criticism was a response to 'the categorical imperative to overthrow all conditions in which man is a degraded, servile, neglected, contemptible being.' In one of his letters Marx wrote, bitterly, that after the Greeks the essential dignity of man disappeared from the world. Historical Christianity too much emphasized man's worthlessness and the vanity of any effort to change his present estate.

"It is clear that Marx's attack on religion is primarily an attack on supernaturalism or other-worldliness which is indifferent to human needs and development. His views are quite in harmony with humanistic and naturalistic philosophies of religion . . . in this respect, as well as others, Marxism and democracy and a liberal religious faith are as one." [11]

In all the historical books and records concerning The Federal Council of Churches which we have examined—books and records written by official historians of the Federal Council—*there is not one scintilla of evidence to show that the question of membership in The Federal Council of Churches has ever been submitted to the men and women in the pews who pay the bills for the local churches, for their preachers and bishops,*

[11] Communist Activities in the New York Area, *Hearings,* House Committee on Un-American Activities, 2238–2239, July 8, 1953.

and for the denominational headquarters and hierarchy. Yet, throughout all the writings on the Federal Council one reads the word "democracy" over and over again in relation to its work. According to the laws of Baptist and Congregational church government, all authority rests in the local church and particularly with the people. *Never once has the question of whether these people wanted to join the Council been submitted to the individual churches.* Rather, denominational leaders have arbitrarily taken their denominations into membership with The Federal Council of Churches.

In Dean Mathews's speech of acceptance of the presidency of the Federal Council, he lightly tossed aside the theological approach of the early church councils and called for a "spiritual message that shall evoke a social passion," and in which the true nature of religion shall be exploited in terms of "brotherhood."

Dean Mathews described the Federal Council's mission as follows:

> We are like men on the bow of some great ship hurtling itself across the boundless ocean. We see no port before us, and no direction. We only hear the throb of the screw and have the feeling that we are going some whither, or are we going some whither or only going? [12]

This brings to mind a similar declaration that was made in Amsterdam, The Netherlands, in August 1948 by Dr. Visser 't Hooft, the general secretary of The World Council of Churches, after it had been formed by the Federal Council leaders of the United States. This was Dr. Visser 't Hooft's description of The World Council of Churches:

> It is a new type of craft, on its maiden voyage, heading for an unknown destination with an inexperienced crew

12 Quoted from *Christian Unity at Work*, p. 44.

speaking different languages, and we embark in the midst of one of the worst storms in history! [13]

This is hardly the kind of ship to which Christians would care to entrust the safety of life and soul. Rather, Christians prefer to know whither they are bound, who the Pilot is, and from what source the chart and compass come. [14]

[13] *The Ecumenical Courier,* World Council of Churches, May 1949.
[14] Cf. hymn "Jesus, Savior, Pilot Me," Hopper and Gould.

4   THE OCTOPUS EXPANDS

Some churches resist Council. Southern Baptist Convention refuses to join. Southern Baptist Seminary succumbs. Churches secede from Northern (American) Baptist Convention. Congregational versus Episcopalian type of church government. State and local councils multiply. The Conference of Interdenominational Executives. The interlocking directorate. Growth of councils. Increase of financial requirements. Sources of Council wealth. Dr. Cadman announces political aims of Federal Council. World Council idea takes form.

WHEN THE LAST FAREWELLS were said after the formal founding meeting of the Federal Council in 1908 in Philadelphia, "the Church of Christ in the United States was united as never before," says Dr. Sanford. He fails to tell us, however, that thousands of churches and a number of major denominations would have no part of the Federal Council. Presumably these churches were to be considered outside "the Church of Christ." Indeed, since 1908, the leaders of the Federal-National Council on the national, state, and local levels have been called upon to use every tactic at their command to silence and discredit pastors and laymen who expose the falsity of the Council system.

According to Dr. Sanford's statistics, The Federal Council of Churches "represented" 17,422,280 communicants in 1914. Yet the Southern Baptist Convention has never joined the

33

Federal, National, or World Council of Churches. In Dr. Sanford's historical account, however, we find this item:

> Individual members of Southern Baptist Churches have been in full sympathy with the aims and purposes of The Federal Council of the Churches of Christ in America. Under the leadership of men like Dr. Mullens of Louisville, Kentucky, president of the largest theological seminary in the United States, and influential laymen like Joshua Levering, of Baltimore, we have reason to anticipate that, in the near future, the great Baptist fellowship of our country will give their united strength in advancing the work of the Federal Council.[1]

The Southern Baptist Convention as a whole can never be taken into the National or World Council of Churches because of the Congregational type of government which prevails in the Convention churches. However, Council leaders have persuaded a number of Southern Baptist churches, singly, to join the local councils of churches in the cities and states and have brought them into the local ministerial alliances also. But in some cities of the South, the Southern Baptist churches have formed their own Baptist Ministerial Associations, or Associations of Baptist Churches, and have refused to collaborate with the local echelons of the Federal, National, and World Councils of Churches.

One method used by the ecumenical leaders to get Southern Baptists to join in with them is to send ministers and professors from theological seminaries of the Northern Baptist Convention (now known as the American Baptist Convention) as visiting speakers to seminaries operated by the Southern Baptist Convention. It is significant that Dr. Sanford, writing in 1916, should have mentioned Dr. Mullens of Southern Baptist

[1] *Origin and History,* p. 324.

Seminary at Louisville as being in sympathy with the aims and purposes of The Federal Council of Churches. In recent years this seminary has come under fire from a number of Southern Baptist ministers and theologians for having invited a parade of liberal clergymen from denominations within the Federal and National Councils of Churches as visiting speakers and professors. These clergymen have been propagandizing the Southern Baptist students continually in favor of the ecumenical movement.

Some Northern Baptist ministers have taken over pulpits in Southern Baptist churches and have inducted the churches into the Northern (American) Baptist Convention. Because the Northern Convention is already in the Federal Council, the victimized Southern Baptist churches have automatically become Council members. It's the old Fabian game. If you can't get the whole thing at once, then get it piecemeal, church by church.

As if to compensate in some degree, the Northern (American) Baptist Convention has lost thousands of churches since it was taken illegally into The Federal Council of Churches. Under Baptist polity, all important questions must be submitted to the local churches for decision. Because this was not done in regard to joining The Federal Council of Churches, thousands of Northern Baptist pastors and their churches have withdrawn from the Northern (American) Baptist Convention rather than submit to an illegal, unwanted, and totalitarian procedure.

It has been perfectly easy for most of these Baptist churches to withdraw. The congregations have decided by majority vote to withdraw from the Convention and so have taken their churches out of the Federal Council and the denomination. Most of these churches have been allowed to keep their property because, under Baptist polity, the property is owned by the local congregation, which has sole authority over it. However, in some instances the Northern (American) Baptist Convention has taken the churches to court and sued them for the property. With few exceptions, the property has been awarded to the denomination instead of to a local church *only* when the local church has owed money to the denomination on a mortgage held by denominational headquarters.

Recently, Baptist groups have tried to insert a "reversionary" clause in their state Baptist constitutions which would stop this withdrawal of Baptist churches from the conventions. This clause applies to any mission or branch church of a regular church in the Convention, if funds for building it have been supplied by the regular church. The clause provides that if this church ever becomes a full-fledged Baptist church within the Convention and later tries to pull out, the property will revert to the Convention because the church was started by a Convention church or with Convention money.

Many churches with the Presbyterian or Episcopalian type of government, in which authority rests in the hands of the denomination, have found to their sorrow that, in withdrawing from The Federal Council of Churches and from the denomination, they could not take their property with them. In most of the court cases involving this type of church, the court has awarded the church property to the denomination. (Exceptions to this rule have been found in the Southern Presbyterian Church, which is more democratic in its procedure.) The result has been that hundreds of ministers and thousands of church members have withdrawn from their denominations, which had brought them into the Federal, National, and World Councils of Churches, and have started over again, meeting in tents or rented stores until they could erect their own independent buildings, place the deed in the hands of their local boards of deacons or trustees, and form *independent* Bible, Presbyterian, Methodist, or Evangelical churches.

On page 466 of the historical account of The Federal Council of the Churches of Christ in America by Dr. Sanford, we find that plank V states one object of the Federal Council to be "To assist in the organization of local branches of the Federal Council to promote its aims in their communities." [2] To illustrate how this plan for organizing state and local units was carried out, we refer to some Biennial Reports of The Federal Council of Churches of the last few decades.

In the 1936 Biennial Report, in the chapter entitled "Field Department" [3] and under the heading "State and Local Councils of Churches," we find that there were 14 state councils holding a cooperative relation with The Federal Council of Churches. We read that a number of these state councils of churches merged with state councils of religious education into single state organizations. In addition to the state council of churches, a plan was initiated in 1934 for forming the Conference of Interdenominational Executives. These executives were representatives of the following interdenominational organizations that were working with The Federal Council of Churches: The Federal Council, The International Council of Religious Education, The Home Missions Council, The Council of Women for Home Missions, The Foreign Missions Conference of North America, The Council of Church Boards of Education, and The Missionary Education Movement. Many Federal Council leaders served simultaneously on the boards of these interdenominational agencies, so that interlocking directorates came into being. After the 1936 Biennial Report was written, the strength of The Federal Council of Churches in the states and local communities had grown so great that, in the 1940 Biennial Report, The Council's Field Department could claim:

2 See Appendix 1 of this book for further documentation.
3 P. 83.

Twenty-one states now have an inclusive type of inter-denominational organization, eight states have both a council of churches and a council of religious education, three states have only a council of religious education, one state has a home missions council and a council of religious education, five states have Sunday School associations, two states have councils of church women, while similar councils are a part of the cooperative organizations in seventeen additional states.[4]

In the same report, The Field Directory for American Protestant Christianity showed 600 ministers' associations, 43 councils of churches in cities over 143,000 population, and five major cities having both a council of churches and a council of religious education.

We come next to the Biennial Report for 1944. The Field Administration report [5] says that four pamphlets were distributed by the Federal Council under the title *Church Cooperation Series*. These pamphlets were "Guidance Materials for Ministerial Associations," "How to Organize a Council of Churches and Religious Education," "How to Finance a Council of Churches," and "Churching the Community Cooperatively—Comity."

With the growth of the state and local councils of churches, cooperating with The Federal Council of Churches through the years, the Department of Field Administration of the Federal Council added more and more personnel, larger quarters, and a bigger budget.

The summary of state cooperative organizations in the 1944 report is as follows:

Thirty-one states now have an inclusive council of churches, three states have both councils of churches and

4 P. 12.
5 P. 37.

councils of religious education, three states have Sunday School associations, three states have home missions councils or conferences, four states have councils of church women only, while twenty-four additional states have a council of church women in whole or in part related to other state councils listed above.[6]

Only four states were listed as having no statewide cooperative organization.

Advice and direction were freely given by the Department of Field Administration in the formation of these local councils of churches. The Field Administration report states [7] that the Directory of American Cooperative Christianity, compiled by the Inter-Council Field Department, showed that there were then 127 city and county councils with employed executive leadership, 239 city and county councils with voluntary leadership, and approximately 1,400 ministerial associations.

In the 1946 Biennial Report, under the Department of Field Administration, the following summary is given: "Thirty-five states have either in whole or in part an inclusive council of churches." [8]

The report further states that full-time executive leadership and budgets running into thousands of dollars were now being consummated in the various state and local councils of churches. The report says there were "156 city and county councils with employed executive leadership, 440 city and county councils with voluntary leadership, 2,176 ministerial associations, and 1,440 state and local councils of church women." A grand total of 634 state, city, and local councils of churches in the United States is recorded. The report further states that gross budget expenditures of all the state, city, and

6 P. 40.
7 P. 41.
8 P. 21.

local councils of churches in 1941 was $1,800,000 and in 1946 $6,100,000.

In the Biennial Report for 1948, under the Department of Field Administration, we find the following summary of state councils of churches:

> Thirty-nine states have inclusive councils of churches, 2 states are in the process of organization, 2 states have home missions conferences, 1 state has parallel councils of churches and religious education, 4 states have councils of church women only. There are 1,775 ministerial associations, 227 state, city, and county councils with employed executive leadership, 485 state, city, and county councils with voluntary leadership, making a total of 712 state, city, and local councils.[9]

After reading these statistics and noting the phenomenal growth of the local and state constituent groups of The Federal Council of Churches, one can readily see the powerful organization which the Council was building up over the years to put across its special propaganda.[10] Decisions could be made at the top level of the Federal Council and filtered right down through the various cooperative agencies, denominations, state, county and city councils of churches, and local ministerial alliances.

Combined budgets of the Federal Council, its related agencies, and these various state and local councils ran into millions of dollars annually. For example, in 1948 the total income of The Federal Council of the Churches of Christ in America was $649,644.29. Total expenditures amounted to $642,383.86. Of the total income, only $232,024 came from the constituent denominations. That means that over $400,000 was obtained from other sources.

9 Pp. 67, 68.
10 See Appendix 2.

Let us see what some of those other sources were: The Julius Rosenwald Fund made a contribution of $30,229.56; the Arbuckle-Jameson Foundation gave $16,975.47; the Russell Sage Foundation gave $2,959.00; the Lewis J. and Mary E. Horowitz Foundation, Inc., gave $2,000.00; The Henry Luce Foundation, Inc. (of *Time, Life,* and *Fortune* fame), gave $1,000.00; the Rockefeller Brothers Fund, Inc., contributed $1,000.00; the Adeline and Carl Loeb Foundation gave $250.00; the Bulova Foundation for the Department of Race Relations gave $150.00; The Gastonia-Jewish Welfare Fund contributed $50.00.

Of special importance is the fact that The Federal Council of Churches had secured a tax-exempt status. The Treasury of the United States had authorized all contributions to the Council to be deductible in income-tax reports.

Now let us look at some startling figures given in the official statement of income and expenses of The National Council of Churches:

> INCOME: *Contributions*—Councils of churches and other organizations, *1952—$400,374.28; 1953—$2,-818,083.19; nine months ending September 30, 1954 —$1,960,079.02.*

Here we see a total of $5,178,536.49 contributed by state and local councils of churches and other organizations within a period of two years and nine months to the budget of The National Council of Churches. This figure is entirely apart from the contributions made by member denominations of the National Council, boards, individual churches, persons, corporations, and foundations.

In spite of these official figures, some Council leaders say that the local councils of churches are *not* working with and promoting the National Council! Do they think that people cannot read official reports?

The report of the Department of Field Administration for 1954 shows beyond a doubt that The National Council of Churches is thoroughly represented in those state and city councils of churches which they have helped to set up. It shows that these councils are merely instruments by which the National Council puts across its propaganda to the church people at the grass-roots level. This fact has been denied time and time again by officials of the National Council. It has been denied by executives of local councils of churches when laymen confront them with the charge that they are affiliated with The National Council of Churches. We leave it to the reader to provide the answer after he has read the report of the Central Department of Field Administration given in Appendix 2.

At this point we will refer to some of the official publications and actions of The Federal Council of Churches in recent years before it changed its name to the National Council of Churches in 1950. (We will discuss this change of name in chapter 5.)

The Federal Council published a little pamphlet entitled "Furthering Christian Unity." In this pamphlet the Council claims to be the accredited agency through which 25 national denominations, comprising 142,354 local congregations, with a membership of 28 million, cooperate in common tasks. The Federal Council, we read, is "the greatest movement of Christian unity in our national life." This is the same pamphlet in which the Federal Council declares that it does not care to go "into the details of doctrine," for doctrine is in the realm of theory as far as the council is concerned. All it is interested in is getting the churches together, regardless of what they believe. "Cooperation" is the theme. Under the subtitle "The Genius of the Council," it tells how its influence is extended from the national denominations down to the local communities:

> A similar process has been at work in local communities, and the furthering of this development is one of the most important responsibilities of the Federal Council. There are now more than 670 city, county and state councils of churches, representing the Christian groups of their own communities and providing community leadership for a united Christian program.
>
> A World Council of Churches is now being formed, modeled on the general pattern of the Federal Council in America, to enable the churches to function more truly, as "one body of Christ throughout the world."

The Federal Council rapidly developed in power and in the range of its political activities. Organized under the laws of New York State as a corporation, it had millions of dollars at its disposal. In 1925, for example, the regular expenditures of the Council ran close to half a million dollars. Besides claiming to speak, at that time, for 28 denominations,[11] it represented a dozen or so cooperating and consulting bodies. Among these organizations, such as the American Civil Liberties Union, its relationships were closer than they were with the denominations which it professed to represent. This was because its political program was coordinated with their activities through strategic interlocking directorates with them.

These political activities included promotion, among other worthy causes, of the slacker's oath, League of Nations propaganda, recognition of Soviet Russia, protection of aliens in America, cancellation of foreign debt, and reduction of tariffs. These objectives generally were advocated by the Socialists.

The Council met once in four years, and while its members

11 The National Council now claims to speak for 30 denominations.

were presumed to be officially designated by the denominations, there is no record of any denomination holding an election to choose delegates to the Council or to give instructions
to the Council. Even if they had elected their own representatives, it would have made little difference. All the business of
the quadrennial meetings was conducted by the "business
committee," which was appointed from the top instead of
elected from the bottom. The "business committee" furnished
the proper resolutions to be approved at the meetings and
made arrangements for the entertainment and the speeches.
There were no minority reports, and the whole thing was
handled like any tightly controlled and well-managed convention. Then, during the four-year interim, the business of
speaking for millions of church members was turned over to
the executive committee, which met once a year.

The Federal Council announced that it was going into
politics in a big way, both nationally and internationally. For
instance, Dr. S. Parkes Cadman, president of the Federal
Council in 1926, announced in the Federal Council's May–
June 1926 bulletin as follows:

> In the first place, the American churches are going
> to grapple courageously with great social and inter-
> national questions. The day is past when any realm of our
> economic, industrial, social, political, or international
> life will be regarded as outside the sphere or responsibility
> of the churches. All over the country, prophetic voices
> are declaring from the pulpit and in ecclesiastical assem-
> blies that the organized group life of society is to be no
> less subject to the rule of Christ than the life of the indi-
> vidual.
>
> When, however, the churches attempt to make their
> influence felt in molding public opinion on great public
> issues, they discover that if they are to do anything effec-

tive, they must act far more unitedly than has hitherto been the case. The realization of this fact has led to a second notable trend in American religious life, namely, the progress of cooperation among the churches. Few things are more noteworthy in the history of American Christianity during the last two decades.

The Council then proceeds to furnish the propagandists who are the "prophetic voices."

Leroy F. Smith and E. B. Jones, in their book *Pastors, Politicians, Pacifists*,[12] point out the significance of Dr. Cadman's pronouncements on behalf of the Federal Council:

In the language of a clergyman, Dr. Cadman outlines a platform for a clerical political party. Evidently, he thinks that this country is ready for the creation of a new third party by himself and the group that controls the Federal Council. Nothing in the realm of secular affairs and politics is excluded in this program. Under his plan the Federal Council would not only take charge of the nation's foreign relations and write treaties, but the administrative council of his organization would prepare tax, tariff, river-and-harbor, goods, and public-building bills. It is presumed that eventually the state Federal Councils would plunge into state politics and the city Federal Councils would go into ward politics.

Dr. Cadman's prophecy has come true. As we read the Biennial Reports of The Federal Council of Churches for many years back, which include the minutes of all their official meetings and the pronouncements of their various committees and commissions, we see that the Federal Council is literally a political party operating within the framework of whatever

12 Pp. 84, 85.

legitimate political party happens to be in power in national, state, and local governments. Federal and National Council leaders are quick to take the credit for any Socialist program which is adopted by the various echelons of civil government and for the formation of any international organization such as the League of Nations and the United Nations. Indeed, some leaders claim that the planning details of these organizations were worked out within the Council by men who later attained high office in the United States government.

5   HOW THE FEDERAL COUNCIL BECAME THE NATIONAL COUNCIL

National Council is born, 1950. How Federal Council's functions were transferred to National Council. Official statement of continuity. Federal Council leaders become National Council leaders. Some left-wing affiliations. Oxnam, Sockman, Adams, Barnes, Bowie, Boyd, Cavert, Dahlberg, Darsie, Douglas, Harrison, Johnson, Landis, Nace, Weigle, Taft, Flemming, Horton, Holt, Dun, and others are held over. Council staff set-up. Its 221 boards and committees. The churchgoers still ignored.

THE NATIONAL COUNCIL OF CHURCHES came into official existence on November 29, 1950, at a constituting convention in Cleveland, Ohio. Delegates from 29 Protestant denominations were in attendance. This information is based on the official pamphlet published by The National Council of Churches, 297 Fourth Avenue, New York, and entitled "The Constitution, General By-laws and Certificate of Incorporation of the National Council of the Churches of Christ in the United States of America."

It is important that we devote some attention to this matter because, when evidence of collectivism is made public concerning The *Federal* Council of Churches, leaders of The *National* Council of Churches disclaim all responsibility, declaring that the Federal Council is no longer in existence and that the National Council bears no relationship to it. We are flogging a dead horse, they say. But nothing could, in fact, be further

from the truth. We read in the constitution and general by-
laws of The National Council of Churches (emphasis added):

> The National Council of the Churches of Christ in the
> United States of America was made possible by the deci-
> sion of 8 interdenominational agencies, all of which had
> had an important part in the historical development of
> cooperation among the churches, to combine their forces.
> These 8 agencies, which by their official action *transferred
> their functions and responsibilities* to the National Coun-
> cil, were:
> > *Federal Council of the Churches of Christ in America*
> > Foreign Missions Conference of North America
> > Home Missions Council of North America
> > International Council of Religious Education
> > Missionary Education Movement of the United States
> > and Canada
> > National Protestant Council on Higher Education
> > United Council of Church Women
> > United Stewardship Council
> Four additional agencies later decided to merge their
> interests in the National Council:
> > Church World Service, Inc.
> > Inter-Seminary Committee
> > Protestant Film Commission
> > Protestant Radio Commission [1]

The language is perfectly clear. The Federal Council of the
Churches of Christ in America was one of the eight agencies
"which by their official action transferred their functions and
responsibilities to the National Council." Further, the eleven
agencies listed with the Federal Council above had always
cooperated and interlocked with the Federal Council. Many

[1] P. 3.

of the officers serving on the Federal Council boards and commissions were also officers in these other eleven agencies.

The Federal Council's activities, objectives, and policies are being continued by the National Council. This is acknowledged in a statement from the December 1950 issue of the Federal Council *Bulletin* (emphasis added):

> *All the work of the Federal Council will continue under the new auspices . . . it is expected that the program will be enlarged as the new organization gains increased support . . . other divisions in the National Council and the general administration of the Council will also draw upon the resources in both personnel and finances.*

Finally, we will list some of the prominent persons in the old Federal Council, together with their positions in the new National Council of Churches and the left-wing affiliations of a considerable number of them.

BISHOP G. BROMLEY OXNAM was the president of the Federal Council, a member of the Board of the Federal Council, one of the most active promoters of the new National Council of Churches, and one of the board members. His Red-front record is contained in the record of the hearing held for him in July 1953 by the Committee on Un-American Activities, U.S. House of Representatives.

DR. RALPH W. SOCKMAN was chosen to preach the first sermon at the constituting convention of the National Council. His Communist-front associations have been the American Youth Congress; the Emergency Peace Mobilization; board chairman of the Inter-Church Committee of the American Russian Institute; the Methodist Federation for Social Action; greetings sent on the occasion of the 31st Anniversary of the Russian Revolution (Communist) under auspices of the

National Council of American-Soviet Friendship; World Youth Conference (sponsor).

EARL F. ADAMS [2] was the chairman of the Field Department of the Federal Council; administrative secretary of the National Council, and director of the Washington office of the National Council. Communist-front association: American Youth Congress.

ROSWELL P. BARNES, associate general secretary of the Federal Council; executive secretary of the Division of Christian Life and Work. Leftist affiliations: Associated Film Audiences (member of the Executive Board); Committee on Militarism in Education (secretary); Committee for Norman Thomas; Norman Thomas Campaign Committee (secretary); Emergency Peace Campaign (national sponsor); Fellowship of Socialist Christians (secretary); National Religion and Labor Foundation; North American Committee to Aid Spanish Democracy; United China Relief; War Resistors League, and World Youth Congress (sponsor).

W. RUSSELL BOWIE, vice chairman, Commission on Worship of the Federal Council; now vice chairman, Department of Worship and Art. Leftist affiliations: American Committee for Non-Participation in Japanese Aggression; American Committee to Save Refugees; American Committee for Protection of Foreign Born; Church Emergency Committee for Relief of Textile Strikers; Church League for Industrial Democracy; Attack the American Legion Lobby in Washington; Citizens Emergency Conference for Inter-Racial Unity; Civil Rights Congress; Committee on Militarism in Education; Coordinating Committee to Lift the Spanish Embargo; Emergency Committee for Strikers Relief; Friends of Italian Democracy; Greater New York Emergency Conference on Inalienable Rights; Harry Bridges Defense Committee; National Citizens Political Action Committee; National Citizens Committee on

2 Deceased 1956.

Relations with Latin America; National Council of the Arts, Sciences and Professions; National Emergency Conference for Democratic Rights; National Federation for Constitutional Liberties; Non-Intervention Citizens Committee; North American Committee to Aid Spanish Democracy; Open Letter on Harry Bridges (signer); Open Letter to President Roosevelt protesting Bridges deportation (signer); *The Protestant* (pro-Communist magazine; signed petition); Schappes Defense Committee; War Resistors League; Washington Committee to Lift the Spanish Embargo, and World Tomorrow Poll, which called for socialism.

BEVERLY M. BOYD, executive secretary, Department of Christian Social Relations in the Federal Council; executive director of the Department of Social Welfare of the National Council. Communist-front association: Russian War Relief, Inc. (chairman of the Richmond committee).

SAMUEL MCCREA CAVERT, general secretary of The Federal Council of Churches; general secretary of the National Council. Leftist affiliations: North American Committee to Aid Spanish Democracy (sponsor); *The Protestant* (pro-Communist magazine; signed appeal, and sponsor of *The Protestant* dinner); War Resistors League (endorsed pamphlet, "Military Training in the Schools and Colleges of the U.S.," an attack upon the reserve officers' training program).

EDWIN T. DAHLBERG, chairman, Department of Evangelism of the Federal Council; vice chairman of the Joint Department of Evangelism of the National Council. Communist-front associations: signed Open Letter to President Roosevelt protesting Bridges deportation; Citizens Committee to Free Earl Browder.

HUGH D. DARSIE, chairman of the Commission on Marriage and the Home, of the Federal Council; recording secretary of the Joint Department of Evangelism of the National Council.

Communist-front association: American Relief for Greek Democracy.

TRUMAN DOUGLAS, vice chairman of the Protestant Radio Commission of the Federal Council; chairman of the Broadcasting and Film Commission of the National Council.

SHELBY HARRISON, chairman of the Department of Christian Social Relations of the Federal Council; chairman of the Central Department of Research and Survey of the National Council. Leftist affiliations: World Peace Conference (sponsor) and Social Work Today Cooperators.

F. ERNEST JOHNSON, executive secretary of the Department of Research and Education of the Federal Council; executive director of the Central Department of Research and Survey of the National Council. Leftist affiliations: Consumers National Federation (sponsor); Institute for Propaganda Analysis (adviser); League for Industrial Democracy; World Peaceways (sponsor).

BENSON Y. LANDIS, associate executive secretary of the Federal Council's Department of Research and Education and secretary of the Federal Council's Committee on Town and Country; acting secretary of the Federal Council's Washington office. In the National Council, executive director of the Department of Town and Country Church and associate executive director of the Central Department of Research and Survey. Communist-front association: Consumers National Federation (sponsor).

I. GEORGE NACE, vice chairman and secretary of the Joint Commission on Planning and Adjustment of Local Inter-Church Relations of the Federal Council; executive secretary of the Division of Home Missions of the National Council. Communist-front association: National Committee to Abolish the Poll Tax (sponsor).

WILLIAM SCARLETT, chairman of the Department of International Justice and Goodwill and acting chairman of the

Committee on Policy, of that department, in the Federal Council; chairman of the Department of International Justice and Goodwill of the National Council. Leftist affiliations: American Committee for Non-Participation in Japanese Aggression (sponsor); Church Emergency Relief Committee; Church League for Industrial Democracy; Committee on Militarism in Education; National Religion and Labor Foundation; *The Protestant* (sponsor of Call for Dinner—forum).

WALTER W. VANKIRK,[3] executive secretary of the Department of International Justice and Goodwill of the Federal Council; executive director of the Department of International Justice and Goodwill of the National Council. Leftist affiliations: American Youth Congress; Emergency Peace Mobilization; Committee on Militarism in Education; League for Industrial Democracy; War Resistors League.

LUTHER A. WEIGLE, president of The Federal Council of Churches, member of the Commission on General Christian Education as executive secretary of the Standard Bible Committee. Leftist affiliations: Committee on Militarism in Education; Coordinating Committee to Lift the Spanish Embargo; National Religion and Labor Foundation; North American Committee to Aid Spanish Democracy; World Tomorrow Poll, which called for socialism (signer); War Resistors League.

We take time at this point to note that Dr. Weigle, formerly of the divinity school of Yale University, was the head of the committee which brought out the Revised Standard Version of the Bible, described as a new translation. Noted Hebrew and Greek scholars, examining the text, found that it was not a translation at all but an "interpretation." It was written by radical liberals of the International Council of Religious Education. Eight of these men have left-wing records, and one of the eight had more than twenty-five left-wing associations.

3 Deceased July 1956.

This Council, actually the education arm of the Federal Council through the years, united with The Federal Council of Churches as a part of the new National Council.

Dr. Weigle has long been active in the ecumenical movement. When, in 1924, the Joint Advisory Committee on Methods and Materials for Religious Education on the Foreign Field was established, Professor Luther Weigle was named chairman. The 1917 report of the American Unitarian Association records that Dr. Weigle collaborated with Professor Starbuck in preparing a series of textbooks for Unitarian Sunday schools. Unitarians reject the Christian doctrine of the Trinity; they do not believe that Jesus Christ is the Second Person of the Trinity or that the Holy Spirit is the Third Person of the Godhead. Unitarians reject altogether the deity of Jesus Christ and do not believe the Bible to be infallible. They consider themselves "freethinkers" or "liberals."

Dr. Weigle is involved also in a translation of the apocryphal writings. The 1954 Biennial Report of the National Council says:

> The Standard Bible Committee continues its work under the effective chairmanship of Dr. Luther A. Weigle. It is engaged now in the latter phases of the translation of the Apocrypha. This work is progressing satisfactorily, the last meeting of the Committee having been held during August at Northfield, Massachusetts. It is expected that the translation will appear in 1957.[4]

Are the Protestant churches of America now to be offered the Apocrypha through a great sales drive, as they were offered the Revised Standard Version of the Bible? What are the Apocrypha?

4 P. 40.

The Winston Simplified Dictionary, advanced edition, gives the following definitions of Apocrypha:

> 1, writings or statements of doubtful authorship;
> 2, in the early church, writings uncertain as to origin and authority; Apocrypha, certain writings originally included in the Old Testament, and still incorporated in the Vulgate, but now generally omitted in the Protestant versions of the Bible.

The Apocryphal books have never been incorporated into the widely used Protestant versions of the Bible. Protestant scholars down through the ages have classified these books as being the imaginative works of authors who were not chosen by the Holy Spirit to record Scripture.

The question now arises: why is The National Council of Churches spending time and money in translating the Apocrypha? Are they to be offered to the Protestant churches as Scripture?

Let us consider another perennial Council member.

Mrs. Douglas Horton, vice chairman of the Division of Christian Life and Work, has been a continuing member of the Federal and National Councils. Mrs. Horton was appointed wartime head of the WAVES, the Women's Division of the U.S. Navy, by President Franklin D. Roosevelt. Her husband, the Rev. Dr. Douglas Horton, is an official of the General Council of Congregational Christian Churches and is very active in the Federal-National Council's work. In 1953 Mrs. Horton was nominated by the Eisenhower Administration as U.S. delegate to the United Nations Social Commission. After the Federal Bureau of Investigation had investigated Mrs. Horton and made its report to the State Department, her nomination to the United Nations Social Commission was suddenly withdrawn. Mrs. Horton has been cited four times in the files of the Committee on Un-American Activities, a fact that was widely publicized after her nomination had been made. She became a member of the Appraisal Committee of The National Council of Churches as an additional duty.

In the 1954 Biennial Report,[5] Mrs. Horton is recorded as having been elected to a two-year term in the General Assembly of The National Council of Churches, beginning November 28, 1954. She is listed[6] as a member of the General Board of The National Council of Churches for 1953–1954, representing the General Council of the Congregational Christian Churches, and as the vice chairman of the Division of Christian Life and Work of The National Council of Churches.[7] One of the departments of this Division is the Department of International Justice and Goodwill. In 1953, the Department sponsored a National Study Conference, as recorded in the 1954 Biennial Report:

> The largest single project of the Department during the past biennium was the Fourth National Study Conference on the Churches and World Order, October 27–30, 1953, at Cleveland, Ohio, over which Mrs. Douglas Horton, department chairman, presided. The Call to the Conference was issued by the president of The National Council of Churches. Some 380 delegates and 50 consultants from 26 communions participated. The Conference discussed five working papers prepared in advance by drafting commissions: 1) Christian Faith and International Responsibility, 2) the United States and the United Nations, 3) the United States and Foreign Economic Policy, 4) the United States and the Less Devel-

5 P. 10.
6 P. 22.
7 P. 71.

oped Areas, and 5) the United States and Collective Security.[8]

The National Lay Committee of The National Council of Churches, composed of businessmen and women over the nation, protested the opposition to the Bricker Amendment by The National Council of Churches. A statement opposing the Bricker Amendment was prepared by the Department of International Justice and Goodwill, of which Mrs. Douglas Horton was the chairman. When this statement was originally presented to the General Board on May 20, 1953, three representatives of the Lay Committee spoke against it, declaring that it was a political and highly controversial matter, and that it did not have sufficient ethical or religious content to require organized Protestantism to take sides in the controversy. After a long debate the statement was finally sent back to the Department of International Justice and Goodwill.

The opponents of the Bricker Amendment within The National Council of Churches did not let it rest there. The Cleveland Study Conference on the Churches and World Order adopted a resolution disapproving of the Bricker Amendment. Also it passed other resolutions, including a denunciation of the McCarran-Walter Immigration Act. The text of the resolutions adopted at Cleveland was mailed to all members of the Congress and received nationwide press attention.

At a later meeting of the General Board, several lay members criticized the whole procedure and denounced the anti-Bricker Amendment statement. Bishop William C. Martin, president of The National Council of Churches, replied that the General Board had never spoken on the Bricker Amendment and had never placed itself on record.

Bishop Martin could only have been speaking with tongue

8 P. 63.

in cheek; for the National Study Conference on the Churches and World Order, over which Mrs. Douglas Horton, the chairman of the Department of International Justice and Goodwill, presided, was officially called by the same Bishop Martin, president of the National Council. It was also convened by the General Board of the National Council, and its programs were planned by an official department within a division of the National Council.

What else were the press and Congress to assume but that this was an official pronouncement of The National Council of Churches against the Bricker Amendment? While denying that it was an official statement adopted by the General Board, officials of the General Board wrote the anti-Bricker statement, cleared it through the Cleveland Study Conference, and handed it out to the Congress and to the press of the nation!

IVAN LEE HOLT next comes under scrutiny. He was president of The Federal Council of Churches and is chairman of the Joint Department of American Communities Overseas of the National Council. Communist-front associations: Coordinating Committee to Lift the Spanish Embargo; Emergency Peace Mobilization; North American Committee to Aid Spanish Democracy; Washington Committee to Lift the Spanish Embargo.

Let us quote from one of Dr. Holt's works:

If Protestantism should turn to a fuller social gospel it would mean not only a denunciation of war but the severance of any connection with it. It would mean not only a willingness to be imprisoned rather than invoke a blessing on armies in the field, but it would mean a withdrawal of chaplains from service with the Army and Navy. It would seek an overthrow of the present capitalistic system. There are those who feel that the profit motive is wrong and that there can never be happiness for mankind until the present economic system gives way to some cooperative scheme . . . it might mean revolution. There are those who, while opposed to the use of force in international relations, would not hesitate to use force in the overthrow of an economic system which they regard as un-Christian and vicious.[9]

Other leading Federal Councilites now in high positions in the National Council are as follows: [10]

CHARLES P. TAFT, president of the Federal Council; now chairman of the Department of the Church and Economic Life of the National Council.

CHARLES T. LABER, chairman of the Division of Foreign Missions.

CAMERON P. HALL, executive director of the Department of the Church and Economic Life.

CHARLES H. SEAVER, recording secretary of the Department of the Church and Economic Life.

ARTHUR S. FLEMMING, chairman of the Division of Christian Life and Work; vice president of the National Council.

E. G. HOMRIGHAUSEN, chairman of the Joint Department of Evangelism.

JESSE M. BADER, executive director of the Joint Department of Evangelism.

HARPER SIBLEY, chairman of the Central Department of Church World Service.

MRS. LESLIE E. SWAIN, co-chairman of the Department of Race Relations of the Federal Council, now Chairman

9 *The Search for a New Strategy in Protestantism,* pp. 31, 32.
10 National Council *Workbook for the Second General Assembly,* Denver, Colorado, Dec. 9-12, 1952.

WORLD-NATIONAL COUNCILS CHAIN OF COMMAND

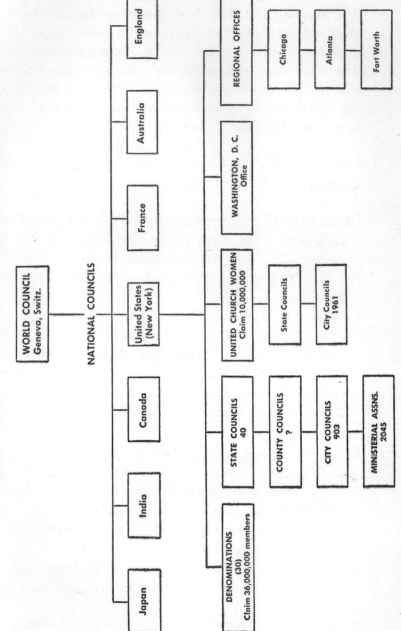

of the Central Department of Ecumenical Relations of the National Council.

ANGUS DUN, vice chairman of the Central Department of Ecumenical Relations.

J. QUINTER MILLER, executive director of the Central Department of Field Administration.

This list should clear up all doubt as to whether the crowd that directed the policies and activities of the old Federal Council of Churches is likewise directing the work of the new National Council. The National Council is merely the Federal Council and its related agencies all working together under one name.

The National Council of Churches' *Workbook* for the General Assembly of that body which met in Denver, Colorado, December 9–12, 1952, was put into the hands of all the delegates attending. In the back of the *Workbook* is found Appendix C, a chart three pages wide, entitled "Lines of Staff Responsibility of Major Units of The National Council of the Churches in the U.S.A." This chart closely resembles a military setup. At the top is the General Assembly, followed by the General Board, the various sections of the General Administration, and then the Central Departments, General Departments, Divisions, Joint Departments, Commissions and Committees, and Divisional Units. This is only the *headquarters* layout of The National Council of Churches.

Also handed out to the delegates was an analytical report, stating that the National Council has *221 boards, committees, and commissions* which supervise the work of the Council at various levels of organization. "There are about 3,600 separate individuals sitting as members of these bodies—some 600 more than the entire Church counted as members at Pentecost—and the report which follows has information on 3,473." [11]

11 P. 2.

The report admits on page 4 that criticism has been directed against the elaborate machinery, the domination of the Council by professionals and "big names," and "the gulf between those who make national decisions and those who sit in the pews or stand in the pulpits." Truer words were never spoken. The men and women in the pews know nothing whatever about The National Council of Churches and its workings. The National Council claims to speak for Protestants on every subject from the United Nations to the Bricker Amendment, yet these questions have never been submitted to the people for a vote, nor have the people ever been consulted by ballot as to whether or not they even wanted membership in the Federal, National, or World Council of Churches.

THE COUNCILS AND THE GOVERNMENT

Councils have won top posts and important friends in Federal government. Dean Acheson. John Foster Dulles. Alger Hiss. Harold E. Stassen. Arthur S. Flemming. Council lobbying. The mysterious Mr. Smith. Council support of government policy. Foreign aid. Immigration. World organizations. Council for Social Action. Lutheran, Congregational, Presbyterian, Methodist, and Protestant Episcopal churches plunge into politics. David Lawrence urges, "Keep the churches out of politics." What Christ said to the Herodians. Tax-exempt foundations make grants to Council, with political overtones. Representative Scherer replies to Congregational Christian Churches. Philip Murray Memorial Foundation makes grant to Council.

THE NATIONAL COUNCIL OF CHURCHES, the groundwork having been prepared by its predecessor, the Federal Council, has captured strategic posts within the United States government and has constructed an active lobbying machine. It has won strong financial support from tax-exempt foundations.

The main speaker at the Constituting Convention of The National Council of Churches in Cleveland, Ohio, November 1950, was the Secretary of State, Mr. Dean Acheson. During this conclave, Mr. Acheson's foreign policy, a significant factor in the loss of China and other sections of the Far East to the Communists, was praised by Council spokesmen at the convention and throughout the country's newspapers. After all, Mr. Acheson was a very important person.

And Mr. John Foster Dulles, a top-ranking officer of the Council, was assisting Mr. Acheson in the State Department. And had not Mr. Alger Hiss, who had worked with Dean Acheson for so many years in the State Department, also served as chairman of an important committee of The Federal Council of Churches in 1948? And had he not used the committee as a propaganda medium for the United Nations? (See page 179.)

Now Mr. Dulles is Secretary of State for the Eisenhower Administration. And Mr. Harold E. Stassen, elected a vice president-at-large of The National Council of Churches, is special adviser to the President on disarmament, with Cabinet rank. Mr. Stassen was formerly president of the International Council of Religious Education, which authorized the writing of a "liberal" new version of the Bible.

Also there is Mr. Arthur S. Flemming, who for a time was assistant in charge of manpower problems in the Office of Defense Mobilization, in the Eisenhower Administration. Mr. Flemming was the president of Ohio Wesleyan University where, in 1942, the Federal Council's Commission on a Just and Durable Peace drew the blueprint for a world government (Chapter 12). He was elected vice president of the Division of Christian Life and Work at the 1950 Constituting Convention.

It is not accidental, nor is it irrelevant, that The National Council of Churches should have, among its officers and chief window dressing, men who occupy high positions in the Federal government. Because the Council has never advocated the spreading of the Christian faith as its primary mission, but has labored toward putting over massive political programs on a national and international scale, nothing could be more logical than to encourage administrators to accept, simultaneously, high positions in the Council and in the government.

It is also logical that, according to the 1954 Biennial Report[1]

1 P. 141.

of the Council, the Washington office of The National Council of Churches should have expanded its responsibilities, services, and facilities. Who is vice chairman of the expanded Washington office? The vice chairman is Mr. Arthur S. Flemming.

The Washington office is headed by the Rev. Eugene Carson Blake, as chairman. Dr. Blake was elected president of The National Council of Churches at its third biennial meeting in Boston, Mass., on November 28, 1954. He is also the stated clerk of the Presbyterian Church in the U.S.A. denomination.

The National Council has vehemently denied that it does any lobbying. "The Washington office as such is not to engage in efforts to influence legislation," the Council announces. But Paragraph 1 of the report of the Washington office defines one of its functions: "By giving prompt and authoritative notice regarding pending legislation and governmental directives and other developments in the national capital affecting the functioning of the churches and their agencies; and by securing official interpretations of legislative and administrative acts when required by the National Council."

These words can be broadened to include almost any conceivable action in the field of national and international affairs. There is no political matter with which the National Council has not concerned itself and which cannot be determined to affect "the functioning of the churches and their agencies."

One cannot but feel uneasy when the Washington office reports mysteriously that a new executive, one Charles M. Smith, has been added to the staff as director of special services. Mr. Smith, the report says, has had many years of government service. But the report does not identify his government position. Mr. Smith, the report adds, carries out research work on topics of major interest to the churches. Whatever he uncovers during his researching is disseminated in "fact sheets" which are sent to a "limited circulation." Who the recipients of these sheets are, is not disclosed in the report.

More openly, for all to see, is the public espousal by church leaders of political measures. Commonplace examples are the following:

CHURCH HEADS BACK IKE ON FOREIGN AID
The Washington Post and Times Herald
Wednesday, May 29, 1957
Associated Press

Spokesmen for Protestant and Jewish organizations generally endorsed the nonmilitary aspects of the foreign aid program before the House Foreign Affairs Committee yesterday.

The Right Rev. Angus Dun, Bishop of the Protestant Church in the Diocese of Washington, testified as the representative of the Protestant Episcopal Church in the United States at the request of the presiding Bishop, the Right Rev. Henry Knox Sherrill. . . .

The Rev. Dr. Ralph W. Sockman, senior minister of Christ Church Methodist, New York City, appeared in behalf of the National Council of the Churches of Christ in the U.S.A. and the Board of World Peace of the Methodist Church.

President's View Supported

Dr. Sockman supported the economic aid legislation substantially as it has been presented by President Eisenhower. "We of the churches are of the judgment that the time for courageous action on the part of our Government has arrived."

The Washington Post and Times Herald
Saturday, April 6, 1957

A three-member deputation of the National Council of

Churches conferred earlier this week with President Eisenhower and Secretary of State John Foster Dulles to "express an interest" in strengthening the mutual assistance program "on the basis of the Christian understanding of the proper role of the United States in the free world."

CHURCHMEN BACK FOREIGN AID AIMS
Chicago Daily News
Friday, April 12, 1957

WASHINGTON—(UP)—The National Council of Churches of Christ in America endorsed the administration's new foreign aid proposals Friday on grounds of moral responsibility, military necessity and "good business."

Dr. Eugene Carson Blake, its president, told a special Senate foreign aid committee that "church people across our land are arising in support of a more dynamic program of technical cooperation and economic aid." . . .

"I assure you," he said, "that theirs will be an increasingly mighty voice in the land on this issue during the days immediately ahead."

The National Council of Churches publishes a *Christian Newsletter on International Affairs*. This publication is a political propaganda sheet on current government policies, and it advocates Socialistic measures and internationalism.

The February–March 1957 issue of this letter tells the story of the general board meeting of The National Council of Churches in Williamsburg, Virginia, on February 27–28, at which was cited "a new situation of utmost urgency . . . with regard to international economic policy."

This situation was defined as the opposition arising over the entire nation against continued foreign-aid spending and the pleas coming to the Congressmen for cuts in the federal budget. The ecclesiastics, alarmed, voted to send representatives to Congress to tell the lawmakers that "the church people" were all for continued foreign aid and technical assistance.

The sounds of the "ayes" had hardly died away when the wheels were set in motion. Press releases were hurriedly prepared, communications were issued to all the constituent denominations and departmental agencies, and the pressure upon Capitol Hill began.

The General Board stated that it "reaffirms the previous position of the National Council on technical assistance, economic aid, and trade policies."

One has to go back into the previous *Newsletters* and the Biennial Reports of the National Council to find out what the "previous positions" are. One will find such "positions" as opposition to the McCarran-Walter Act and the plea to have it amended so as to let down the immigration bars and eliminate certain safeguards; support of visits of Red delegates to the United States; higher appropriations for foreign aid and less for national defense (March 1956 *Newsletter*); churchmen's pilgrimages to Washington for briefing on current legislative affairs; support of GATT, ILO, OTC, and other world organizations, in taking tariff powers away from the United States Congress; federal aid to education; opposition to Congressional investigations of subversion.

The propaganda drive of the National Council is carried out by the constituent members, the denominations, state and local councils of churches, women's groups, etc. Once the top echelon of command has decided what it wants to do, the program is filtered down through the sympathizers entrenched in the constituent chains of command. For example, the Council of Christian Social Progress of the American Baptist Convention draws up resolutions similar to those drawn up by the General Board. It urges churches to study them. Then: "We further urge that individuals and groups in our churches take positive [political] action; that they write to national and local legislators expressing their convictions." The "convictions" will be decided by the General Board of the National Council, which communicates them to the denominations, which work through their Social Action groups to get the people to write Congress for this or that program, which should not be questioned by laymen because the clergy decided it and, therefore, it is holy, just, and righteous.

The February–March 1957 National Council *Newsletter* reports, in another instance, that the National Lutheran Council meeting in Atlantic City passed its judgment on the McCarran-Walter Immigration and Naturalization Law and called for amendments to the law. These crippling amendments, according to Congressman Francis Walter, who wrote the act, would weaken the security of the United States. The same *Newsletter* reports that the Methodist Women's Division of Christian Service joined the chorus and called for revision of the McCarran-Walter Act, and that a new director of World Relations for the United Church Women was appointed to direct an "educational program in the area of international relations. Under national guidance this is carried out through nearly 2,000 state and local councils of church women, with an estimated 10,000,000 members, throughout the country." Mrs. Esther W. Hymer, the new director, is identified as a former UN observer and an "expert" of the Foreign Operations Administration's advisory council.

The Congregational Church has been split wide open over the activities of its Council for Social Action. The furor raised by contributing laymen and some clergymen became so great that the leaders of the denomination were called upon to investigate the Council's activities. They whitewashed the charges; to do otherwise would have indicted clerics and denominational wheels who were in "good standing" within the church machinery. Now the Congregational hierarchy has forced a merger with the Evangelical and Reformed denomination in the current drive for a world church (the ecumenical movement). The Social Resolutions adopted by the General Council of the Congregational Church at Omaha, June 20–27, 1956, is the National Council of Churches program right down the line. The General Council even voted to set up a Washington office, whose purpose is "to speak on behalf of the Council for Social Action to issues before our national Congress." Who says the churches are not engaged in lobbying activity?

The Presbyterian Church in the U.S.A. (Northern Church) has gone all out for the Social Action program. Denominational leaders are telling church members who protest that they are questioning the program of God Himself. Seminars, study courses, and conferences are held all over the country on this Social Action program; the works of notorious Communist-fronters, Socialists, and enemies of the American free-enterprise system are used as authorities on "social questions."

The pattern is exactly the same with the Protestant Episcopal Church. Its National Council has available a bundle of literature on Social Relations. It is called "Christian" Social Relations, but upon examination most of the material is seen to deal with secular affairs. Economic security, "selfish individualism," reconciliation with the Soviet Union, support of world government, and the limiting of national sovereignty are matters of prime concern.

In connection with what amounts to an interlock between the Federal government and The National Council of Churches, Mr. David Lawrence wrote an editorial in the April 2, 1954, issue of *U.S. News & World Report,* entitled "Keep the Churches Out of Politics." He reminds churchmen that a basic tradition in this country is to keep church and state separate. "Lately," he says, "some of the National Church organizations have begun to meddle in politics. If the trend is not arrested, it can only lead to a loss of faith in churches and in clergymen who profess to teach Christianity." Many sermons preached on Sunday, he continues, are more concerned with political questions and political figures than with the subject of Christianity. If it keeps up, he says, laymen will soon be asking each other, "Is yours a Republican or Democratic Party pulpit?"

> A case in point [he argues] is The National Council of the Churches of Christ in the U.S.A., which has just issued a statement demanding that Congress adopt certain rules and regulations which the National Council would prescribe with reference to the handling of Congressional investigations. The phraseology of the document is copied in large part from the language of political spokesmen who are making partisan use of such proposals. Granted that there is a need for such reforms, why does the National Council feel that laymen are incompetent to fight that battle and that the prestige of such a big church organization must be dragged into the mire of partisan politics?

He ends his editorial: "This is the time, of all times, for clergymen to teach Christianity and not to become sinners themselves in the unmoral precincts of present-day politics." We can add a hearty "Amen" to what Mr. Lawrence has said. The business of the Church is outlined in the New Testament. The New Testament does not teach that the churches are to go into politics or to try to change the political life of the world. Rather, the message as given by Christ, the Head of the Church, to His followers was to go into all the world "and preach the Gospel" (Mark 16:15). And to the Herodians He said, "Render therefore unto Caesar the things which are Caesar's; and unto God the things that are God's" (Matt. 22:21).

As The National Council of Churches has won massive political support within the Federal government, so it has won impressive subsidization from tax-exempt foundations. These two facts are not unrelated. By law, and as expressly stated in their charters, tax-exempt foundations are forbidden to advocate or oppose political legislation on any level. Also The National Council of Churches and its constituent bodies are tax exempt, with the same limitation. But The National Council does advocate and propose political legislation. It lobbies in Washington, it has its representatives doubling as government officials, and it carries on political propaganda through its regional, state, county, city, and local councils.

Technically and in spirit, therefore, the National Council has violated a basic condition of its tax-exempt status. Likewise, the question must be raised as to whether a foundation which is tax exempt and which makes grants of money to the politically active National Council is violating the letter and spirit of its charter, contrary to the law of the land.

At least two major foundations have made such grants. The Ford Foundation's subsidiary, The Fund for the Republic (which claims independence from the Ford Foundation but which is intimately related), in its annual report of May 31, 1955, shows a donation of $10,000 to The National Council of Churches, made in November 1954.

If this were merely an isolated fact, it would be interesting enough. But it is not isolated. Dr. Ray Gibbons, director of the Council for Social Action, an official body of the Congregational Christian Churches, wrote a letter, dated January 10, 1957, to Representative Gordon H. Scherer. The letter said that "a number of religious agencies" were prepared to "take vigorous action" against the House Committee on Un-American Activities unless it halted its investigation of The Fund for the Republic."

Representative Scherer replied on January 25 in part as follows:

When you point out that the groups you represent have large constituencies, it is apparent that you intend to use the voting power of these groups against the members of The Committee on Un-American Activities if the investigation is not halted. . . . You advance no reason why the Committee should discontinue its investigation except that the groups you represent have a financial interest at stake by reason of the fact that grants are now being made by The Fund for the Republic for their projects.

In September 1954 the press carried an announcement from the headquarters of the Philip Murray Memorial Foundation that the foundation had made a gift of $200,000 to The National Council of Churches in honor of the late president of the CIO and the Steelworkers Union. The presentation was made by Walter P. Reuther, president of the CIO, to Bishop William C. Martin, Methodist, of Dallas, Texas, president of the National Council. Half the amount given was to be used in the Council's educational program and half to establish a library and research center on religion and economics at the National Council's headquarters in New York City.

We can only conclude, from the evidence adduced in this chapter, that controlling elements of the U.S. government, of the monolithic National Council of Churches, of the great denominations, and of powerful foundations are bound together in an impregnable interlock. They are engaged in a massive campaign to supplant the individualistic Gospel of the Galilean with a great collectivistic machine designed for political and economic ends. Where political forces move in on church affairs, the preaching of the Christian doctrine of individual salvation is of necessity silenced.

Peace versus pacifism. Christ the Prince of Peace. Councils prefer pacifism. The "new internationalism." Federal Council "always extremely active in any matter against national defense." Commission on Peace and Arbitration. Carnegie Endowment for International Peace. Church Peace Union founded by Carnegie. Henry A. Atkinson's role. Hendrix, Lynch, Mathews, Mott. Peace conference at Constance. Its failure. World Alliance for International Friendship Through the Churches. The Alliance a propaganda agency for League and UN. Peace Union deplores armament. Federal Council disarms United States. Council backs League. World made safe for democracy.

THERE IS a great difference between peace and pacifism. There is also a great difference between the mission of the churches in seeking peace and the legitimate functions of secular governments in promoting cordial relations between nations.

The Bible refers to Christ as the Prince of Peace. The angels' message to the shepherds in the field of Judea declared: "Peace on earth toward men of good will." This was upon the occasion of the birth of the Prince of Peace. The message would imply that there are men who are not of good will; therefore, they do not know what real peace is. This is in keeping with the Prophet Isaiah's words: "But the wicked are like the troubled sea, when it cannot rest, whose waters cast up mire and dirt. There is no peace, saith my God, to the wicked" (Isaiah 57:20, 21).

No reasonable person is against all efforts to bring about world peace; but the mission of the churches is not to enter the area of politics and use its prestige and machinery for promoting political alliances, world government, and nonviolent resistance campaigns against required national-defense programs. The mission is to preach "the peace of God which passeth all understanding" (Philippians 4:7), which only comes when individuals accept the person of the Prince of Peace. Until the heart of each individual is changed, there can be no peace in this world.

Dr. E. Stanley Jones, an evangelist for The Federal Council of Churches and a Methodist missionary, spent many years in India, supposedly for the purpose of converting the heathen, among whom was the late Mahatma Gandhi. Instead of Dr. Jones influencing Gandhi toward Christian conversion, the reverse took place. Dr. Jones admits this in his book *Mahatma Gandhi*. Dr. Jones became a disciple of *Satyagraha*, or pacifist resistance, as practiced by Gandhi and his followers.

Dr. Jones went so far as to ask Gandhi to come to the United States and organize the people in a resistance movement against military preparedness. He called Gandhi "God's trump card" and the man through whom God was working in the twentieth century. He admits that Gandhi would not accept the Christ or the God of the Bible; but the fact that Gandhi was a pacifist made him a "natural Christian" instead of an "orthodox" one.

Dr. Jones suggests that we should allow the Russians to throw us in jails (they would get tired of building jails and would become ridiculous) or even to butcher us for five years, if they invade our shores. He believes that at the end of five years they would get tired of butchering nonviolent resisters and throw in the towel.

The fact is that Dr. Jones has not given any evidence to

show that the Communists have become tired of butchering anyone since 1917.

When clergymen engage in advising young men not to register for military service, and urge church people to refuse to make the weapons of national defense, their so-called "peace" efforts approach treason against the government under which they are granted freedom to preach. This type of activity gives aid and comfort to the enemy.

Various leaders in the councils of churches seem to put all-out confidence in the United Nations as the last hope for world peace, judging from the voluminous material which they disseminate on this subject to the churches and to the secular press. Sunday-school lessons, sermons, youth papers, retreat talks, conference speeches praise the glories of the UN to the skies, while omitting the traditional exposition of Bible doctrines. Women's societies within the churches are given entire courses on such subjects as "The UN and US" (study pamphlet published in 1957 by the Presbyterian Church in the U.S.A.).

What should be obvious to these leaders is that the UN didn't see fit to give the Prince of Peace a seat in its assembly or on the Security Council. In fact, as the book of the Revelation says (3:20), Christ was left outside the door. Many of the capitalist nations did not want to offend the Communist nations by admitting the Lord. How can members of the clergy, of all people, put such confidence in the UN's ability to bring about world peace in the light of this fact?

The Church of Jesus Christ is commanded by Him to preach the Gospel. If the churches carry out this mission, men's hearts will be turned to peace; for men make up governments and nations. This is the business of God. If "Caesar" wants to make pacts, alliances, and agreements with worldly organizations, that is "his" business. From the beginning, the

Councils have ignored Christ's injunction to keep separate the respective functions of church and state.

The Rev. Charles S. Macfarland, secretary of The Federal Council of Churches, devotes a section of his book *Christian Unity at Work* to the report of the Commission on Peace and Arbitration, headed by the Rev. Frederick Lynch, secretary. The subtitle of the report is "The Church and the New Internationalism." Dr. Lynch states that "war as a means of settlement of international disputes is anti-Christian in its very nature. The Federal Council has always insisted that leadership in the cause of international arbitration should be assumed by the churches." Here we find Dr. Lynch laying a foundation for the participation by The Federal Council of Churches in international affairs.

At this point there should be read into the record a report of the Office of Naval Intelligence which appeared in the *Congressional Record* of the House of Representatives proceedings, dated 1935. Of course, the present-day National Council leaders are always quick to try to defend their position when an exposure like this is made. The former secretary of The Federal Council of Churches, Dr. Samuel McCrae Cavert, has said that this report was written by "a very minor official in the United States Naval Intelligence." The intelligence services are not so much concerned with whether a "major" or "minor" official wrote a report as they are with whether or not the report is true. The report is absolutely true, for the official records of The Federal Council of Churches, as recorded in its own Biennial Reports, show that it was very actively against promoting the national defense of the United States.

Here is the report as it appeared in the *Congressional Record* (emphasis added):

(C) Organizations which, while not openly advocating the "force and violence" principles of the Communists, give aid and comfort to the Communist movement and Party. Among the strongest of these organizations are: . . . (b) The Federal Council of the Churches of Christ in America: this is a large, radical, pacifist organization. It probably represents 20,000,000 Protestants in the United States. However, *its leadership consists of a small radical group which dictates its policy*. It is always extremely active in any matter against national defense. [1]

Dr. Lynch says, on page 198 of Dr. Macfarland's historical account, that "the Federal Council has always been first in America to speak" against war. If Dr. Lynch had told the whole truth, he would not have confined his statement to "war" but would have included all that had to do with defense, militarily speaking, against war!

The Federal Council of Churches created the Commission on Peace and Arbitration on October 17, 1911, and appointed a number of clergymen to it. Dr. Lynch says: "These men responded heartily to the call for immediate work, and in cooperation with the agencies of the Carnegie Endowment for International Peace, soon succeeded in reaching every church in the United States with resolutions and with appeals to the United States Senate." Dr. Lynch further states that, as a result of this campaign, put on by the Federal Council, the churches of the United States "flooded Congress with petitions and personal letters." The Federal Council here takes credit for awakening thousands of ministers to the importance of the "peace movement." It "secured thousands of sermons on arbitration, and the establishment of a permanent Supreme Court of Nations." Dr. Lynch says that, following his graduation from Yale University and its divinity school, while in his pastorate in New York City he was identified with many national and international movements and was upon the directorates of

[1] *Congressional Record,* 1935, p. 13503.

other important movements for "social uplift." He made many trips to Europe and met "influential peace workers of the various nations."

The time shifts to 3:00 o'clock on the afternoon of February 10, 1914; the scene is the home of Andrew Carnegie, the multimillionaire steel magnate. The story is told by Dr. Macfarland in his book *Pioneers for Peace Through Religion*,[2] which is based on the records of the Church Peace Union over the years 1914 through 1945. The Union was founded by Mr. Carnegie. Dr. Macfarland's book about it is dedicated to Mrs. Andrew Carnegie, to William P. Merrill, the president of the Church Peace Union, and to Henry A. Atkinson, the general secretary.

The Rev. Henry A. Atkinson has quite a record. He was affiliated with the American Committee to Save Refugees,[3] cited as a Communist front;[4] the American Round Table on India, cited as "a Communist front headed by Robert Norton, a well-known member of the Communist Party";[5] the American Russian Institute[6] and its branches in New York, Philadelphia, and Southern California (including Los Angeles), all listed by the Attorney General as Communist;[7] the American Youth Congress,[8] cited as subversive and Communist by Attorney General Tom Clark;[9] the League of American Writers,[10] cited as subversive and Communist by the Attorney General;[11] and the *Protestant Digest,* described as "a magazine which has faithfully propagated the Communist Party line under the guise of being a religious journal."[12]

2 Fleming H. Revell, New York, 1946.
3 House Report of the 78th Congress, Second Session, 1944, Appendix IX.
4 Special Committee on Un-American Activities Report, March 29, 1944.
5 California Committee on Un-American Activities, 1948 Report.
6 House Report of the 78th Congress, Second Session, 1944, Appendix IX.
7 April 27, 1949.
8 House Report of the 78th Congress, Second Session, 1944, Appendix IX.
9 Dec. 1947 and Sept. 1948.
10 House Report of the 78th Congress, Second Session, 1944, Appendix IX.
11 June and Sept. 1948.
12 Special Committee on Un-American Activities Report, March 29, 1944.

This was the secretary of the organization which was to spend Mr. Carnegie's millions in the cause of "peace."

In the foreword to his book Dr. Macfarland writes, "The year 1914 marks the turning point in history." It marked "the beginning of a trend on the part of the churches in their attitudes toward the state, especially in relation to international peace." He then describes the volume as being a history of the role which the churches played in international affairs. He credits the Church Peace Union with an important part in the development of the ecumenical movement and the founding of The World Council of Churches.

The meeting in Andrew Carnegie's home was historic. Men from various Protestant and Jewish groups were present. The first president of The Federal Council of Churches, Bishop E. R. Hendrix of the Methodist Episcopal Church South, was there. So was the Rev. Frederick Lynch, a Congregationalist, secretary of the Federal Council's Commission on Peace and Arbitration. Dr. Shailer Mathews, Dean of the divinity school of the University of Chicago, second president of the Federal Council, and identified in Dr. Macfarland's book as being "widely known as the chief interpreter of the Social Gospel," was in attendance. Dr. John R. Mott, wrongly alleged to be the father of the ecumenical movement, was another participant. Unitarians and Universalists sat down with these radical leaders of The Federal Council of Churches—in the home of Andrew Carnegie, a Swedenborgian who did not accept the great doctrines of the Christian faith.

Dr. Macfarland says that the guests were selected because of "their broad social outlook . . . and all believed profoundly in the social mission of the Church." They were the founders, then and there, of the Church Peace Union, and to them Mr. Carnegie turned over two million dollars in five-percent bonds, to be spent in the cause of "peace."

"From this time on," writes Dr. Macfarland, "the Church

Peace Union became the 'hub' about which revolved a world-wide movement." [13] As we shall see, the Church Peace Union played a major role, along with the Federal Council, in establishing The World Council of Churches.

Mr. Carnegie's idea was to bring together German, British, and American churchmen in a conference at Constance, Germany, on or about August 1, 1914. (An entirely separate peace conference for Roman Catholics had been planned for Liège, Belgium, at the same time. The group did not meet in Liège, because peace was suddenly blown to smithereens when the Germans attacked that city.) The Protestant meeting in Constance was about to convene; delegates were arriving from France, Germany, Switzerland, Denmark, Norway, Sweden, Bulgaria, and the United States. But many delegates failed to arrive from the United States, Great Britain, Italy, Austria, Hungary, and Belgium: trains were turned back at the frontier, because war had begun. Several American delegates were arrested by the Germans and kept in prison for a while. Thus the first peace conference under the auspices of the Church Peace Union was ended before it began.

After the break-up of the scheduled conference, some delegates were able to slip through the German lines by devious routes and make their way to London. There they organized the World Alliance for International Friendship Through the Churches. Perhaps they thought that a change of name would work magic and bring peace after all. Later on we will see that the Church Peace Union and this World Alliance merged and became a propaganda agency first for the League of Nations and then for the United Nations.

Dr. Macfarland, in his book *Pioneers for Peace Through Religion,* ties The Federal Council of Churches in closely with the various pacifist movements. Many officers of the Federal Council served simultaneously on the boards of pacifist organ-

[13] *Pioneers for Peace Through Religion,* p. 23.

izations. Dr. Macfarland says, "The Church Peace Union had a large, if not a major, part during the critical year of 1914 in the effective establishment of the Council." [14]

Dr. Macfarland admits that Andrew Carnegie did not have great insight in world affairs. In the early part of 1914 he considered war to be a thing of the past; he was not prepared for the great shock which took place in August of the same year. Even when war came, he believed that Kaiser Wilhelm was basically a man of peace and that the war was caused by the German military caste. Dr. Macfarland admits that the Council leaders followed the "tenets of the Liberal School, which counted on moral progress and the essential goodness of human nature to help us overcome any serious difficulties that might threaten."

Dr. Macfarland reports: "During a considerable part of the war, the American Council of the World Alliance and the Commission on International Justice and Goodwill of the Federal Council constituted a joint body under the title of the World Alliance, with a headquarters where the machinery and the Federal Council might be readily available. The Church Peace Union was a counseling body and made appropriations for the work of the combined organizations." [15] In place of the one organization, the Church Peace Union, which started out in such a grandiose manner in February 1914, there now are three, all financed by Mr. Carnegie.

Dr. Macfarland comforts those who were in the Church Peace Union from 1914 to 1916 with the thought that, although the Union failed to stop the war, yet "even the messages and resolutions were not without their educational values."

Midway in the war, in 1916, before American entry, the Church Peace Union sent a resolution to President Wilson

14 *Ibid.*, p. 39.
15 *Ibid.*, p. 47.

"deploring increased armament." *If the Church Peace Union
had had its way, the United States probably would have had no
defense whatever during World War I. The Union's procedure was exactly the same as that which The Federal Council of Churches used during the eventful years leading up to
World War II.* If the Japanese hadn't failed to follow up the
successful attack upon Pearl Harbor with an attack upon the
United States, the United States might have been crushed because of the efforts of the Federal Council pacifists, who successfully propagandized against adequate defense. Again we
refer to the Office of Naval Intelligence report. [16]

The Church Peace Union also went on record in 1916
against military training in the schools. When it seemed that
few people were paying any attention, the Union decided to
turn over such pronouncements in the future to "larger and
more representative bodies, such as the World Alliance, and
the Commission on International Justice and Goodwill of
the Federal Council." The Church Peace Union continued
to subsidize both organizations.

One of the Federal Council of Churches' leading lights in
the peace movement was Sidney L. Gulick. He had been sent
to Japan, came back to attend the meeting at Constance, Germany, and returned to the United States and wrote a book
entitled *The Fight for Peace.*[17] This book was widely distributed during the war years, along with the so-called *Peace-
makers Manual,* special Sunday-school lessons on international
peace, and other educational handbooks for use by pastors,
class leaders, Sunday-school teachers, and men's brotherhoods.
The Church Peace Union and its cooperating agencies even
went into the theological seminaries with their propaganda
and offered essay prizes.[18]

[16] See p. 77 of this book.
[17] Fleming H. Revell, New York, 1915.
[18] One of these was won by Dr. Reinhold Niebuhr.

Dr. Macfarland's book shows the role of the Church Peace Union, the World Alliance, and The Federal Council of Churches in promoting a League of Nations. This is exactly the role which the Federal Council was to play during the early days of World War II. Today the Council is taking credit for getting the United States into the United Nations, as we shall see later.

Here is Dr. Macfarland's account:

All this came to the notice of the governmental United States Speakers' Bureau and that agency requested the Church Peace Union to act for the Bureau in its education among the clergy in the churches. This led in December 1917 to a reconsideration of plans and methods, resulting in the initiation of an autonomous educational body. The following report was approved:

Paragraph 1. That the Church Peace Union undertake during the year 1918 to present to conferences of clergymen and other Christian workers, and to the churches of the United States, the various proposals now engaging the attentions of the leading statesmen and thinkers of the world looking towards some "concert" or "League of Nations" which shall insure the judicial settlement of international disputes and adjust a permanent peace.

Paragraph 2. That the Church Peace Union accept the invitation of the Committee on Public Information of the Administration to cooperate with them in educating the people of the United States in the aims of this war, basing our interpretation of those aims on the messages and addresses of the President of the United States to whose declared policy we pledge our support, and that we also offer our services to Colonel Edward M. House in laying before the public the results of the study of his assistants along lines of world organization for a lasting peace.

Paragraph 3. That we accept the invitation of the Committee on Public Information of the Administration to appoint a representative of the Church Peace Union to membership upon its advisory committee.

Paragraph 4. That we appoint a committee of five from our trustees, with power, which shall be so constituted that it can hold frequent meetings, to conduct the campaign outlined above, but which shall act in close cooperation with the Executive Committee.

Paragraph 5. That we approve the request of the League to enforce peace, which with its highly developed organization and eminent members can be of great service, to cooperate with us, and request them to appoint a committee of five to act with the committee appointed by the Church Peace Union.

Paragraph 6. That we welcome the offer of the joint committee of the World Alliance for Promoting International Friendship Through the Churches and the Commission on International Justice and Goodwill of The Federal Council of the Churches of Christ in America to put their machinery in this campaign, especially in conserving the results of the meetings in study groups, in sermons, and in the distribution of literature bearing upon the general subject.

Paragraph 7. That the Church Peace Union appropriate $65,000.00 for this work.[19]

Here we see the church bodies aligning themselves with the power of the Federal government; *they cry for separation of Church and State but will not hesitate to use the power of the State in putting over their particular programs.*

[19] *Pioneers for Peace Through Religion*, pp. 56, 57.

As soon as World War I came to an end, the administration of the Church Peace Union was changed. The Rev. Henry A. Atkinson, whose Communist-front record we have already discussed on page 79, was elected general secretary in December 1918, and the Rev. Frederick Lynch was made educational secretary. At the same time, Dr. Atkinson was recommended to the World Alliance as its executive. Dr. Lynch, a ranking member both of The Federal Council of Churches and of the Church Peace Union, was sent to Paris to attend the Peace Conference, and a cable was sent to President Wilson, also in Paris, wishing him success in establishing the League of Nations. The leaders of The Federal Council of Churches and the Church Peace Union plunged headlong into the task of backing up President Wilson and propagandizing for his League of Nations and his 14 Points throughout the country.

> There was unanimous agreement in the committee that the best thing that the Church Peace Union could do for this coming year was to try to present, in every city in the United States of any considerable size, which may be a center for bringing in clergymen from neighboring towns, the idea of the League of Nations and a World Court, and other features of a constructive peace program that might be considered at the peace conference of the nations.[20]

Dr. Macfarland reports that a letter was sent out to all speakers, during the campaign of the National Committee on the Churches and the Moral Aims of the War, urging them to put major emphasis on the League of Nations. Then he asks the question:

> How far could this body be said to represent the churches?

20 *Ibid.*, p. 68.

Officially, not at all. One can only say that its association with the Federal Council was close, that the membership of the associates was made up of representative church leaders and that they included denominational officials, *that at least tacitly, and in some instances by action, it has the general approval of all concerned.*[21]

Much liaison work was done directly with Col. Edward M. House, President Wilson's personal assistant.

Space does not permit the revelation of all the organizations and individuals through which these politico-pacifist churchmen worked. They were in the halls of government, they were making speeches all over the country before clubs, women's groups, and forums, always propagandizing for the League of Nations.

Dr. Macfarland laments that, although "public opinion" was overwhelmingly on the side of the League of Nations, public opinion was overridden by the United States Senate arbitrarily.

The Council leaders failed to prevent World War I, they failed to persuade the United States to join the League of Nations, but the pacifist leaders of The Federal Council of Churches, the Church Peace Union, and the World Alliance for International Friendship Through the Churches comforted themselves with the thought that the world had been "saved for democracy" and that the League of Nations was actually in existence, through the initiative of the United States.[22]

21 *Ibid.*, p. 70.
22 For the postwar development of the international pacifist organizations, see Appendix 3 of this book.

The social-service movement. Dr. Ward and the Socialistic concept of Christ. Church Association for the Advancement of Labor. Department of Church and Labor. Role of the Methodist Church. Infiltration of Methodist Church by Marxists. Methodist Federation for Social Service. Bishop Oxnam pushes social reform Dr. Walter Rauschenbusch creates "The Kingdom of God" on earth. Brotherhood of the Kingdom. Dr. Rauschenbusch visits the Webbs. He changes the emphases and direction of American Protestantism. Socialism the end, religion the means. Commission on the Church and Social Service in partnership with A.F. of L. Labor conditions investigated countrywide. Dr. Ward disseminates socialism through Sunday schools and missionary education movement. Commission on Church and Country Life. Social service becomes international. Its realm of operation.

COLLECTIVIST PROPAGANDA penetrated American Protestant churches many years before the Bolshevik Revolution in Russia or the organization of the Communist Party in the United States in 1919. In fact, it was flourishing in the churches before the Party members were known as such.

Let us turn to *A Yearbook of the Church and Social Service in the United States*,[1] prepared for the Commission on the Church and Social Service of The Federal Council of the Churches of Christ in America by the Rev. Harry F. Ward. In

[1] Copyright 1916 by the Commission on the Church and Social Service of The Federal Council of Churches and published by the Missionary Education Movement of the U.S. and Canada, New York, 1916.

an introductory note signed by Dr. Ward and dated January 1, 1917, we find the following:

> This yearbook is an attempt to bring together, from various sources, information which may be needed by religious and social workers concerning the social service movement in the churches.
>
> Those who can furnish corrections and additional information are earnestly requested to send them to the office of the Federal Council Commission on the Church and Social Service, 105 E. 22nd Street, New York City.

On page 9 the Rev. Charles S. Macfarland is listed as secretary of this Federal Council Commission. Then follows a list of denominations connected with The Federal Council of Churches which have church social-service organizations. Among them are the Baptist, Congregational, Methodist Episcopal, Presbyterian, Protestant Episcopal, Christian, Disciples of Christ, Friends, German Evangelical, Lutheran Evangelical, Methodist Episcopal (South), Reformed in the U.S., and the United Presbyterian. There is another list of denominations which are identified as being connected with The Federal Council of the Churches of Christ in America but which have no organized social-service agencies.[2]

Dr. Ward's thesis, stated on the first page, is that the social-service movement in the churches goes back to the religion of Israel and that the constructive sociology of the Bible is the "fundamental idea of brotherhood." He says that the prophets were the moving spirits in the working of this idea into the national life; they presented religion in social terms; they were

[2] The Free Baptist, the National Baptist Convention, Seventh Day Baptist, Evangelical Association, Methodist Episcopal African, Methodist Episcopal Zio African, Methodist Episcopal in America (Colored), Methodist Protesta t, Mennonite Moravian, Presbyterian in the U.S.A. (Southern), Reformed in America, Reformed Episcopal, Reformed Presbyterian, United Brethren, United Evangelical, and Welsh Presbyterian.

almost indifferent to its ceremonial side but turned with passionate enthusiasm to moral righteousness as its true domain; they proclaimed a primitive democracy based upon an approximately equal distribution of the land. Dr. Ward says that "when the nation of Israel lost its political self-government and training, apocalyptic dreams of bookish calculations, together with the narrow religious individualism, took the place of the sane political program and the wise historical insight of the great prophets."

Under the subhead "Social Message of Jesus," Dr. Ward says that "the social program and the social hopes of the prophets were fulfilled in Jesus." He says that Jesus' ministry was largely concerned with human needs, and that this central teaching of the Kingdom of God is a *collective* conception involving the whole social life of man. "Christ's whole teaching, like his life, is social," Dr. Ward declares. "Jesus was not a mere social reformer. He has been called the first Socialist." [3] (He is quoting Dr. Peabody and his book *Jesus Christ and the Social Question*.)

Dr. Ward sets the theme for all his later conclusions, namely, that Jesus Christ was not interested in theology or in religious ceremony but was interested primarily in the social needs of mankind. Dr. Ward says that, later on, belief in another world and "sacramental and ritual superstitions drifted in from contemporary heathen society." He says that *doctrine* came from "Greek intellectualism."

In discussing the Reformation movement, Dr. Ward ranks the doctrinal declarations of Luther and John Huss as secondary and makes these men out to be great social reformers first of all. He says that the peasants' rising in 1525 in Germany "embodied the social ideals of the common people." Under the subhead "The Evangelical Revival," Dr. Ward says, quoting from T. C. Hall's book *Social Meaning of Modern*

[3] *A Yearbook of the Church and Social Service in the United States*, p. 15.

Religious Movements in England: the birth of Methodism "became a social factor of first significance." Under the next subhead, "Modern Social Prophets," Dr. Ward says:

> The next step in the social expression of religion was the work of that group, some of whom called themselves Christian Socialists, who prove once again that the wider social outlook is more invariably the condition for the prophetic gift. The men of our own age who have had something of the prophets' vision and power of language and inspiration have nearly all had the social enthusiasm and faith in the reconstructive power of Christianity. Maurice and Kingsley, Ruskin and Carlyle, Lamennais and Mazzini, and Tolstoy were in their measure true seers of God, and they made others see.[4]

In the documentation (see Chapter 9) of testimony given by former members of the Communist Party before Congressional committees concerning the collaboration of certain radical Protestant ministers with these members before they left the Party, this espousal of Socialist teachings on the part of the ministers was to be called "prophetic religion."

Under the subhead "The Missionary Awakening," Dr. Ward concludes that, when missionaries began to go to the heathen lands, they found themselves compelled "to apply the Gospel to social conditions," and "the direct spiritual successors in the English group of modern social prophets were the men who developed the Settlement Movement and the Forward Movement in modern city church work."

Dr. Ward continues: "In the United States the pioneers of Christian social thought to whom a tribute of honor is due are Washington Gladden, Josiah Strong, and Richard T.

4 *Ibid.,* p. 19.

Ely."[5] He says that the Church Association for the Advancement of the Interests of Labor (the C.A.A.I.L.), organized by a few ministers in 1887, was probably the first organization of Social Christianity in this country. The next organization, called the Brotherhood of the Kingdom and formed in 1893, was known as "one of the earliest organizations of Social Christianity in the country. Its early members were all Baptists." The Presbyterian Church in 1903 established the Department of Church and Labor.

Dr. Ward states that the honor of making the first "ringing declaration" in a national convention belongs to the Methodist Episcopal Church, and that since 1892 every General Conference has been memorialized by some minor body pleading for action. The year 1908 seems to be the fateful year, for he says that no fewer than thirteen annual conferences, besides various preachers' meetings, presented memorials. Dr. Ward says:

> The Committee on the State of the Church presented a brave and outspoken report, culminating in a kind of bill of rights for labor, and ending in a splendid summons to all the militant forces of this great church to do their part in the pressing duty of the hour.
>
> Immediately after the Methodist General Conference in December, 1908, The Federal Council of the Churches of Christ in America was organized in Philadelphia, representing and uniting 33 Protestant denominations. This organization marked an epoch in the history of American Protestantism. But no other session created so profound an interest as that devoted to Social Service. The report of the commission was heard with tense feeling, which broke into prolonged and enthusiastic applause at the close. The bill of rights adopted by the

5 *Ibid.*, p. 20.

Methodist Conference was presented with some changes and adopted without the slightest disposition of halting at any point. Nearly every great denominational convention since that time has felt the obligation to make a serious pronouncement on social questions. In several cases the Social Creed of the Federal Council was adopted; for instance, by the Congregational Council in 1910. When any change was made, it was in the direction of increased emphasis.[6]

Note the influence which the Methodist Church had, from the beginning, on the organization of The Federal Council of Churches and on getting the Council to adopt the Methodist Social Creed. Perhaps this explains why, when a speaker comes to a particular city and begins to expose Communists within the churches, Methodist preachers are in the forefront of those who attack the speaker and make vehement denials that communism has penetrated the church in any manner. It will be shown, as we go further into the documentation, that the Methodist Church has been infiltrated by the Marxists more thoroughly than any other major denomination. In recent years the Methodist Church has been put on the defensive as laymen of the church have begun to awaken to the fact that their great church machinery is being used not to teach the great doctrines of the Christian faith or to win men and women to Christ but rather as a Marxian social-action organization.

We leave Dr. Ward's book for a moment. According to the June 22, 1950, issue of *The Christian Advocate,* official monthly publication of the Methodist Church, the Methodist Federation for Social Service was formed in 1907. Dr. Harry F. Ward was one of the five founders. This was just one year before The Federal Council of the Churches of Christ in

6 *Ibid.,* p. 21.

America was founded, which later adopted the creed of the Methodist Federation for Social Action. Dr. Ward was the Methodist Federation's secretary for thirty-five years.

The Federation was given official status in 1912 by the General Conference of the Methodist Church, which declared:

> We recommend that the General Conference recognize the Methodist Federation for Social Service as the executive agency to rally the forces of the church in support of the measures approved in the adoption of this report, and that three bishops be appointed upon the Council of Federation as in the past.

Now, back to Dr. Ward's book, *A Yearbook of the Church and Social Service in the United States:*

> One of the first results of the formation of The Federal Council of the Churches of Christ in America was the organization of a Commission on the Church and Social Service. This has coordinated the work of the various denominations, and in this field there have been taken the most significant steps toward realizing the fundamental unity of Christendom. It is significant that in 1906, when the Congregationalist, The United Brethren and the Methodist Protestant bodies, together comprising over a million members, were on the point of entering into organic union, a creed was adopted in which one of the five articles was wholly devoted to the social duty of the church: "We believe that, according to Christ's law, men of the Christian faith exist for the service of man, not only in holding forth the Word of Life, but in the support of works and institutions of pity and charity, in the maintenance of human freedom, in the deliverance of

all those that are oppressed, in the enforcement of civic justice, in the rebuke of all unrighteousness."[7]

Dr. Ward then goes on to say that the denominational agencies adopted certain methods for disseminating what became known as the "Social Gospel." They produced and circulated printed matter. They conducted information bureaus which suggested reading, sources for sermons and speeches, and workable plans for local community service by churches. And they carried on widespread speaking propaganda, country-wide in its influence, which extended and intensified the influence of the church in many quarters.

An interdenominational alliance of social-service agencies arose, and its Secretarial Council held regular meetings, with the result that literature of one denomination was made available to all, a common body of printed material was developed, methods were standardized, and a joint educational scheme was promoted. Dr. Ward referred to the period of this activity as "seed sowing" and said that broad, concrete results were to be expected from then on.

Dr. Ward makes a very important statement which we will later see corroborated by his pupil, the controversial Bishop G. Bromley Oxnam:

> It may fairly be said that one result of social-service activities in the churches in the past few years *is a changed attitude on the part of many church members concerning the purpose and function both of the church and of Christianity.* A social consciousness and a social conscience have been developed in the churches. Their social will is strengthening and they are determined to make the Gospel real, to carry it to the uttermost conclusion in the social order as in the individual life.[8]

7 *Loc. cit.*
8 *Ibid.*, p. 23.

It is here that Dr. Ward reveals that the primary purpose of the churches, recognized down through the ages as that of preaching that men and women were sinners and needed a Savior, Jesus Christ, and that personal salvation was an individual responsibility which had to be met by the individual in one way or another, was now being replaced with the doctrine of collectivism. Men and women now would be reformed not by individual decision but by the institution of *social* action and *environmental* change. This was making "the Gospel real." *The one great fallacy of this whole theory is that "society" is made up of individuals, and "society" as a whole cannot be changed unless the people who make it up are changed individually. If people are changed individually, "society" will not need changing.*

It is time to turn to a work entitled *Personalities in Social Reform* by Bishop G. Bromley Oxnam.[9] Bishop Oxnam was a pupil of Dr. Harry F. Ward and was employed by him in taking dictation for some of Dr. Ward's books. (We shall go into Dr. Ward's pro-Communist record at length in chapter 9.)

Bishop Oxnam devotes five chapters in this book to what he calls "social reformers." In Chapter One, "The Scholar as Social Reformer," he identifies "the scholar" as the husband-and-wife team of Sidney and Beatrice Webb, the Fabian Socialists of England. He devotes forty-one pages of eulogy to these Socialist patron saints. Chapter Two is entitled "The Minister as Social Reformer." The minister is identified as Walter Rauschenbusch. Chapter Three is entitled "The Administrator as Social Reformer." The administrator is David E. Lilienthal, former head of T.V.A. (who has since changed his philosophy in several respects). Chapter Four is entitled "The Saint as Social Reformer," and, surprisingly enough, the saint turns out to be Mohandas Gandhi of India, who denied the deity of Christ and would not accept Him as his

9 Abingdon-Cokesbury Press, New York and Nashville, 1950.

personal Savior. Chapter Five is entitled "The Missionary as Social Reformer," and the missionary is identified as Albert Schweitzer, an ultramodernist theologian of Germany who denied practically all the major doctrines of Christianity while making a name for himself as an authority on Bach, a philosopher, and a medical doctor.

We are concerned solely with Chapter Two, in which Dr. Oxnam discusses Dr. Walter Rauschenbusch, the minister as social reformer. Dr. Oxnam does not hesitate to show us that Walter Rauschenbusch is not a conservative or orthodox theologian. On page 52 he uses the biblical words "redemption" and "regeneration," but not in the biblical or dictionary sense. He tells us that Dr. Walter Rauschenbusch prayed for a share in the work of "redemption"; that he wrote a book that changed the thinking of American Christianity, and that his teaching, preaching, and writings *summoned the religious forces of the nation for the regeneration not of the individual but "of society."* Here we see the collectivistic thesis of Dr. Ward entering into the picture once more. Dr. Rauschenbusch was a graduate of the University of Rochester and, in 1885, of the Rochester Theological Seminary. Dr. Oxnam says: "He had planned to go to India as a missionary for the American Baptist Mission Society, but his professor in Old Testament and Hebrew questioned his liberal views, and he was rejected." [10]

Dr. Rauschenbusch saw Jesus Christ in the same way that Harry Ward did, not as one who would come to save sinners from their sins but as one who had a "social passion" for society. Dr. Rauschenbusch, however, brought something new into the picture. He knew that, if he identified socialism as such in his preaching and teaching, many people in the church would not accept it and would revolt. So he gave it some window dressing. He entitled his socialism "The Kingdom of

[10] *Personalities in Social Reform,* p. 58.

God" on earth. (In this same manner, Socialist and Communist propagandists in the church, instead of identifying socialism by name, always have dressed it up in religious terminology so that the people who sit in the pews or read their works and who, by and large, do not evaluate what they hear or read, will accept it as being authoritative because a theologian or a minister has said it.)

Dr. Oxnam tells us that Dr. Rauschenbusch was driven back to the Bible and that he reached this conclusion: "The views most men held on wealth were at variance with teachings of the Book. In the New Testament he found the principles that confirmed his passion; they were the principles of Jesus. The Kingdom idea enthralled him." Dr. Rauschenbusch asked the question, did not the Kingdom of God involve getting justice for the working man and would this not be carrying out God's will on earth as it is in Heaven? [11]

Dr. Oxnam says that in 1891 Dr. Rauschenbusch made his third trip to Europe and devoted himself to the study of the teachings of Jesus and of sociology. He quotes Dr. Rauschenbusch as saying, *"I felt a new security in my social impulses,"* and points out his conclusions: that church union (a plug for The Federal Council of Churches and the ecumenical movement as far back as 1891), political reform, reorganization of the industrial system, and international peace were all implicit in the Kingdom of God on earth. Dr. Rauschenbusch included the words "social" and "society" in everything he wrote; Bishop Oxnam said that Dr. Rauschenbusch's literary gift developed and "shook the very foundations of society"; that "Chapter Five of *Christianity and the Social Crisis* reveals Rauschenbusch at his greatest power, save only for the *Prayers of the Social Awakening,*" etc.[12]

Dr. Rauschenbusch wrote: "On the other hand, we differ

11 *Ibid.,* p. 59.
12 *Ibid.,* p. 62.

from many Christian men and women [who] believe that if only men are personally converted, wrong and injustice will gradually disappear from the construction of society. It does not appear so to us." [13]

Dr. Oxnam says: "In 1892, Rauschenbusch and his friends organized the Brotherhood of the Kingdom, one of the first organizations of social Christianity in this country. It sought to give spiritual fellowship to a small group of men who had experienced a social awakening akin to that of the prophets." [14] Their efforts were bent toward the "social aims of Christianity."

Dr. Oxnam has given us the clearest information available on how Marxian Socialists, under the guise of Christianity, took over the machinery of the major Protestant churches in this country, lock, stock, and barrel. We find the following (emphasis added):

> Dr. A. W. Beaven, a former President of the Federal Council of Churches of Christ in America, wrote Mrs. Walter Rauschenbusch in 1937, after there had been time enough to survey the contribution of this professor [Rauschenbusch] to religion and to reform: "It is clear, it seems to me, that the greatest single personal influence on the life and thought of the American Church in the last fifty years was exerted by Walter Rauschenbusch. Probably the three most influential men in American church history upon the thought of the church have been Jonathan Edwards, Horace Bushnell, and Walter Rauschenbusch."

13 *Ibid.*, p. 68.
14 *Loc. cit.* Dr. Oxnam employs a very clever literary device in his writings and lectures. Again and again, in advancing a Socialistic theory, Dr. Oxnam quotes other writers; and when he is called to task for having promoted such a theory, he always can say, "Well, I didn't say it, so-and-so said it." He uses this device throughout *Personalities in Social Reform*.

"The Social Creed of the Churches," adopted first by the Methodist Episcopal Church, is dated 1908. The Federal Council of Churches of Christ in America was founded in 1908, and Walter Rauschenbusch participated in its establishment. Sharpe concludes, "He not only taught history, he made history. *The stream of American Christianity has broken from the 'old bottom' of individualism and has channeled a new course through the social bad lands of poverty, slums, excessive wealth, industrial inequity and economic injustice.* Rauschenbusch changed both the emphases and the direction of American Protestantism." [15]

What right had Dr. Rauschenbusch to change "both the emphases and the direction of American Protestantism"? Who gave him the authority to do so?

We are told on page 75 of Bishop Oxnam's book that Dr. Rauschenbusch visited Sidney and Beatrice Webb, the leaders of Fabian socialism in England, in 1907. The Fabian Socialists had adopted the military tactics of the Roman general Quintus Fabius, who taught that one should not engage the whole enemy at one time in one place but rather should lure him out piece by piece until he is utterly destroyed. Seeing that the British machinery of government could not be captured at once, the Fabians sent their followers into all the major spheres of British society, persuading men and women to accept the Socialist outlook. They finally captured the government when the Socialist Labour Party, under Ramsay MacDonald, defeated the Conservatives. The Labour Party again won out, under Clement Attlee, driving out Winston Churchill's Conservative Party.

"Socialism," says Dr. Rauschenbusch, "is the most solid and militant organization since Calvinism, and it is just as dog-

15 *Ibid.*, pp. 73, 74.

matic."[16] John Calvin, of course, was one of the Reformers who preached Christian faith in no uncertain language. He taught the eternal security of the believer in Christ. Calvin taught that the individual had to have a personal relationship with Christ, as the Bible teaches. And now we have seen how Dr. Walter Rauschenbusch, Dr. Harry F. Ward, and the leaders of the social-action movements in the churches decided to do away with Christian individualism and turn to outright collectivism, using the church as their instrument. In 1893 Dr. Rauschenbusch said: "The only power that can make socialism succeed, if it is established, is religion. It cannot work in an irreligious country."[17] Socialism, then, was his first concern. Religion was only a means toward attaining socialism. And, like all other false prophets who have infiltrated religion through the centuries, he used a "front," or disguise. This disguise, as we have seen, was "The Kingdom of God." The Kingdom was not pictured as a spiritual society into which men and women had to be born as individuals through a personal relationship with Jesus Christ as Savior, but as a collectivist society which would be brought about by slum clearance, eradication of poverty, redistribution of wealth, correction of industrial inequities, and the bringing about of "economic justice."

One of the first commissions brought into being by The Federal Council of the Churches of Christ in America, when the Council was organized in Philadelphia in 1908, was the Commission on the Church and Social Service.[18] Some thirty

16 *Ibid.*, p. 75.
17 *Ibid.*, pp. 76, 77.
18 Dr. Ward says that he was the editor of the first edition of the *Social Creed of the Churches* and that he wrote the edition which was accepted by The Federal Council of the Churches of Christ in America in 1908. He further identifies himself as secretary of the Methodist Federation for Social Service; professor of social service in the School of Theology of Boston University; and associate secretary of the Federal Council's Commission on the Church and Social Service.

denominations and communions, as constituent bodies of the Council, carried out their social-service program through this commission.

The Commission on the Church and Social Service elected the Rev. Charles S. Macfarland as its secretary in the spring of 1911, and its offices were associated with those of the Federal Council. Dr. Macfarland later became the general secretary of the Council. Two later meetings of this Commission on the Church and Social Service were held in November 1911 and December 1912, in Chicago. At that time, six secretaries of social-action committees of various denominations were made associate secretaries of the Federal Council's commission. Among them were the Rev. Henry A. Atkinson, secretary of the Congregational Commission on Social Service, and Dr. Harry F. Ward, secretary of the Methodist Federation for Social Service.

This Commission, from the very beginning, acted as a clearing house for social-action material for the major denominations within The Federal Council of Churches, putting out literature in common and cooperating at every possible point both nationally and locally. Cooperation later was sought with the Industrial and Social Service Departments of the International Committee of the Y.M.C.A., the Industrial Department of the Y.M.C.A., and the Young Peoples Society of Christian Endeavor.

This newly formed Commission of the Federal Council began to work hand-in-glove with the officials of the American Federation of Labor. It even designated a Labor Sunday. It conducted investigations of industrial conditions in various cities of the country, as in South Bethlehem, Pennsylvania; Muscatine, Iowa; sections of Michigan, Colorado, and Massachusetts; and Paterson, New Jersey. With the Federal Council Commission for 1915 are listed a number of names that became well known later on for their support of the Communist-front movement in the United States. One member, *Dr. Harry F. Ward, has been identified under oath by many witnesses before United States Congressional committees as a member of the Communist Party.*

In his *Yearbook of the Church and Social Service in the United States* Dr. Ward states that what was begun in the formation of the Methodist Federation for Social Service in 1908 was officially approved by the General Conference of the Methodist Church in 1912. He says:

> This statement pledges the church to cooperate in a general campaign for church welfare, public health, social purity, organized recreation, industrial safety, a living wage, and international peace; also, in the movements against poverty, overwork, and crime, through civic action to effect all these purposes. It also binds the church unceasingly to labor for the realization of social action, and the Methodist Federation for Social Service is declared to be the executive agency to rally the forces of the church in support of the measures thus approved.
>
> In acceptance of this commission the Federation enlarged its work and put into the field a secretary, the Rev. Harry F. Ward, part of whose time it had previously engaged.[19]

Dr. Ward then relates how he and his colleagues disseminated the word throughout the Methodist Church over a period of years by writing material for Sunday-school lessons and for the Missionary Education Movement. Seminar courses were added to Boston University's School of Theology, a Methodist School. Lectures on labor problems were held in Boston, and a resolution of thanks to the Boston University School of Theology was offered by the I.W.W. (Industrial

[19] *Yearbook,* p. 47.

Workers of the World) and by men of the American Federation of Labor.

Having discussed the work of the individual denominations in the field of social service, Dr. Ward confirms the fact that "local forms of The Federal Council of Churches came into being." Local councils of churches were organized, as in Dallas, Texas; Louisville, Kentucky; and Atlanta, Georgia. The Council promulgated the new Social Gospel through these lower echelons.

The Federal Council of Churches was not content with reaching the big cities. At its annual meeting in December 1914 the Executive Committee of the Council created a new commission to direct its rural work. On December 20 the Commission on Church and Country Life was formed, and Ohio was picked as the experimental ground for penetrating the small country churches.

Dr. Ward tells us that the social-service program expanded also into the international field. He says: "The Federal Council has a separate organized Commission on Peace and Arbitration of great influence, which has been instrumental in bringing about the organization of the Church Peace Union and the World Alliance of the Churches." [20] The Federal Council leadership played a primary role in the establishment of the Church Peace Union, which was actually the organic beginning of what was later to be known as The World Council of Churches. "The spirit of the Social Gospel in connection with foreign mission work," writes Dr. Ward, "had become in many respects more influential than the work of the churches at home."

Dr. Ward urged at the time that the various denominational secretaries be ready, whenever possible, to cooperate in campaigns of "Social Service Evangelism," under the auspices of The Federal Council of Churches. The churches were urged

[20] *Ibid.*, p. 89.

to work for the following: pure water supply, food inspection in public markets, legislation for mortuary and vital statistics, legislation for tenement buildings and sanitary codes, municipal or mission lodgings, workhouse and state farms, playgrounds and comfort stations, social centers and public schools, working men's compensation laws, laws limiting working hours for women, and enforcement of labor laws. The churches also were counseled to investigate the social cost of saloons and the cost of living; to help determine minimum-wage standards; to discourage Sunday work and demand one day's rest in seven, and to improve industrial education in the public schools.

In short, the church was to turn itself into a social-service enterprise that would have little resemblance to the church which Christ founded to spread the gospel of the redemption of men's souls.

9

COLLABORATORS
WITH
COMMUNISM

Dr. Atkinson, Dr. Ward, Dr. Taylor, the Rev. Webber, the Rev. McMichael all work together. *The Protestant*. People's Institute of Applied Religion. Testimony on Dr. Ward's furtherance of communism. Dr. Ward works with Browder, Jerome, and Manning Johnson. Benjamin Gitlow testifies on Dr. Ward's work with Communists and collaborators. Dr. Ward's pro-Red speeches in China. American League Against War and Fascism, headed by Dr. Ward, is key to Communist infiltration of the churches. Dr. Ward professor of Christian Ethics at Union Theological Seminary for twenty-five years. Dr. Ward praised by Lamont and Browder. Manning Johnson testifies on how the Communist Party recruits clergymen. New York's Lusk Committee finds Union Theological Seminary and St. Stephen's College to be centers of revolutionary Socialistic teaching. Dr. Ward chairman of Civil Liberties Union. Dr. Ward assigns Communist students to Party work. Bishop Oxnam's record. He attacks Congressional investigations. He pays tribute to Dr. Ward. Miss Winifred Chappell.

The Commission on the Church and Social Service, of which the Rev. Charles S. Macfarland was secretary, was to become one of the most controversial commissions of the entire Federal Council of Churches setup. Through this commission came many pro-Socialist and pro-Communist pronouncements.

The commission organized a Secretarial Council consisting of one representative from each of the denominational social-action organizations. Two of the three most prominent representatives were the Rev. Henry A. Atkinson, secretary of the

Congregational Brotherhood, and the Rev. Harry F. Ward. Both men have been identified under oath before Congressional committees by former top members of the Communist Party as collaborators with the Communist conspiracy.

The third prominent member is the Rev. Alva W. Taylor of Nashville, Tenn. In the April 1946 issue of the *Social Action Bulletin* of the Communist-front Methodist Federation for Social Action, he has a lead article entitled "Utopia of Jesus." This article follows the Communist Party line. He signed the letter of the American Council on Soviet Relations, a Communist front, calling upon the President to declare war on Finland as demanded by the Soviet Union and the Communist Party. He signed a Communist appeal in 1943 calling for a dissolution of the Dies Committee. He was an editorial adviser of *The Protestant,* a magazine notorious for serving as an instrument for the Communist infiltration of religion. He was a sponsor of the People's Institute of Applied Religion, a Communist organization, together with many well-known Communist leaders and with such Methodist Federation stalwarts as the Rev. Charles C. Webber, the Rev. Jack R. McMichael, and Dr. Harry F. Ward. The People's Institute received financial support from a foundation identified as Communistic—the Sound View Foundation. All the officials of the Sound View Foundation were Communist Party members, according to testimony given by Mr. Benjamin Gitlow, a member of the American Communist Party in 1919. Dr. Taylor also signed an appeal to Governor Dewey to grant a pardon to a Communist professor convicted of perjury and sent to prison. In addition, Dr. Taylor—a professor of Christian Social Ethics at Vanderbilt University—served as the secretary-treasurer of the Communist-dominated Southern Conference for Human Welfare.

In his article in the Methodist Federation's *Social Action Bulletin,* according to testimony given by Mr. Gitlow before the Committee on Un-American Activities of the United States House of Representatives, meeting in New York in July 1953,

> Professor Taylor advocates changing the church into an instrument primarily "organized to promote social reform." He insists that the church be more than a school for Christian living by converting it into "the advance guard of a new and untried idea."
>
> The Communists, too, consider themselves "the advance guard of revolution of new and untried ideas." Professor Taylor advocates turning the church into a political organization, which "would make politics a means of ministry."

What Mr. Taylor says in this article, written in 1946, is wholly in keeping with the objectives of the social gospelers as expounded by Dr. Harry F. Ward, whose "Social Creed" was adopted first by the Methodist Episcopal Church in 1908 and in the same year by The Federal Council of Churches at its formation.

Leaders of The Federal Council of Churches have tried in recent years to deny that Dr. Ward had anything to do with the Council. Now, with all due respect to the personal characters of these men, it can be safely said that either they are deliberately telling an untruth or they are woefully ignorant of the facts as recorded in the history of their own movement. *Dr. Harry F. Ward has had tremendous influence on the Federal and National Councils of Churches and on hundreds of young men studying for the ministry under his direction in Union Theological Seminary and in the Boston School of Theology.* For this reason we are now going to devote a considerable portion of our documentation to Dr. Ward's record.

As we have seen, Dr. Harry F. Ward was associate secretary of the Federal Council Commission on the Church and Social

Service and secretary of the Methodist Federation for Social Service. In these connections, we shall turn to a series of three volumes entitled "Part Six, Seven, and Eight of Investigation of Communist Activities in the New York City Area, Hearing Before the Committee on Un-American Activities, House of Representatives, 83rd Congress, First Session, July 7 and 8, and July 13 and 14, 1953." Testimony was given at this hearing under oath by various witnesses. The hearing was in executive, or closed, session, and the testimony was not at first made available to the public. But when some of the leaders of The National Council and The World Council of Churches began to attack the Congressional committee and emphatically declared that communism had not penetrated the ranks of the clergy, the committee decided to release the entire testimony to the American public and let it judge for itself.

We turn to page 2266 and read the testimony of Mr. Manning Johnson, formerly a top member of the Communist Party. The questions are asked by Robert Kunzig, chief counsel for the committee. (Emphasis throughout is added.)

Mr. KUNZIG: Mr. Johnson, before we leave this point I note that the name Harry Ward has appeared in so many of these various organizations and groups. It seems as if there is almost an interlacing tie-up of one to the other and, not in any one particular religious sect or denomination, but through various sects and denominations. Have you any comment to make on this situation?

Mr. JOHNSON: Yes, I have. *Dr. Harry F. Ward, for many years, has been the chief architect for Communist infiltration and subversion in the religious field.*

Mr. CLARDY (Rep. KIT CLARDY, MICH.): That, you think, explains why we find his name turning up practically in all the Communist-front or Communist organizations.

Mr. JOHNSON: Absolutely correct.

Now let us turn back to page 2169 of Mr. Johnson's testimony.

Mr. KUNZIG: Mr. Johnson, who was the chairman of this American League Against War and Fascism?

Mr. JOHNSON: The Rev. Harry F. Ward.

Mr. KUNZIG: Do you know him personally?

Mr. JOHNSON: Yes, I did.

Mr. KUNZIG: When you were a member of the Communist Party, did you know him as a member of the Communist Party?

Mr. JOHNSON: *Yes, he was a member of the Communist Party while I was a member.*

Mr. KUNZIG: Did you meet with him as such?

Mr. JOHNSON: Yes, I did.

Mr. KUNZIG: Would you characterize him as a prominent member of the Communist Party?

Mr. JOHNSON: I would say that *he is the Red Dean of the Communist Party in the religious field.*

On page 2212 of Mr. Johnson's testimony we find the following:

Mr. JOHNSON: Earl Browder and Dr. Harry F. Ward both belonged to the same party and the same Communist Party fraction within the American League Against War and Fascism.

Our next pertinent testimony is found on page 2138. The witness is Mr. Leonard Patterson, also a former leader of the Communist Party.

Mr. KUNZIG: What positions did you hold in the Communist Party, itself, Mr. Patterson?

Mr. PATTERSON: I was a member of the District Committee and District Bureau of the Communist Party of the Philadelphia District in the year 1931. At the same time I was District Organizer of the Young Communist League. I was a member of the Section Committee of the Communist Party of Baltimore in 1934, 1935; and in the latter part of 1935 to 1937, the time I went out of the Communist Party, I was a member of the District Committee of the Philadelphia Communist Party. I also held a position as a member of the Central Committee of the Negro Commission of the Communist Party in 1933, part of 1934, and other positions I held in the Party.

Mr. SCHERER (Rep. GORDON SCHERER, OHIO): Let me ask: *did you ever know in your work in the Communist Party a Rev. Harry F. Ward?*

Mr. PATTERSON: *Yes.*

Mr. SCHERER: Did you know him well?

Mr. PATTERSON: *Yes, I worked with him.*

Mr. KUNZIG: Would you explain to the Committee just how you worked with him and where?

Mr. PATTERSON: In New York City, I believe, in 1933 or early 1934—I believe it was 1933—Dr. Ward, Earl Browder, myself, Victor Jerome, Manning Johnson, and other top leading members of the Communist Party were assigned to a top fraction. In other words, a top policymaking body of the Communist Party—by the Central Committee of the Communist Party to prepare—

Mr. SCHERER: You say Dr. Ward was a member of that fraction?

Mr. PATTERSON: I said that—to prepare for a conference to sponsor a broader conference against war and fascism to be held later on in the year 1933—I believe the year is

1933 or 1934. This top policy body met at 799 Broadway, where many of the Party front organizations met at that time, and again there was a conference held in Chicago. I believe that was the Second Congress Against War and Fascism. . . . I believe that was in 1935, I might be a little wrong in the date, but research will show, and there we also had a meeting of the fraction while the Congress was there and I was together with Dr. Ward in the top fraction meeting in Chicago also.

Mr. KUNZIG: This is a top fraction meeting of the Communist Party?

Mr. PATTERSON: Yes; a meeting where only selected top leading Communist Party members could attend. It was a policymaking body.

Mr. KUNZIG: Rev. Harry F. Ward was present?

Mr. PATTERSON: *He was present and an active member of that body.*

Mr. KUNZIG: And therefore you know Rev. Harry F. Ward as a member of the Communist Party, as a very important member of the Communist Party?

Mr. PATTERSON: Yes.

Mr. SCHERER: Was he still a member of the Party at the time you left the Party?

Mr. PATTERSON: To my knowledge, yes, he was still active in the Communist Party front organizations like the National Negro Congress. In fact, I believe in 1935 or 1936 they had a meeting of the congress in Philadelphia, and he was present there and also participated in Communist Party fractions.

Mr. SCHERER: As far as you know, at the time you left the Party, he was still a member of the Party?

Mr. PATTERSON: Yes.

Now we shall turn to page 2057 of this record. The testimony is given by Joseph Zack Kornfeder, a former Communist Party leader and a graduate of the Lenin School of Political Warfare in Moscow, the most advanced training school of the Communist conspiracy.

> Mr. KUNZIG: Mr. Kornfeder, you testified briefly regarding your knowledge of what the Communists did to religious groups and religious denominations while you were present at Moscow attending the Lenin School. You have also testified as to the tactics applied in Moscow to destroy the church from the outside and from the inside. You have also testified that in the United States two organizations, the Methodist Federation for Social Action and the People's Institute of Applied Religion, practiced the tactics which you acquired knowledge of in Moscow in order to destroy religion in the United States. You have also testified that you have personal knowledge of the value of the Rev. Harry F. Ward in the Communist attempt to infiltrate religion in the United States. I think that is all I have.
>
> Mr. SCHERER: Does the name of Harry F. Ward and other early leaders in the antireligious movement as related to the Communist program appear in the social-action movements of the various denominations in the United States?
>
> Mr. KORNFEDER: Yes, it does; it also appears—Harry Ward's name—in some of the speeches in a laudatory manner of Earl Browder . . . he is, really, and the stuff he writes indicates that he is, the theoretical and political leader of this method of operation.

Earl Browder was the head of the Communist Party in the United States at that time.

Next, we turn to pages 2075–2077 for the testimony under

oath of Mr. Benjamin Gitlow, a charter member of the Communist Party in the United States in 1919 and its candidate for the vice presidency of the United States in 1924.

Mr. GITLOW: The Russian Communists were the first to exploit ministers of the United States and, through them, the church organizations, for the purpose of spreading propaganda in favor of Communist Russia, and for the building up of a pro-Soviet sentiment among church people in America and among Americans generally.

I will, if I may, make mention of a few of the prominent American religious leaders who were used for that purpose in the early 1920's: Dr. Kirby Page, Dr. Sherwood Eddy, Jerome Davis, *Dr. Harry F. Ward,* the Rev. Albert Rhys Williams, and others. . . .

Mr. KUNZIG: Did the Communist Party of the United States in the early 1920's enlist the support of church people for its campaigns and in support of the Communist Party, its activities in Soviet Russia?

Mr. GITLOW: It certainly did, for the number of ministers that actively supported the Communist Party in those days, though not as large as it is today, was, nevertheless, impressive. The outstanding clergymen among them were *Dr. Harry F. Ward,* Bishop William Montgomery Brown, Jerome Davis, William B. Spofford, and Albert Rhys Williams. . . .

To be specific: before the creation of the front organizations, the ministers who carried out the instructions of the Communist Party or collaborated with it were limited in numbers.

The outstanding ones among them were, besides *Dr. Harry Ward,* Dr. William B. Spofford, Jerome Davis, Rev. Tucker P. Smith,[1] Rev. Irwin St. John Tucker,

1 Tucker P. Smith was not a minister.—Author

Rabbi Judah L. Magnes, the Rev. John Haynes Holmes, Rev. Sydney Strong, Rabbi Stephen S. Wise.

Mr. KUNZIG: Do you mean to say that Dr. Ward engaged in Communist propaganda when he was in China in 1925?

Mr. GITLOW: Certainly. I would like to read a few excerpts from a series of lectures he delivered in China at that time, if I may.

Mr. KUNZIG: You may.

Mr. Gitlow then read a number of Dr. Ward's pro-Communist speeches delivered in China in 1925.[2]

Mr. GITLOW: All the lectures delivered in China by Dr. Ward had for their main purpose the bolstering up of the position of the Communist movement in China and winning support of the Chinese intellectuals and Christians in China for the Chinese Communist Movement and for Soviet Russia.

Page 2082:

Mr. KUNZIG: Do you attach any special significance to Dr. Ward's lectures in China?

Mr. GITLOW: I only presented Ward's lectures delivered in China in 1925 because they were discussed at length in Moscow and at the Comintern. The Comintern leaders were of the opinion that clergymen, with Dr. Ward's point of view, using the cloak of religion, could render service of inestimable value to the Communist cause in China and to Soviet interests. Besides, the missions and church institutions of China could be used, in the opinion of the Comintern, to cover up Communist espionage activity in China. Clergymen, who served in various capaci-

2 See Appendix of this book.

ties in China, and who deliberately followed the Communist Party line or who were duped into following it, formed an important branch of the conspiracy to turn China over to the Communists. They not only gave assistance to the Communists in China but *they also carried on effective propaganda in the United States to influence public opinion for their point of view.* Later in my testimony I will show how the Methodist Federation for Social Action was tied into the Communist conspiracy.

The lectures which Dr. Ward made in China date back to 1925, beginning just after he had been to Moscow. Preparation for the fall of China to the Communists was being made in the early 1920's, when the Kremlin's Colonial School for training leaders in the take-over of other countries was functioning fully, although China was not won by the Communists until late 1949. The Communist program is a long-range one. It may take many years to implement its tactics and strategy, but its objectives never change.

This clergyman, Dr. Harry F. Ward, not only had a powerful influence in the American churches, through The Federal Council of Churches, softening up his own country with Communist propaganda, but he went overseas to help to prepare China, with its 500 million souls, for eventual capture by communism. Men in the pulpit will not tell their people these things, and the people do not even know that testimony upon them is available.

We continue the testimony from pages 2084 and 2085 of the record.

> Mr. KUNZIG: What kind of an organization was the Methodist Federation for Social Action, and how did it differ from a Communist-front organization?
>
> Mr. GITLOW: The Methodist Federation for Social Ac-

tion, originally called the Methodist Federation for Social Service, was first organized by a group of Socialist, Marxist clergymen of the Methodist church headed by Dr. Harry F. Ward. Dr. Ward was the organizer, for almost a lifetime its secretary and actual leader. He at all times set its ideological and political pattern. Its objective was to transform the Methodist Church and Christianity into an instrument for the achievement of socialism. It was established in 1907, 12 years before the organization of the Communist Party in the United States in 1919. The outbreak of the Bolshevik Revolution in Russia in November 1917 had a tremendous effect upon the Socialist ministers of this organization and especially upon Dr. Ward. When the Communist Party was organized in 1919, Dr. Ward was already a convinced Communist with a few insignificant minor reservations. By 1920 he was already, though not yet a member of the Communist Party, cooperating and collaborating with the Communist Party. This collaboration of Dr. Ward with the Communist Party was reflected in the expressions and activities of the Methodist Federation for Social Action. The inner hard core of the Methodist Federation consisted, up to the time Jack R. McMichael, a member and leader of the Young Communist League, was elected its executive secretary, after Dr. Ward had relinquished his post, of a Communist cell headed by Ward, which functioned under the direction of the Communist Party.

Mr. KUNZIG: What were the connections between the Methodist Federation for Social Action and the two Communist-front organizations you mentioned that played such an important role in the Communist infiltration of religion?

Mr. GITLOW: In the first place the Methodist Federation for Social Action was affiliated with and collaborated more closely with the American League Against War and Fascism, and the American League for Peace and Democracy, and the American Youth Congress. It was no accident that Dr. Ward, the organizer and leader of the Methodist Federation, became the chairman, and served in that capacity for many years, of both the American League Against War and Fascism and the American League for Peace and Democracy. Rev. Jack McMichael was the chairman for many years of the American Youth Congress.

Mr. KUNZIG: Did Dr. Ward use his position as chairman of the American League Against War and Fascism to aid the Communist conspiracy for the infiltration of the churches?

Mr. GITLOW: He did.

Page 2092:

Mr. KUNZIG: Did the Communists infiltrate the Methodist Church?

Mr. GITLOW: In the infiltration of the Methodist Church, the Communists were highly successful. *To detail the extent of the Communist infiltration of the Methodist Church, the people who served the Communists in the church consciously and those who were its stooges would take several hundred pages of testimony.*

Mr. KUNZIG: Who were the principal individuals involved in the Communist infiltration of the Methodist Church?

Mr. GITLOW: The principal individuals involved in the Communist conspiracy to subvert the Methodist Church for Communist purposes are: *Dr. Harry F. Ward,* Rev. Jack R. McMichael, Rev. Charles C. Webber, Rev. Alson

J. Smith, Dr. Willard Uphaus, Margaret Forsyth, Rev. Lee H. Ball. . . .

Mr. KUNZIG: What organization, in your opinion, played a most important part in the Communist infiltration of religion?

Mr. GITLOW: In my opinion the Methodist Federation for Social Action. *First, it set the pattern for setting up similar organizations in the other Protestant denominations.* It, in fact, *assumed the leadership of the so-called social action movement in the Christian churches,* and greatly influenced their ideas and the programs they adopted and their activities. It maintained the closest relations with all of them and often collaborated with them. In addition, the Methodist Federation for Social Action officially affiliated with some of the most important Communist-front organizations. Those with which the Methodist Federation for Social Action did not officially affiliate, the organization usually endorsed, sponsored or supported through its *Social Questions Bulletin* or through the recognized leaders of the federation.

We turn to page 2170, for further testimony from Mr. Manning Johnson. Mr. Kunzig is asking Mr. Johnson about the methods which the Communist leaders in the United States used to win over church people.

Mr. JOHNSON: I would first like to read to you what William Z. Foster has to say on this matter:

"Communists must ever be keen to cultivate the democratic spirit of mutual tolerance among the religious sects and the people's mass organization. A still greater lesson for us to learn, however, is how to work freely with religious strata for the accomplishment of democratic mass objectives, while at the same time carrying on our basic Marxist-Leninist educational work.

"A very serious mistake of the American left wing during many years, and one it would not have made had it understood Marx and Lenin, has been its attempt arbitrarily to wave aside religious sentiments among the masses. Reactionary forces have already known how to take advantage of this shortsighted sectarian error by instigating the religious masses against the left wing. In recent years, however, the Communist Party, with its policy of 'the outstretched hand,' has done much to overcome the harmful left-wing narrowness of former years and to develop a more healthy cooperation with the religious masses of the people in building [a] democratic front."

Continuing along this line, the Communist leaders instructed us in the use of deceit in dealing with religious elements.

Mr. KUNZIG: Was deceit a major policy of Communist propaganda and activity?

Mr. JOHNSON: Yes, it was. They made fine gestures and honeyed words to the church people which could be well likened unto the song of the fabled sea nymphs luring millions to moral decay, spiritual death, and spiritual slavery. An illustration of this treachery, I might point out, is smiling, sneaky Earl Browder, for example, who was vice chairman of the American League Against War and Fascism, greeting and praising ministers and other church workers participating with him in the united-front, antiwar activities, while secretly harboring in his heart only contempt for them and for the religion they represented.

Now, in order to train others in the use of such deceit, he wrote, and I quote from *What Is Communism?*, 1936:

"It is true that we have learned to be much more careful about the quality of our mass work in this field We take pains not to offend any religious belief. We don't want to close the minds of religious people to what we have to tell them about capitalism, because of some remark or action offensive to their religion. We can well say that the cessation of ineffective, rude, and vulgar attacks on religion is a positive improvement in our work."

The major organizational form of the united front in which the churches were involved was the American League Against War and Fascism, which has been headed by the Reverend Harry F. Ward. That organization was the key Communist Party front. There was no other Communist Party front in all of the solar system of organizations of the Communist Party that involved so many ministers, churches, and religious organizations. In fact, this organization was the key to the infiltration of the church, and as a result of the successful infiltration and penetration they were able to involve these ministers in every other Communist front through the years, even down to the present time.

Page 2177:

Mr. KUNZIG: Mr. Johnson, how do you account for the large number of clergymen in religious organizations involved in this American League Against War and Fascism?

Mr. JOHNSON: The majority of the ministers in the American League Against War and Fascism were involved by Harry F. Ward, and the organization which he was connected with, known as the Methodist Federation for Social Action; also, the People's Institute of Applied Religion, and other Communist-front organizations operating in the religious world. The Methodist Federation for Social Service later became the Methodist Federation for Social Action. This program was widely circulated throughout church organizations.

Pages 2201 and 2202:

Mr. KUNZIG: Mr. Johnson, could you give us further detailed testimony about the Methodist Federation for Social Service which, I understand, later changed its name to the Methodist Federation for Social Action?

Mr. JOHNSON: The Methodist Federation for Social Service or the Methodist Federation for Social Action, headed by the Rev. Harry F. Ward, whom I have already identified as a Party member, was invaluable to the Communist Party in its united-front organizations campaign. It was invaluable because through it the Party was able to get contacts with thousands of ministers all over the country. . . .

I might add that quite a few ministers, for example, participated in the united front known as the American League Against War and Fascism, and later called the American League for Peace and Democracy, in which many ministers were involved. In fact, they were so deeply involved through Harry F. Ward that they became the spokesmen, the advocates, the builders, and the leaders of this most important Communist front that engaged in everything from simple assault on a government to espionage, sabotage and the overthrow of the Government of the United States.

On page 2228 of this testimony is a reproduction of an article in the *Daily Worker* of Thursday, May 7, 1953. This was received in evidence by the committee as Manning Johnson Exhibit No. 21. It reads:

DR. HARRY F. WARD'S ACHIEVEMENTS RECOUNTED AT DINNER IN HIS HONOR
(By David Platt)

Dr. Harry F. Ward, one of America's noblemen, who will soon reach his 80th birthday, was guest of honor at a dinner at the Hotel McAlpin the other night. The affair was sponsored by *New World Review*, a progressive monthly devoted to circulating the truth about the Socialist and People's Democracies abroad.

The magazine brought out several hundred friends and former students of Dr. Ward, and some of those who knew him well, like Rev. Jack McMichael, of the Methodist Federation for Social Action; Corliss Lamont; Paul Robeson; Frederick Field; and Jessica Smith, editor of *New World Review*, told the others of how Dr. Ward's teachings enriched them personally and how his tremendous work for brotherhood, peace, and justice has influenced the nation as a whole.

"His influence on the churches of this country is incalculable," said Rev. McMichael, one of Dr. Ward's former students at Union Theological Seminary, in his stirring account of the life of this "rare scholar and man of action."

When you see ministers taking a courageous stand on civil liberties and peace, it is because of the inspiration of Dr. Ward's work. . . .

Other speakers noted the enormous amount of activity that Dr. Ward has been involved in during the past half century.

He is the author of 15 books since 1913 and has a new one coming out soon.

He was for years chairman of the American League Against War and Fascism and the American League for Peace and Democracy.

He was general secretary of the Methodist Federation of Social Service from 1911 to 1944.

He was professor of Christian Ethics at Union Theological Seminary for 25 years and chairman of American Civil Liberties Union from 1920 to 1940. . . .

Jessica Smith pointed out a few more things about Dr. Ward, such as his activity in the British labor movement as far back as 1889. He knew the British labor leader Tom Mann, she said, and was himself a worker when he came to America as a young lad of 17.

He was a rancher and a teamster and worked with Sidney Hillman in the great garment strike that brought about the birth of the Amalgamated Clothing Workers Union.

He knew William Z. Foster and Eugene Debs.

He studied the works of Marx and Engels and learned what was the basis of the thinking of these Socialist giants.

He went to the Soviet Union in 1924, and in 1931 spent a whole year there studying the incentives of socialism, out of which came his book *In Place of Profit.*

How did Dr. Ward find time to do all the things he did? The answer, said Corliss Lamont, is to be found in a poem by Alfred Tennyson, "His strength was as the strength of ten because his heart is pure!"

The entire audience broke into applause when Dr. Ward came to the mike. [He said:]

"It is war that is destroying the Bill of Rights and undermining the Constitution. War is bringing fascism to our doorstep. War is submerging peace. War is taking money needed for education and health and subverting the social well-being of the whole Nation. These are the things we must make the people see. Let that be our answer to the Department of Justice." (Tremendous applause!)

Page 2229:

Mr. JOHNSON: Now, I would also like to quote from a pamphlet entitled "Socialism—What's in It for You?" by A. B. Magil, New Century Publishers (an official publishing house of the Communist Party in the U.S.A.). A. B. Magil has for years been a national leader of the Communist Party in the United States.

Now, Magil in this pamphlet states the following, and I quote:

"There are religious people who, far from considering socialism a menace, see in it the fulfillment of the ethical principles of their faith. It is this that has attracted to socialism distinguished clergymen like the Dean of Canterbury, Dr. Harry F. Ward, Professor emeritus of Christian Ethics at Union Theological Seminary, and the Reverend Eliot White, formerly of the Grace Episcopal Church of New York."

The next quote deals with Harry F. Ward and is taken from a pamphlet written by Earl Browder in 1936 and called "Democracy or Fascism?" (Workers Library Publishers). This pamphlet is made up from the report of Earl Browder to the ninth national convention of the Communist Party in 1936. I was present at the ninth national convention of the Communist Party in New York City held at Manhattan Center on 34th Street when this report was made. I was a delegate, and it was at this convention I was elected to membership on the national committee.

In the report Browder mentioned the splendid work of Dr. Harry F. Ward as one of the finer types of comrades or Party members. He stated that

"It is impossible to speak of the American League and its work without noting the outstanding contribution of its tireless and devoted chairman, Dr. Harry F. Ward."

Mr. CLARDY: By American League, of course, you mean the American League Against War and Fascism?

Mr. JOHNSON: Yes, the American League Against War and Fascism. I continue:

"Such selflessness and consistent service to a progressive cause as Dr. Ward has given *will always receive the unstinted recognition and support of the Communist Party.*"

Mr. CLARDY: You have of your own knowledge placed Dr. Ward in the Party, and you have so testified repeatedly before us. Now, what you have been giving us is some documentary confirmation of precisely what you, yourself, have testified to.

Mr. JOHNSON: That is correct.

Concluding this portion of the testimony given to the Congressional committee, we turn to page 2278 and read the very pertinent summary of testimony given by Mr. Manning Johnson:

Mr. KUNZIG: At the conclusion of your testimony here, Mr. Johnson, could you give us a summary of the overall manner in which the Communists have attempted to infiltrate and poison the religious organizations of America wherever possible?

Mr. JOHNSON: Once the tactic of infiltrating religious organizations was set by the Kremlin, the actual mechanics of implementing the "new line" was a question of following the general experiences of the living church movement in Russia, where the Communists discovered that the destruction of religion could proceed much faster through infiltration of the church by Communist agents operating within the church itself.

The Communist leadership in the United States realized that the infiltration tactic in this country would have to adapt itself to American conditions and the religious make-up peculiar to this country. In the earliest stages it was determined that with only small forces available it would be necessary to *concentrate Communist agents in the seminaries and divinity schools.* The practical conclusion drawn by the Red leaders was that *these institutions would make it possible for a small Communist minority to influence the ideology of future clergymen in the paths most conducive to Communist purposes.*

In general, the idea was to divert the emphasis of clerical thinking from the *spiritual* to the *material* and *political*—by political, of course, is meant politics based on the Communist doctrine of conquest of power. Instead of emphasis towards the spiritual and matters of the soul, the new and heavy emphasis was to deal with those matters which, in the main, led toward the Communist program of "immediate demands." These social demands, of course, were of such a nature that to fight for them would tend to weaken our present society and prepare it for final conquest by Communist forces.

The Communists had some small forces in the seminaries and under the leadership of Harry F. Ward. These were quickly augmented by additional recruits and siphoned into the divinity institutions by manipulations of Communist cells in the seminaries. This infiltration into seminaries was expedited by the use of considerable forces the Communists had in educational institutions which were eligible for hire by divinity organizations.

The plan was *to make the seminaries the neck of a funnel through which thousands of potential clergymen would issue forth, carrying with them, in varying degrees, an ideology and slant which would aid in neutralizing the anti-Communist character of the church and also to use the clergy to spearhead important Communist projects.*

This policy was successful beyond even Communist expectations. The combination of Communist clergymen, clergymen with a pro-Communist ideology, plus thousands of clergymen who were sold the principle of considering Communist causes as progressive, within 20 years furnished the Soviet apparatus with a machine which was used as a religious cover for the overall Communist operation ranging from immediate demands to actually furnishing aid in espionage and outright treason.

The Communists have an advantage in religious organizations due to the fact that their forces within religious groups are well organized as a totalitarian group which, operating as a highly mobile force, works unceasingly toward a premeditated program. This gives this destructive element a great tactical advantage over all others in the religious organizations who deal with religion as individuals, operating ethics on the basis of an individual conscience before God.

In the early 1930's the Communists instructed thousands of their members to rejoin their ancestral religious groups and to operate in cells designed to take control of churches for Communist purposes. This method was not only propounded, but was executed with great success among large elements of American church life. Communists operating a double-pronged infiltration, both through elements of Communist-controlled clergy and Communist-controlled laymen, managed to pervert and weaken entire strata of religious life in the United States.

Communists in churches and other religious organizations were instructed to *utilize the age-old tradition of the sanctity of the church as a cover for their own dastardly deeds.* Through Reds in religion, we have a true, living example of the old saying: "The Devil doth quote the Scripture."

The Communists learned that the clergymen under their control served as a useful "respectable face" for most of their front activities. In this way the name of religion was used to spearhead the odious plots hatched by the agents of anti-religious Soviet communism.

Communist strategists counted the effectiveness of their forces not so much on numbers alone, but on the importance of *individuals loyal to communism in key spots* where a small group can influence large numbers and create havoc by controlling a sensitive spot. Thus, one professor of divinity, lecturing to future clergymen, who in turn will preach to thousands of churchgoers, is, in the long run, more dangerous than 20 Red preachers, singing the praises of communism from the pulpit.

The same can also be said of a Communist agent operating an important position in a *church publication* which reaches large multitudes of churchgoing public. One practical effect of Red influence in church publications is to tip off scores of pro-Soviet clergymen, who are only too glad to receive sermon material through the medium of a church publication.

The large backlog which the Communists have in the *writing and journalistic field* makes it easy for them to infiltrate religious publications and organize new publications representing the Communist slant in church circles.

It is an axiom in Communist organization strategy that if an infiltrated body has 1 per cent Communist Party members and 9 per cent Communist Party sympathizers, with well-rehearsed plans of action, they can effectively control the remaining 90 per cent who act and think on an individual basis. In the large sections of the religious field, due to the ideological poison which has been filtered in by Communists and pro-Communists through seminaries, the backlog of sympathizers and mental prisoners of

Socialistic ideology is greater than the 10 per cent necessary for effective control.

In 1919 the New York State Joint Legislative Committee to Investigate Seditious Activities within the state was set up. This committee was headed by state Senator Clayton R. Lusk. It produced a monumental work of four volumes of over 1,000 pages each, giving evidence of the infiltration of subversive forces within the State of New York. This committee report was published on April 24, 1920. On the subject of Communist infiltration, Part One has this to say:

There are two dangerous centers of Revolutionary Socialist teaching of a university type in ecclesiastical institutions. One is the Union Theological Seminary of New York, where Christian Ethics are taught by Dr. Harry F. Ward; the other is St. Stephen's College at Annandale, N.Y., where the president is the Rev. Iddings Bell, and the professor of economics the Socialist, Dr. Edwards. . . .

Dr. Ward is the author of *The New Social Order,* in which he shows a decided sympathy for Socialist social forms and is friendly to Bolshevism in Russia. He also wrote *The Labor Movement,* which contained addresses delivered before the Boston School of Theology, when he was professor of social science at that institution. He expressed in it approval of the I.W.W. [Industrial Workers of the World]. It is reported in a recent issue of the *National Civic Federation Review* that he gave his endorsement to the new gospel of Bolshevism, which he considers a spiritual movement replacing the outworn Christianity of the Russian Orthodox Church. He characterized the cognate I.W.W. "philosophy" as the most ideal and practical Christian philosophy since the days of Jesus Christ, and as expressing the ideas of Christ much more closely than any church of the present day.

The activities of Dr. Ward, as shown in other parts of this report, are entirely consistent with this point of view. He is chairman of the American Civil Liberties Union, which champions the I.W.W., and presided over the I.W.W. meeting of Feb. 9, 1920, held at the Rand School, to raise money for the defense of the I.W.W. murderers of the four members of the American Legion at Centralia. He has also been prominent in numerous pacifist and radical societies such as the Fellowship of Reconciliation, the Emergency Peace Conference and People's Council, the Liberty Defense Union.

The pro-Bolshevik articles which Dr. Ward contributed to *The Social Service Bulletin* of the Methodist Federation for Social Service were considered particularly objectionable because the *Bulletin* was circulated not only by the Methodist Church but by the Congregational, Northern Baptist, and other organizations. They called attention to Dr. Ward's textbooks circulated by the Graded Sunday School Syndicate. Dr. Ward is also connected with the Y.M.C.A., the Y.W.C.A., and the Inter-Church World Movement.

The Philadelphia Annual Conference of the Methodist Church protested against the pro-Bolshevism of Dr. Ward being circulated in the name of the denomination. Such specialists in Bolshevism as Lieutenant Klieforth and Wm. English Walling have characterized Dr. Ward's statements as downright falsehoods or distorted facts, and as a kind of Bolshevism far worse than the Bolshevism of Russia.[3]

As one can see from this report, the American public was

3 Pp. 1115, 1116.

warned as far back as 1920 about Union Theological Seminary as a breeding ground for Bolshevik teaching. Dr. Harry F. Ward was professor of Christian Ethics there for twenty-five years. He was also a lecturer at the Boston School of Theology in Boston University, a Methodist institution.

As we turn back for a moment to page 2142 in the record of the Investigation of Communist Activities in the New York City Area by the Committee on Un-American Activities, we find a startling piece of information in regard to communism's penetration of Union Theological Seminary. Mr. Kunzig is questioning Mr. Leonard Patterson (emphasis added):

> Mr. KUNZIG: I would like to ask you one further question. Did you ever see any examples of young ministers sent out to churches by the Union Theological Seminary who were Communists?
> Mr. PATTERSON: Yes.
> Mr. KUNZIG: Would you describe that to the committee?
> Mr. PATTERSON: Yes. While I was in Baltimore, two members who had graduated from Dr. Ward's Seminary came down to Baltimore for assignment to their ministerial duties; at the same time they came for assignment for their Communist duties from the section committee of the Baltimore section of the Communist Party.
>
> They were Party members when they got there. They explained that *they were recruited as Party members by Dr. Ward while they were studying under him.*

When this testimony was given to the Committee on Un-American Activities in July 1953, the names of these two ministers were not mentioned. However, on March 25, 1954, when the committee conducted a hearing in Baltimore, their names were revealed. Press dispatches appearing in the Chicago *Tribune* of March 26 identified them as the Rev. Joseph S.

Nowak, former pastor of the Portage Park Presbyterian Church of Chicago, and the Rev. John A. Hutchison. The Rev. Nowak admitted membership in the Communist Party. He said that he quit it after four months. The Rev. Hutchison, when confronted by the committee with Manning Johnson's testimony, denied that he had had anything to do with Communist activity; however, the Rev. Nowak testified against his friend; the Rev. Hutchison, he said, helped to organize Communist-front activities in Baltimore, worked closely with Communist officials, and had attended at least one Communist meeting.

The Baltimore activities of the Rev. Nowak and the Rev. Hutchison were described by Earl C. Reno, a former Communist who was Party organizer in Baltimore from 1936 to 1937, and Leonard Patterson, who was the Young Communist League director in Baltimore during the same period.

Mr. Reno said that the Rev. Nowak and the Rev. Hutchison came to Communist Party headquarters in 1935. They had just been graduated from Union Theological Seminary, he said, where they had been "well grounded in Marxism."

Union Theological Seminary for many years has been one of the "darlings" of the Federal, National, and World Councils of Churches. Many Council leaders have been trained in this seminary on Morningside Heights in New York, and others have been affiliated with it as faculty members and frequent lecturers. The seminary has entertained Earl Browder, the former head of the American Communist Party, as one of its speakers. During his talk there, he acknowledged the fact that ministers were working closely with the Communist Party.

On September 30, 1952, amid great fanfare, The Revised Standard Version of the Bible, copyrighted by The National Council of the Churches of Christ in the United States of America (successor to the Federal Council) was presented to the American public. Union Theological Seminary was involved, for on the jacket flap is carried the following statement: "The members of the committee since 1937, listed in order of the date of appointment with indication of their assignments to the Old Testament and New Testament sections, are . . ." A list of 22 names follows. Four are from Union Theological Seminary. Two of these four, James Moffatt and Frederick C. Grant, have been connected with subversive organizations, according to the files of the Committee on Un-American Activities of the House of Representatives.

In the *American Mercury* magazine of November 1953 appeared an article entitled "Red Infiltration of Theological Seminaries" by Dr. J. B. Matthews. Dr. Matthews is one of the world's greatest authorities on Communist strategy and tactics. He, himself, is a graduate of Union Theological Seminary and holds three degrees in theology. In his article, which defines the extent to which communism has infiltrated the seminaries, Union Theological Seminary crops up frequently with such names as George A. Coe, Harry F. Ward, Paul Scherer, Robert Hastings Nichols, and Arthur L. Swift, Jr. All were members of Union's faculty and at one time or another were involved in left-wing activities.

Bishop G. Bromley Oxnam, one of the most powerful present-day figures in the ecumenical movement, has had a very controversial and colorful career. He has been a bishop of the Methodist Church in Omaha, Boston, New York, and Washington, D.C. He has been secretary of the Council of Bishops, president of DePauw University in Greencastle, Indiana, a Methodist school; former president of The Federal Council of Churches of Christ in America; president for North America of The World Council of Churches; and a member and officer of the Communist-front Methodist Federation for Social Action. There has been no more vehement critic of Congressional investigations than Bishop Oxnam. For years he has attacked committees of the Congress investigating Communist infiltration of all major spheres of American society.

The extent of Communist penetration of the church system of the United States was brought out into the open when the chairman of the Committee on Un-American Activities, the Hon. Harold Velde, of Illinois, announced over the Mutual Broadcasting System in 1953 that certain left-wing clergymen were to be investigated by the Committee on Un-American Activities. The committee, he said, could no longer sit back and see this activity going on without warning the people about it.

Bishop Oxnam mocked the committee continually, until finally he was put on the spot by the testimony of former undercover agents of the F.B.I., including Herbert Philbrick and Edward and Martha Edmiston, all of whom had identified ministers working in the top ranks of the American Communist Party. Bishop Oxnam had argued that the F.B.I., not Congressional committees, should do the job. He knew that the F.B.I. could not release the names of those engaged in subversion; the F.B.I. is the private detective agency of the Department of Justice and is not allowed to reveal information to the public.

Congressional committees, however, may disclose publicly the names of individuals and organizations which are collaborating with the Communist conspiracy in the United States. This, Bishop Oxnam and other "liberal" leaders of the ecumenical movement did not want done; it would alert the American churchgoing public to the fact that wolves in sheep's clothing had been using organized Protestantism as a cover-up for spreading the "Social Gospel" and had been working hand-in-glove with communism.

And so, in an attempt to make the best of an existing situation, on July 21, 1953, at 2:00 P.M., Bishop G. Bromley Oxnam appeared as a witness before the committee *at his own request.*

He was not under subpoena, although the committee might have exercised its rights and subpoenaed him. The investigation was called to a halt, on the bishop's insistence, at about midnight of the same day. Had he been subpoenaed, the committee members could have examined him more thoroughly than the voluntary nature of his appearance permitted them to do. They could have questioned him on the writings and statements he had produced over a period of years in behalf of left-wing programs and organizations.

Bishop Oxnam's relations with Dr. Harry F. Ward were brought out at one point during the hearing. Mr. Kunzig asked Bishop Oxnam about Dr. Ward's chairmanship of the American Civil Liberties Union, then followed with a question about the bishop's connection with Dr. Ward. Bishop Oxnam replied:

> Professor Ward came to the Boston School of Theology, I believe, in 1914. I was a student. He was a brilliant teacher. He was an inspirational personality. He made an extraordinary contribution to the students of that institution. I was very, very fond of him. I took dictation from him as a part-time secretary in the dictation of one of his books. I knew his family. Professor Ward was a leader in the social movement of the Methodist Church and over a long period of time rendered, I believe, very valuable service. . . . Now, then, he was an inspirational teacher, to whom I owe very, very much. He was a dear personal friend. When he shifted his views, as I believe, I had to break with Professor Ward. He understood it.[4]

Bishop Oxnam said he broke with Dr. Ward in *1928.* The committee then produced a newspaper article showing that, at a meeting in Kansas City on *May 15, 1939,* of the Methodist

---

[4] *Hearings,* House Committee on Un-American Activities, July 21, 1953, p. 3725.

Federation for Social Action, the bishop was alleged to have paid high tribute to the Federation and to its secretary, Dr. Ward. After being pressed closely on this point, Bishop Oxnam finally admitted (page 3729):

> For a moment I said some words in praise of Dr. Ward, his service to the church in days gone by, and the like.
>
> You see, while I had personally come to the conviction that I could no longer go along with him, I don't think when you're dealing with a friend of many years, who's had distinguished leadership in the church, that you're called upon publicly to call him a Communist under the circumstances of that particular meeting.

Representative Clardy of Michigan said (page 3730) that he was puzzled to think that Bishop Oxnam should make such kind remarks about Dr. Ward after he discovered that he was a Communist. Bishop Oxnam replied that he didn't say Ward was a Communist. He said that Dr. Ward took the Communist position "as to objective." He also said that, back in those days, "I don't think we thought of this situation as we do now."

Over Bishop Oxnam's persistent and vehement protests, Mr. Kunzig, the chief counsel, was able to enter into the record the testimony of Manning Johnson identifying Dr. Ward as a member of the Communist Party. Bishop Oxnam admitted that Ward was a member of the Methodist Federation for Social Service from its beginning in the year 1907. (It should be kept in mind that Bishop Oxnam was president of The Federal Council of the Churches of Christ in America while also a member of the Methodist Federation for Social Service—later called the Methodist Federation for Social Action.)

In 1952 the Methodist General Conference passed a resolution calling upon the Methodist Federation for Social Action to drop the name Methodist and move from the Methodist headquarters building in New York City. This action was initiated by laymen within the church. The Federation refused to drop the name Methodist and it continued to stay on in the Methodist headquarters at 150 Fifth Avenue, New York, for a considerable length of time. While it is not an "official" organization of the Methodist Church, its membership has been composed largely of Methodist officials, who have given it an official blessing ever since the organization was started. The Methodist General Conference failed to censure any of the officials of the church who promoted the work of the Federation and many of whom have been its officers.

Mr. Kunzig demonstrated (page 3738) that Bishop Oxnam was a member of the Methodist Federation for Social Action for many years after he had supposedly broken with Dr. Ward in 1928. Bishop Oxnam admitted that he did not write a letter of resignation until 1946. Dr. Ward had been an officer in the organization until 1940. Bishop Oxnam, then, was involved in the organization with this member of the Communist Party for at least twelve years. Also, he had served for years in the same organizations with members of his own denomination, such as Miss Winifred Chappell, known to be a member of the Communist Party, and the Rev. Jack R. McMichael, charged in Benjamin Gitlow's testimony with being involved in the Communist conspiracy to subvert the Methodist Church for communism.

10

**THE PLANNERS
AND CONTROLLERS**

Bishop Oxnam presides over Church and Economic Life conference. Victor and Walter Reuther the experts. Mrs. Perkins walks out. Conference votes for equalizing taxation. Something about the Reuthers. Left-wingers solicit for Council. The Council urges that cooperatives replace free enterprise. Murray Lincoln looks to the coming revolution.

WHEN THE Church and Economic Life Department held a conference in Detroit, Michigan, in February 1950, Bishop Oxnam presided. Victor and Walter Reuther of the United Auto Workers, C.I.O., were the chief experts for The Federal Council of Churches on labor relations.

As recorded in the Detroit papers, Mrs. Frances Perkins, a delegate to the convention and Secretary of Labor under President Franklin D. Roosevelt, couldn't tolerate the conclusions brought in by the various study groups in the final session. She rose and said:

> Why should we meet with a lot of half-baked people to discuss things they know nothing about? The clergy's duty is to guide people in the knowledge of God and not in politics and economics.[1]

[1] Detroit *Free Press*, Feb. 20, 1950, p. 9.

Howled down by the disciples of collectivism, she left the meeting in disgust.

Dr. George S. Benson, president of Harding College, Searcy, Arkansas, an economist, lecturer, and newspaper columnist, wrote a special report on the conference which was released to newspapers throughout the country. He wrote (emphasis added):

A politico-economic credo which should be disturbing to all straight-thinking Americans has been adopted by a group of prominent Protestant churchmen assembled in Detroit under the sponsorship of The Federal Council of the Churches of Christ in America. The Associated Press reports that the churchmen voted to recommend to the public "the extensive use of taxation to reduce inequalities in income." This advocacy is contrary to the fundamental principles of the American way of life and our historic American concept of taxation.

Taxation in America was conceived as a fair and sound method of financing government—and for no other purpose—but Socialists long ago found it to be their handiest instrument for achieving abolition of private property and subjugation of a people. The boldest Socialists call taxation their "weapon." The book *Elements of Socialism* by Spargo and Arner (Macmillan) says (page 352): "Taxation is, of course, a form of confiscation, but we have long been acustomed to it and it makes it possible for the process of confiscation to be stretched over such a long period of time as to make it easy and almost unnoticeable."

When it is understood that *delegates to the Detroit Convocation came from 30 states and represented the leading 22 Protestant denominations and 10 allied religious bodies,* the economic principle advocated becomes one of the most significant formal actions taken by an American ecclesiastic body since the founding of religious freedom on these shores more than 300 years ago. It moreover serves to emphasize how far astray intelligent, well-meaning people may be led . . . *their economic credo adopted at Detroit comes straight from Karl Marx.*[2]

Why were Victor and Walter Reuther chosen to fill such prominent roles as advisers on economic and labor matters to The Federal Council of Churches? Victor and Walter Reuther wrote, on January 20, 1934, while they were living and working in the Soviet Union, a letter which ended with the words: "Carry on the fight for a Soviet America." [3]

Several years ago a film issued by the United Auto Workers Union, entitled *The Brotherhood of Man,* was offered to schools all over the country and shown by many of them. This film was produced under Communist influences. It was based on the pamphlet entitled "The Races of Mankind" and co-authored by Ruth Benedict and Gene Weltfish, both of whom had notorious Communist-front records. The War Department banned it and refused to let it be shown to servicemen.

Miss Gene Weltfish was for many years professor of anthropology at Columbia University. She was head of the Congress of American Women, which the Committee on Un-American Activities condemned in a 114-page report. She had appeared at Communist rallies behind the Iron Curtain as head and American representative of this Communist-front organization. Prominent alumni of Columbia University had frequently protested over her presence on the faculty staff, but not until Professor Weltfish appeared before the Senate Com-

[2] Bunkie (Louisiana) *Record,* March 4, 1950.
[3] The letter in full is entered in the official record, under oath, of the Committee on Un-American Activities of the U.S. House of Representatives and is reproduced in Appendix 5 of this book.

mittee on Internal Security, headed by Senator William E. Jenner of Indiana, was action taken against her. When she was asked the $64 question, "Are you now or have you been a member of the Communist Party?", she invoked the Fifth Amendment and refused to answer. Dr. Grayson Kirk, president of Columbia University, soon terminated Miss Weltfish's services.

The screen version of this film release by the C.I.O. was written by Ring Lardner, Jr., in collaboration with John Hubley and Phil Eastman, all three of whom have records of Communist-front affiliation. Lardner was one of the Hollywood Ten who were cited for contempt of Congress.

The film was produced under the auspices of the National Education Department, United Auto Workers. The director of the department was Victor Reuther, brother of Walter Reuther, president of the United Auto Workers.

Now let us bring the Reuther matter up to date in regard to The Federal Council of Churches. Two years after the Council met in Cleveland, in November 1950, and changed its name to the National Council, the Division of Christian Life and Work, Department of Economic Life, distributed a letter signed by three officers of the C.I.O. These were Walter P. Reuther, president of the United Auto Workers, John G. Ramsay, public relations director of the Organizing Committee of the C.I.O., and Ted F. Silvey, secretary of the National C.I.O. Community Services Committee. This letter was sent out on the stationery of The National Council of Churches and mailed to members of the C.I.O. throughout the United States. The letter, with the National Council officers on the letterhead, follows:

THE NATIONAL COUNCIL OF THE CHURCHES OF CHRIST IN THE UNITED STATES OF AMERICA

Division of Christian Life and Work
Department of Economic Life

279 Fourth Ave.　　　　　　　New York 10, N.Y.

The Rt. Rev. Henry Knox Sherrill
President

　　　　　　　　　Charles P. Taft
　　　　　　　　　Department Chairman

Rev. Samuel McCrea Cavert
General Secretary

　　　　　　　　　Rev. Cameron P. Hall
　　　　　　　　　Department Director

　　　　　　　　　November 10, 1952

Dear Sirs and Brothers:

We who are writing you are not only active in the CIO but have also worked closely with the Department of the Church and Economic Life of the National Council of Churches.

Labor and the Churches should stand shoulder to shoulder in the fight for justice and brotherhood in industrial and economic life.

We are glad to report the real contribution to this cause being made by the department of the Church and Economic Life, with which we have had close personal contact. As illustrations of the activities of this interdenominational church body we cite—

Its Labor Sunday Message which commended unions for assisting "free unions in Europe, Asia and other areas to organize and raise living standards of working people and to oppose the efforts of Communists to gain control of the unions of workers in free democratic nations."

Its strong public statements in support of "an unsegregated church in an unsegregated society" and in opposition to universal military training.

Its denunciation of "the attempt to enforce conformity or to silence people by character assassination, guilt by association, or the use of unfounded charges."

Its continuing promotion of a study among the churches of the problems of inflation, its evils and injustices.

Its important conference on the Christian and His Daily Work, the chairman of which was Al Whitehouse of the United Steelworkers. The conference had its delegates and speakers from Labor, industry, farmers, consumers and the churches.

Each year Rev. Cameron P. Hall, Director of the Department, brings ministers to CIO Conventions to hear its speakers and get acquainted with its leaders.

As a labor union always in the thick of the fight for justice and brotherhood, we feel sure you will want to make a contribution to this work which is entirely dependent upon voluntary support. Some internationals are contributing $100, with one at $600; some councils and locals are giving $50 or more; others, $25; and some smaller amounts. Whatever you can send from your treasury will be deeply appreciated.

Please use the enclosed envelope and make checks payable to the National Council of Churches.

Sincerely yours,

/s/ Walter P. Reuther
President, UAW–CIO

/s/ John G. Ramsay
Public Relations Director
Organizing Committee CIO

/s/ Ted F. Silvey
Secretary,
National CIO
Community Services
Committee

Here we see The National Council of Churches using left-wing labor-union leaders to solicit funds from their union councils and locals throughout the United States. Ironically enough, the author picked up a copy of this letter in Nashville, Tennessee, in December 1952, when the C.I.O. was conducting a strike against the Kraft Foods Company in that city. The late Mr. James L. Kraft, an ardent supporter of The National Council of Churches and one of its chief fund raisers, had just sent out telegrams and letters urging leading businessmen in Nashville to send their donations to The National Council of Churches promptly, as the Council had fallen short of meeting its budget and was in great need of financial support. This business leader was asking businessmen to support an organization which takes to its bosom left-wing labor leaders who, in turn, were using the National Council's stationery to solicit funds to support the National Council while they were striking against the businessmen from whom the National Council was also asking support.

In 1942 The Federal Council of the Churches of Christ in America, through its Department of Christian Social Relations, put out a little pamphlet entitled "Social Ideals of the Churches." This had been passed by the Quadrennial Meeting of The Federal Council of Churches in Indianapolis on December 8, 1932, and the abridged edition in 1942. The pamphlet went through three printings, in 1933, 1934, and 1942, and was sold at five cents per copy. In it, The Federal Council of Churches convicts itself of its collectivistic schemes. On pages 6 and 7 the churches are told what principles they should stand for. Among these are "subordination of speculation and the profit motive to the creative and cooperative spirit."

Now, anyone knows that you cannot have a free-enterprise system without a profit motive. Russia does have a cooperative system—and the people cooperate *or else*. People do not go into business in the United States today merely for the sake of brotherly cooperation. They go into business in competition with other businessmen to make a profit. Competition brings a better product and a lowering of prices, so that today the United States of America has the highest standard of living and the American housewife has the finest products, which make her life the easiest of any housewife on the face of the earth.

To illustrate fully what the Federal Council leaders meant by the "cooperative" spirit, we include in Appendix 6 of this book the entire text of an article written by Mr. Pearson L. Linn, of Freedom Acres Farm, Ohio, for the Bucyrus (Ohio) *Telegraph-Forum* of December 29, 1950. We believe it to be one of the most all-inclusive studies on the Federal Council's "cooperative" idea ever made.

In another article which Mr. Linn published in the Bucyrus *Telegraph-Forum,* he gave the following information concerning the Federal Council's role in the field of cooperatives:

Cameron P. Hall is the executive secretary of the Department of the Church and Economic Life of The Federal Council of Churches—the man who perhaps speaks with more influence as a representative of the Federal Council than anyone else. What more is there to know about Cameron P. Hall? For your information, Cameron P. Hall wrote to the Senate Interstate and Foreign Commerce Committee recommending the appointment of John Carson (Co-op League John Carson) to the powerful and important Federal Trade Commission. John Carson was long connected with the Cooperative League as one of its chief propagandists. This Cooperative League is the American branch of the International Cooperative Alliance, which hopes to set up an "International Cooperative Commonwealth." This is to be done by destroying "the present competitive regime of private enterprise" and replacing it with a "cooperative system" or a "cooperative order" for which Dr. Jones so urgently seeks. Cameron P. Hall made this recommendation to the Senate Committee on Federal Council of Churches stationery and in this manner lent the prestige of the political power of the Federal Council's 27,000,000 members to John Carson that he might get an important key position to regulate "competitive private enterprise," which his previous employer had international commitments to exterminate and supersede with a "cooperative system" or "cooperative order."

Cameron P. Hall, in his letter to the Senate Committee recommending John Carson, recommended Mr. Carson on the grounds that "his experience and outlook would admirably serve the people of this country as a member of the Federal Trade Commission." Now, what was John Carson's outlook? Was it his statement that "that world, the world of competitive profit capitalism, began to have its death rattles in 1929, and it has been in convulsions ever since," or was it because of his statement ". . . we must then create a society wholly contrary to our present capitalistic conceptions—what is that society—is it a family society or a nonprofit society?" Was not Mr. Carson's love and affection for a "nonprofit society" or a cooperative order the reason for Mr. Hall lending the prestige of 27,000,000 unsuspecting Protestant church members? How gullible are we?

Let us bore in. Who besides Cameron P. Hall from the Federal Council of Churches testified in behalf of John Carson? The *Congressional Record* informs that the Rev. James Myers . . . long-time Industrial Secretary of the Federal Council, recommended the appointment. This is the same Rev. James Myers who is well known for his advocacy of total cooperation as an end in itself.

And Benson Y. Landis, executive secretary of the Committee on Town and Country of The Federal Council of Churches as well as a well-known long-time supporter and advocate of the cooperative movement which seeks the "cooperative order," as the title of his book *A Cooperative Economy* indicates.

And Rev. Nelson Cruikshank, director of social-insurance activities for the American Federation of Labor, and member of the Federal Council's Department of the Church and Economic Life, who said in his testimony in behalf of John Carson that he found that he and Carson found themselves "interested in the same things."

And Jerry Voorhis, member of The Federal Council of Churches' Department of the Church and Economic Life, as well as executive secretary of the Cooperative League of the USA, which is the American member and agent of the International Cooperative Alliance, whose Constitution says in no uncertain tones that it ". . . seeks

. . . to substitute for the present competitive regime of private enterprise a cooperative system. . . ."

And so it is that we find Cameron P. Hall, and Rev. James Myers, and Dr. Benson Y. Landis, and Rev. Nelson Cruikshank and Jerry Voorhis—all important "Big wigs" in The Federal Council of Churches—seeking appointment to a position which could mean life or death to "competitive private enterprise" for a man who had declared as late as 1945 that "the world of competitive profit capitalism" has been dying since 1929, and a man who had said also as late as 1945 that we must ". . . create a society wholly contrary to our present capitalistic conceptions."

It can, therefore, be said that these prominent persons in The Federal Council of Churches certainly "go to bat" for one of the brethren from the "cooperative world" when he seeks to regulate the "competitive order" which so many of them indicate by their writings that they despise. On the face of the record—the *Congressional Record*—it can be further said that at least some of these Federal Council of Churches leaders do not hesitate to use the offices, the supplies, the prestige and the political power of the Federal Council's 27,000,000 members to get one of their friends into a key position from which he can and will regulate the "competitive private enterprises" of The Federal Council of Churches' 27,000,000 members. This is indeed an odd situation but it's in the record—the *Congressional Record*—for all to see.

Let us go still deeper into the Federal Council of Churches structure to see what makes it tick. Let us consider the Federal Council's Department of the Church and Economic Life, from which much of this "cooperative order" or "cooperative system" stuff stems. Who are some of the people who make up the Department and what do they believe? Surely, if there were just one of these leaders or believers or spokesmen for the cooperative "movement" or "cooperative order" or "cooperative system" in this key group, it would be sufficient if it were a comparatively representative body; but what do we find?

We find not only Cameron P. Hall, Nelson Cruikshank and Jerry Voorhis, whom I shall again refer to later, but also a great number of others. In addition to these, there is Mr. E. R. Bowen, former executive secretary of the Cooperative League, which is the American member, spokesman and agent for the International Cooperative Alliance, which in turn not only wants to cooperatize the world, but also has, according to latest official data available, most of its members from behind the Communist "Iron Curtain."

And John H. Davis, executive secretary of the National Council of Farmer Cooperatives.

And Carl R. Hutchison, long-time Educational Director of the Ohio Farm Bureau cooperative organizations, which organizations furnish the Cooperative League with its president and the International Cooperative Alliance with its vice president, namely, Murray D. Lincoln. At least as early as 1941 the Ohio Farm Bureau announced that its economic program was the cooperative ownership and control from retail to production.

And Raymond W. Miller, former head of the American Institute of Cooperation. It was Mr. Miller's American Institute of Cooperation which collected the data which enabled the September *Ohio Farm Bureau News* to report that in one big co-op "only 21 per cent of the men members knew how membership was obtained" and "only three per cent knew how the board of directors of the central organization was elected." No doubt but that the same thing could be said about the 27,000,000 members of The Federal Council of Churches.

And Bishop G. Bromley Oxnam, former president of the Federal Council of Churches, who is well known for his writings expressing favoritism of a cooperative order over a competitive order, and who, according to an Associated Press release from Columbus, Ohio, on November 21, 1946, said to the Ohio Farm Bureau's annual meeting that, and the AP release follows in part:

"Power must be brought under democratic control," declared the bishop, who is president of The Federal Council of Churches of Christ. "Justice must be established by democratic process. The first of these steps," he said, "will involve fundamental revisions in concepts of sovereignty. The second will involve similar revisions in our concept of property."

Do the members of the clergy think that Bishop Oxnam, in talking to this Ohio branch of the International Cooperative Alliance, was talking about keeping what we have? Let us not be silly.

This concludes our quotation of Pearson L. Linn's article on cooperatives.

Just who is Murray D. Lincoln? According to the Columbus (Ohio) *Evening Dispatch* and the Columbus *Citizen*, in their respective issues of September 9, 1946, and September 11, 1946, Mr. Lincoln has some very definite ideas about the capitalistic system. Here is part of these newspapers' summation of his speech before the National Cooperative Congress at its biennial convention in the Deshler-Wallick Hotel:

In a speech generously sprinkled with denunciations of the "profit motive" and "free enterprise" in American business, while praising key political and economic policies which come to be identified with the CIO, Mr. Lincoln urged cooperatives to be prepared to assume control and management of the nation's business and agriculture in the coming "revolution" as the only "acceptable alternative to chronic insecurity on one hand or statism on the other."

He declared the American public "today is at the mercy of a profit-minded business system which is determined to exact the greatest possible from the consumer."

The Federal Council's "subordination of speculation and the profit motive to the creative and cooperative spirit" is merely Point 1 under the principles which "the churches should stand for" in the pamphlet "Social Ideals of the Churches."

Another point is this: "Social planning and control of the credit and monetary systems and the economic processes for the common good."

The Federal Councilites do not say who is to do the planning and the controlling. There have to be planners and controllers over the rest of us. Could it be that these collectivistic churchmen think they will be in the seats of economic authority when this type of economy comes in? What did Quisling think he would get out of turning Norway over to the Nazis? What did Anna Pauker think she would get out of turning Rumania over to the Communists? What did World Councilite Dr. T. C. Chao of China think he would get out of helping the forces of Communist Mao Tse-tung to take over free China? They all thought they would be in the seats of power. But when the invaders were through using them, they were liquidated.

Let it not be forgotten that the planners and controllers are as subject to sin in the form of bribery, corruption, mink coats, and deep freezes as are those whose lives are being planned and controlled.

Point 3 in the Federal Council's program is "a wider and fairer distribution of the wealth." But who is going to decide what is a fair share of the wealth and what is not? Who will determine how much should be taken from one and given to another? Who will determine how it should be distributed?

In its publication *The Church and Economic Life, Basic Christian Principles and Assumptions,* a statement adopted by the Executive Committee of the Federal Council in September 1948, we are told that the fact that a certain economic system exists doesn't necessarily make it right or by virtue of divine providence. The Church, therefore, is to engage in "revolutionary criticism" of economic systems. The statement reads (emphasis added):

> We should now recognize that God's providence works both for the modification or *destruction* of some old forms of economic institutions and for the creation of some new forms. . . . The mere fact of rapid and radical change in recent centuries has made it difficult to regard any particular economic institutions as final or as ordained of God. . . . These external events enable the Church to have a better understanding of the revolutionary *social criticism* that is implicit in its own teaching.

The Federal Council, having made these false assumptions, proceeds to use them as a basis for attacking the American free-enterprise system. No biblical basis is given. The Council leaders are their own authorities on economics.

A final quotation from this publication on economics:

> All forms of power should be subject to criticism by those whose lives are most affected by them. It is true of irre-

sponsible economic power, as it is of irresponsible political power, that it corrupts those who exercise it.

The Executive Committee of the Federal Council has made a notable omission in this statement. "Irresponsible ecclesiastical power" should have been added to the list, for this form of power easily "corrupts those who exercise it," perhaps even more than economic or political power; much mischief can be committed under the cloak of religion. History abounds in examples.

11

CHURCH WOMEN
ARE COLLECTIVIZED TOO

General Department of United Church Women. Mrs. (Rev.) James D. Wyker, its president, travels with her minister husband on behalf of cooperatives. Rev. Wyker signs Communist appeals. "Bethlehem and Rochdale." Wykers give their all to cooperative movement. Secular activities of Mrs. Wyker's Church Women. Church Women rope in President Eisenhower. They choose anti-Christian Dr. Ferré as devotional speaker.

IN THE *Workbook of the Second General Assembly* of The National Council of Churches appears the report of the General Department of United Church Women. The president of the Council of Church Women at this time (1952) was Mrs. James D. Wyker.[1] Mrs. Wyker is the wife of the Reverend James D. Wyker of Ohio, who gave up his pulpit so that he and his wife could travel throughout Ohio trumpeting for cooperatives. Both have been ordained by the International Convention of the Disciples of Christ denomination.

In January 1943 the Rev. James D. Wyker signed an appeal sponsored by the National Federation for Constitutional Liberties. This organization has been cited as both subversive and Communist by Attorney General Tom Clark and by Attorney General Francis Biddle and was classified as "one of the viciously subversive organizations of the Communist Party"

[1] See Appendix 6 for her activities.

by the Committee on Un-American Activities of the House of Representatives. The Committee[2] labeled the National Federation as among "a maze of organizations [was] spawned for the alleged purpose of defending civil liberties in general but actually intended to protect Communist subversion from any penalties under the law." The California Committee on Un-American Activities, in a report dated 1948,[3] classified this front as "one of the most important Communist-front organizations in the United States. While following the Communist Party line meticulously, the organization has been helpful to Communists who wish to evade and defy government agencies investigating subversive activities." The Federation's appeal, supported by the Rev. Wyker, was a "message to the House of Representatives" opposing renewal of the Dies Committee.

On April 22, 1943, an open letter was addressed to President Franklin D. Roosevelt on behalf of Communist labor leader[4] Harry Renton Bridges. A portion of the letter is as follows:

> My dear Mr. President:
> I am addressing you on behalf of the clergymen, whose names are attached.
> We respectfully ask that you set aside the deportation order against Harry Renton Bridges, President of the International Longshoremen's and Warehousemen's Union, Congress of Industrial Organizations, and afford him full opportunity to become a citizen of the United States of America.

One of the signers of this letter was the Rev. James D.

2 House Report No. 1115, Sept. 2, 1947, House Committee on Un-American Activities, p. 2.
3 P. 327. See also p. 201.
4 According to the *Cumulative Index*, House Committee on Un-American Activities, 1956.

Wyker. This open letter in defense of Harry Bridges was cited as a Communist front by the Committee on Un-American Activities in a report dated March 29, 1944. It was also cited as a Communist front in the California Committee on Un-American Activities report of 1948.

Dr. J. B. Matthews, in his article "Red Infiltration of Theological Seminaries," published in the *American Mercury,* November 1953, gives additional citations in regard to the aid and comfort given the Communist movement by the Rev. James D. Wyker. Having exposed the fake "world peace appeal," Dr. Matthews says the Peace Information Center, a Communist outfit, claimed James D. Wyker, then of the Bible College of Missouri (Disciples), as one of the signers. Dr. Matthews says the St. Louis *Post-Dispatch* of October 23, 1951, carried an advertisement which was an "open letter" to Attorney General Howard J. McGrath in defense of the Civil Rights Congress, a Communist organization. Among the signers of this pro-Communist "open letter" was the Rev. James D. Wyker.

Dr. Matthews also points out that on January 19, 1951, the Communist-front organization which has been agitating for the repeal of the Internal Security Act of 1950 (the McCarran-Walter Act) released an "open letter" signed by the Rev. James D. Wyker and others.

Mrs. Wyker, who with her husband now lives in Mount Vernon, Ohio, besides having been president of the United Council of Church Women has been elevated to the post of vice-president-at-large of The National Council of Churches.

In a pamphlet entitled "Bethlehem and Rochdale" by Benson Y. Landis, another cooperative-minded Federal Council of Churches official, now in the National Council, we read:

In North Jackson, Ohio, Reverend James Wyker, a clergyman of the Disciples of Christ, minister for 12 years of the Federated Church in his community, has resigned and accepted a position as educational director of the Logan County, Ohio, Farm Bureau, where he will stress education for cooperative organizations.

Mr. Landis admits in this pamphlet that he and the Wykers made a study of the works of Sidney and Beatrice Webb, the English Fabian Socialist leaders, and of George Bernard Shaw, Henry A. Wallace, Walter Rauschenbusch (the Socialist minister),[5] and Toyohiko Kagawa, a modernist and Socialist churchman of Japan.

The report on Mr. Wyker's department gives a list[6] of the "activities" which Mrs. Wyker and her staff have outlined for the women of the churches over the country. Here are some of them:

> United Nations Speakers Training Institutes
> United Nations Seminars
> Visits of Church Women to United Nations
> Luncheon for Women Delegates to the Seventh General Assembly of the United Nations
> Study of Relationships of Women, National, State and Local, in Relation to the National Council of Churches
> How to Organize a Local Council of Church Women
> Suggested Constitution for a Local Council of Church Women
> Bible Observance—New Revised Standard Version of the Holy Bible
> United Nations Day
> UNESCO Gift Coupons
> UNICEF
> CROP

[5] See pages 96–101.
[6] *Workbook for the Second General Assembly,* report of the United Council of Church Women, p. 78.

Cooperation with Committee on Equal Pay of Woman's Bureau, White House Conference on Children and Youth, and Continuing Committees. Committee on Christians and Jews (representing Protestant Women), Committee on Joint Cooperation in Defense Areas, Committee on Civilian Defense

The list includes a series of activities under the general heading of "Legislative Action":

Opposing Universal Military Training
In Favor of a Bill to Revise the Immigration Laws [this is the attack on the McCarran-Walter Immigration Law which the Communists seek to destroy]
In Favor of Fair Employment Practices Commission (enforced FEPC)
In Favor of More Adequate Public-assistance Program
Federal Aid to Schools
In Favor of Support for United States Appropriations for the United Nations
In Favor of support for United States Appropriations for UNICEF
Warning as to the Implications of the Bricker Resolution [The National Council opposes the Bricker Amendment]
Urging Ratification of the Covenant on Genocide

The United Council of Church Women says that "a scrutiny of current national legislation is maintained in order that church women may be informed on all pertinent legislation. Recommendations are made to state and local councils when local action is needed to influence public opinion." [7]
In other words, the Council maintains a network over the country which reaches down to the local level, enabling this

[7] 1954 Biennial Report, p. 110.

handful of women to "influence public opinion." The United Council of Church Women claims 2,000 local councils, which are "directed by local women in local areas for local community betterment and enrichment."[8]

Just how propaganda against the Bricker Amendment, in favor of foreign spending, against the immigration laws, and for or against many other national and international political actions upon which the national leaders have taken a stand without consulting the local church women can contribute to "local community betterment and enrichment" is beyond comprehension. The local church women actually are being used as members of a vast propaganda machine to influence the Congress, the President, and the United States Supreme Court on strictly political issues:

> When the national committee met in February 1954 they voted to help local chairmen emphasize education on current legislation. The national office was asked to prepare: information on world trade, equal pay for equal work, church and state relationships, aid to education, and bills affecting children.[9]

Advice was given to the various local councils on "national legislation," "industrial relations," "civil liberties," "adequate public housing," "discrimination," and "attacks on our rights and freedom." The headquarters circulated a pamphlet by Rhoda McCulloch entitled "Loyalty and Freedom." This was the usual left-wing attack on the investigation of subversives by the committees of Congress; according to the 1954 Biennial Report, it was written because the United Church Women were "deeply aware of the danger of hate groups and of mccarthyism to the reputation of the United States in other

8 *Loc. cit.*
9 *Op. cit.,* p. 111.

parts of the world, and of the appeal of these groups for a return to isolationism and extreme nationalism."

The Council of Church Women has disseminated, on every level, literature on the United Nations, world order, UNICEF, appropriations for aid to Communist-sympathizing India for her "economic development," ratification of the Genocide Convention, renewal of a reciprocal-trade-agreements program, and many other political and economic themes which, whether good or bad, are wholly unrelated to God and personal salvation.

Although continually trumpeting for separation of church and state, such groups as the United Church Women never hesitate to use heads of state to lend prestige and publicity to their religious, semireligious, and nonreligious propaganda. The main speaker at the Sixth Biennial Assembly of United Church Women at Atlantic City, October 5, 1953, attended by more than 5,000, was the President of the United States, Dwight D. Eisenhower; the President apparently did not choose to abide by the precedent set by President Theodore Roosevelt, who prudently declined invitations to attend meetings of the early Federal Council of Churches.

A noticeable omission in the official report of this Sixth Assembly is the name of Dr. Nels F. S. Ferré, the featured devotional speaker each morning for the women gathered in Atlantic City. No Protestant theologian, so called, had ever denied fundamental Christian doctrine more consistently than Dr. Ferré. Dr. Ferré, a Christian minister, has written two books in recent years which are anti-Christian in the extreme. In *The Christian Understanding of God* [10] he relates a vile Nazi theory on the birth and character of Christ. Jesus, he suggests, was the product of a hired German soldier stationed in a Roman garrison near Nazareth who got in trouble with a woman named Mary. "Who can deny that such a conjecture

[10] Harper & Bros., New York, 1951.

could be true?" asks Dr. Ferré. He declares that Jesus was not sinless, although the Bible declares Him to be sinless, and he says that He probably picked up some of His teachings from the mystics of the Orient and the Middle East during His wanderings in the silent years of His life.

Another book by Dr. Ferré, *The Sun and the Umbrella,* [11] is one of the most unqualified attacks on major Christian doctrines written in this country. He ridicules belief in the Bible, the incarnation, the virgin birth, the blood atonement, the resurrection, and the return of Christ. There is no extreme to which Dr. Ferré has not gone. Invitations to him to speak have been canceled by religious groups after ministers and laymen had learned of his assaults on Christianity.[12]

Dr. Ferré has been professor of philosophical theology at the Vanderbilt University School of Religion. Leaders of the National Council have hailed him—and introduced him—as one of the great theologians of the day. And the United Church Women selected Dr. Ferré as an appropriate person to conduct their devotional sessions in Atlantic City.

As the writer of the present book travels throughout the country, good, loyal, American Christian women come up to him and ask: "What do you know about the United Council of Church Women? They have a local group here in our city and we don't like the sound of their program. It doesn't sound either American or Christian. What do you think?"

11 Harper, 1953.
12 Canton, Ohio, and Lake Junaluska, N.C.

MR. DULLES AND SOME COLLECTIVISTIC CHURCHMEN

Mr. Dulles heads Commission on a Just and Durable Peace. His influence in internationalizing and secularizing the Federal, National, and World Councils. He is assisted by Arthur Flemming. He urges limitations on national sovereignty. He charges U.S. with irresponsibility. He credits Council with influencing country in favor of UN. He underlines "the failure of our society, as organized." Rockefeller subsidizes Friends of the World Council. Role of the Council at San Francisco Conference. The UN is formed, with Council backing. Mr. Dulles writes Bishop Oxnam's statement on Soviet-American relations. Statement critical of U.S., praises Soviet. Mr. Dulles and Alger Hiss work together in Council. The leftist activities of Dr. Van Kirk. Council churchmen support Covenant on Human Rights and Genocide Convention. Council undermines anticommunism in Asia, misrepresenting its nature. Dr. Mackay urges recognition of Red China and the sending of churchmen there.

IN THE Federal Council pamphlet entitled "Furthering Christian Unity" is a section, "International Understanding," which says:

The Council's Commission on a Just and Durable Peace, made up of thoughtful leaders of special competence in international affairs, under the chairmanship of the distinguished lawyer, Mr. John Foster Dulles, has shown that a united influence is possible.

National study conferences have been held for the purpose of formulating programs on which the churches can stand together. Study groups in local churches have been formed in order to develop an informed conscience on international problems, throughout the nation. Such influential statements as the "Six Pillars of Peace," "Soviet-American Relations," and "Crossroads of Foreign Policy" have given a sense of direction to Christian thinking. Christian missions on World Order have been held in cities across the continent. A mobilization of the churches for support of the European Recovery Program (The Marshall Plan) has been conspicuously effective.[1]

Now, because The Federal-National Council of Churches boasts of its influence in international affairs, it would be well to lay some of its pronouncements before the American church-going public who put into the boxes on Sundays their tithes and offerings, a portion of which goes to support the Council.

President Eisenhower's Secretary of State, Mr. John Foster Dulles, has been connected with the Federal-National-World Council of Churches movement for many years and has been one of its most prominent leaders. He was active in the movement as long ago as July 1937, during the Conference of Christian Leaders and Economists held in Geneva, Switzerland, when preparations were being made for the Second Dicennial World Conference on Faith and Order which was to be held in Edinburgh, Scotland, on August 3. At Edinburgh, plans would be laid for the formation of The World Council of Churches.

During World War II, John Foster Dulles, then a New York lawyer, was appointed chairman of the Federal Council's Inter-Church Commission to Study the Bases of a Just and Durable Peace. In early March 1942 The Federal Council of Churches held a National Study Conference on the campus of Ohio Wesleyan University, at Delaware, Ohio, under the auspices of the Commission on a Just and Durable Peace. The president

1 P. 10.

of the university, Arthur Flemming, was recently a high official of the Defense Department in the Eisenhower Administration.

Three hundred and seventy-five delegates of 30 denominations of the Federal Council met at this conference. Among them were 15 bishops of five denominations, seven seminary heads, including those of Yale, Chicago, Princeton, and Colgate-Rochester, eight college and university presidents, practically all the ranking officials of The Federal Council of Churches, and such well-known laymen as John R. Mott and Harvey S. Firestone, Jr. Methodist Bishop Ivan Lee Holt described it as the most distinguished American church gathering that he had seen in 30 years.

Chairman John Foster Dulles submitted the report, which had been approved by the members of his committee. *It was the most shocking report that has ever come out of any church group.* Intended to be Protestantism's "super" program for a just and durable peace after World War II, it included the following recommendations: 1, ultimately a world government of delegated powers; 2, complete abandonment of United States isolationism; 3, strong, immediate limitations on national sovereignty; 4, international control of all armies and navies; 5, a universal system of money; 6, worldwide freedom of immigration; 7, progressive elimination of all tariff and quota restrictions on world trade; 8, a democratically controlled international bank.

Chairman Dulles placed much of the blame on the United States for World War II and accused it of shortsighted selfishness in its own policies after World War I. He declared that the United States would have to turn over a new leaf if the world were to enjoy a lasting peace. He said (emphasis added):

> *It should be a matter of shame and humiliation to us* that actually the influences shaping the world have largely been irresponsible forces. Our own positive influence has

been impaired because of concentration on self and on
our short-range material gains. . . . If the future is to be
other than a repetition of the past, the United States must
accept the responsibility for *constructive action* commensurate with its power and opportunity. . . .

The natural wealth of the world is not evenly distributed. Accordingly, the possession of such natural resources . . . is a trust to be discharged *in the general
interest.* This calls for more than an offer to sell to all on
equal terms.

That this program should be adopted by these 375 self-styled
overseers of Protestantism in the United States is beyond human comprehension. How many people, sitting in the churches
of the denominations which these Socialist clergymen claim
to represent, knew that such a program was being adopted—
in the name of religion—and that they, the laymen, were paying the bills for it?

As if this were not enough, Dr. William Paton, co-secretary
of The World Council of Churches (which was not scheduled
to be formed until 1948 in Amsterdam but which the Federal
Council leaders took for granted had already been formed),
said, "Collectivism is coming, whether we like it or not."

The report went even further. Here is *Time* magazine's
summary of it:

Some of the conference's economic opinions were almost
as sensational as the extreme internationalism of its political program. It held that a "new order of economic life is
both imminent and imperative"—a new order that is sure
to come either "through voluntary cooperation within
the framework of democracy or through explosive political revolution." Without condemning the profit motive
as such, it denounced various defects in the profit system

for breeding war, demagogues and dictators, "mass unemployment, widespread dispossession from homes and
farms, destitution, lack of opportunity for youth and of security for old age." Instead, "the church must demand economic arrangements measured by human welfare. . . ."[2]

"Full-time educational opportunities, economic security and
retirement, adequate health service and an obligation to work
in some socially necessary service" were also demanded.

The conference stated that many duties at present performed by local and national governments "can now be effectively carried out only by international authority." Individual
nations, the conference declared, must give up their armed
forces except for the preservation of domestic order and must
allow the world to be policed by an international army and
navy. This new international organization would have "the
power of final judgment in controversies between nations, the
regulation of international trade and population movements
among nations." It would be "a duly constituted World Government of delegated powers: an international legislative body,
an international court with adequate jurisdiction, international administrative bodies with necessary powers, and adequate international police forces and provisions for enforcing
its worldwide economic authority."

The full report of this one-world meeting covered eight
pages in the March 25, 1942, issue of the radical *Christian
Century*. The Federal Council of the Churches of Christ in
America made reprints, available at 10 cents a copy from its
headquarters at 297 Fourth Avenue, New York.

If there is any doubt as to why certain liberal churchmen
have been elevated to high positions in recent administrations
in Washington, it should be made known to Protestant church
members that these left-wing leaders of The Federal-National

2 *Time*, March 16, 1942. See Appendix 7 for highlights of *Time*'s report.

Council of Churches have been using the vast machinery of an ecclesiastical organization to undermine the sovereignty of the United States, to plug for world government, to espouse Marxian socialism, and to condemn every person and every organization which exposes what they're doing, including Congressional committees and individual clergymen. These churchmen and church-connected politicians are aligned with the enemies of the United States, whether willfully or otherwise.

In June 1943 the Commission on a Just and Durable Peace of The Federal Council of Churches met in Princeton, New Jersey, with its chairman, John Foster Dulles. It endorsed the "Six Pillars of Peace," which was a plea to proceed with a world political organization. Mr. Dulles later implied, in his address before the biennial meeting of The Federal Council of Churches on November 28, 1944, that this pronouncement had a great effect upon the country at large and upon the State Department—that it actually influenced the Dumbarton Oaks Conference in Washington, D.C., which laid the groundwork for the United Nations. In his speech, as quoted in the 1944 Biennial Report, he said: "In looking back to appraise the influences which led to the Dumbarton Oaks Conference, it can fairly be said that the Protestant churches have played a decisive part." [3]

The same report covers the work of the International Justice and Goodwill Department; concerning the Department's Commission on a Just and Durable Peace, the report declares (emphasis added):

> Very early in the year, the commission turned its mind to the problem of world organization. Interest in this subject had been enormously increased by the declaration of *the Moscow Conference* which stressed the necessity of

[3] P. 23.

creating at the earliest possible moment a general international organization. The Commission formulated and the Executive Committee of the Federal Council approved a statement entitled "World Organization—Curative and Creative." The attention of the churches was called to the need of choosing between "international organization designed merely to perpetuate by repression the particular structure of the world which will emerge from the war, and international organization which, in addition to such use of force under law as is a requisite of order, discharges tasks that are curative and creative." People in and out of the churches were urged to "remain united and vigorous to achieve such international organization and American participation therein." Shortly thereafter the commission made public an appeal addressed to the President, the Congress, and the people of the United States, which declared that "if international organization is to achieve a durable peace, it must be planned from the beginning to become universal in membership and redemptive in purpose." This statement, signed by more than 1,000 Protestant leaders, was given to the press and mailed to the President and members of Congress.[4]

We see The Federal Council of Churches plugging here for the United Nations and using its vast propaganda machine as it did following World War I, when it blanketed the United States with propaganda in favor of the League of Nations. This time, however, the chairman of the commission which drew up the reports was John Foster Dulles, who later was to have a position in the State Department under Secretary of State Dean Acheson; assist at the Dumbarton Oaks Planning Conference for the United Nations organization; serve as a

[4] P. 91.

delegate in San Francisco at the birth of the United Nations; become a delegate to the founding of The World Council of Churches in Amsterdam in August 1948, and serve as Secretary of State, directing the foreign policy of the United States. How many members of the United States Senate, when Dulles's name was up for confirmation, knew his record with The Federal Council of Churches?

Meanwhile, the so-called peace organizations, while outside the framework of the Federal Council, were working in close cooperation with it. And John Foster Dulles was a member of the Carnegie Endowment for International Peace. This should be kept in mind in the light of what will be revealed in regard to John Foster Dulles by other Biennial Reports of The Federal Council of Churches.

From a political point of view, few Republicans who have hailed Mr. Dulles as one of their great leaders know what he said in his statement to the Commission on a Just and Durable Peace at Princeton. The statement was printed in pamphlet form under the title "Long Range Peace Objectives." On page 10 we read (emphasis added):

> President Roosevelt has dealt boldly and dramatically with domestic problems. *Recognizing the failure of our society, as organized,* to adapt itself to new conditions and to meet the imperative needs of human beings, he has effectively grappled with the problem and has not hesitated to break with tradition *and to alter fundamentally the entire structure of our economic order.* As to much that he has done, there is disagreement. But *few would seek to undo the great social reforms he has effected.*

Let us pass from the work of the Federal Council to that of The World Council of Churches, and observe the continuing role of John Foster Dulles.

The string of United Nations conferences on political matters which started off in Hot Springs, Virginia, in June 1943 *culminated in the conference which opened in San Francisco on April 25, 1945.* The United Nations was a suitable vehicle on which all the orthodox religious "one worlders" could ride. *While satisfying the public with purported insistence on the separation of Church and State,* they based their propaganda to the constituents of their denominations on the necessity of accepting the collectivist program developed by the United Nations planners.

Even though the provisional committee which was for so many years the controlling factor of The World Council of Churches was established during the 1937 Oxford and Edinburgh conferences,[5] *it was not until the close of 1945 and the early months of 1946* that the World Council was able to swing into high gear in working for the worldwide program for a controlled economy furnished by the United Nations planning cult.

In December 1945 John D. Rockefeller, Jr., donated a million dollars to the Friends of The World Council of Churches. Several months later, in February 1946, a meeting was held in Geneva, Switzerland, by this same provisional committee. Here it was announced that an international religious training center was to be set up in Geneva. Instruction would be given to students all over the world to prepare them for leadership in interchurch activities. At the same time the Council appointed the Commission on International Relations. *The New York Times* of February 25, 1946, reported the purpose of the commission: "To stimulate the churches of all nations to a more vigorous expression of the demand of the Christian conscience *in relation to the political* policies of governments."

Again the name of John Foster Dulles crops up, along with those of Dr. Reinhold Niebuhr and Bishop G. Bromley Oxnam, both of them notorious for their left-wing affiliations and

5 See Appendix 3.

collectivist pronouncements. *The New York Times* quoted John Foster Dulles as follows:

> We are aiming at a top organization, international in character, to coordinate the thinking and action of Protestant denominations through their national organization. We will attempt to make it do for religion what labor does through the World Federation of Trade Unions.[6]

At this point we again refer to the history of the Church Peace Union as recorded in the book *Pioneers for Peace Through Religion* by Charles S. Macfarland, second secretary of The Federal Council of Churches and a member of the Church Peace Union. In the chapter entitled "The World's Best Chance for Peace in Our Time," Dr. Macfarland says (emphasis added):

> The San Francisco Conference, with representatives from 50 nations, was the most important meeting of our generation. The purpose of the conference was to form a general organization to safeguard the peace and promote the common welfare of nations and their people. The plan agreed upon at Dumbarton Oaks forms the agenda, but beyond the mechanism and the proposals there were many major issues at stake. At San Francisco the State Department made another innovation which is truly revolutionary, for Secretary Stettinius invited 42 national nongovernmental organizations in the United States each to name one delegate and two associates to be *officially* related to the Conference. The churches and religious agencies were strongly represented by: American-Jewish Committee, American Jewish Conference, Catholic Association for International Peace, *Church Peace Union,*

6 July 30, 1946.

Federal Council of the Churches of Christ in America,
National Catholic Welfare Conference. In spite of cynics
the consultants were really consulted, and *the results of
the thinking and influence of the representatives of the
religious agencies are evidenced in the charter itself.* Com-
parison of the charter with the major statements of various religious groups, particularly with the pattern for
peace, indicates the important contribution made by these
organizations. A hundred and twenty-six representatives
served as consultants to the American delegation. The
State Department made all the arrangements for travel
and hotel accommodations, and gave the delegates official
credentials.

*The conference laid the foundations for a new world
order.*[7]

Dr. Macfarland shows that the Church Peace Union adopted
a statement which was presented to the Foreign Relations
Committee of the United States Senate. Then, after The Federal Council of Churches had done the same thing, John Foster
Dulles, one of its representatives, became an official delegate
to the conference which set up the United Nations at Dumbarton Oaks and, later, to the organizing meeting in San Francisco.

Dr. Macfarland seems to revel in the great triumph of the
Council propaganda agencies which helped to form the United
Nations:

This action [ratification of the UN Charter by the United
States Senate] by our Senate means much to us as a nation
and to the world. It means the end of isolationism and
puts on record before the world its solemn promise that
from now on the United States will play its part in everything that helps promote friendship, good will, justice,

7 *Pioneers for Peace Through Religion,* p. 232.

and world peace. The records of the Church Peace Union could not be written without giving emphasis to its more than 31 years of effort to just such a result.[8]

In October 1955 the American Legion National Convention met in Miami, Florida. The featured speaker on the opening day was the Secretary of State, John Foster Dulles. Mr. Dulles admitted that, since the end of World War II and since the United Nations has been in existence, *nine hundred million people have been taken behind the Iron Curtain by the Communist leaders of the Soviet Union.* And the left-wing churchmen still believe that the United Nations is promoting "friendship, good will, justice, and world peace."

In this connection, Bishop G. Bromley Oxnam made an interesting revelation during his testimony before the Committee on Un-American Activities of the House of Representatives, on July 21, 1953. Bishop Oxnam had been asked by the committee's chief counsel about the pro-Communist book *Behind Soviet Power* by Jerome Davis, identified by two witnesses before the same committee as a member of the Communist Party. Bishop Oxnam had sent copies of this book to twenty-two thousand Methodist ministers over the United States with a covering letter signed by the bishop, as president, and by R. E. Diffendorfer, as executive secretary, of the Division of Foreign Missions of the Methodist Church. In this letter Bishop Oxnam suggested that the ministers read, in conjunction with this book, which he said "makes a substantial contribution to understanding of Russia," a statement issued by The Federal Council of the Churches of Christ in America and entitled "Soviet-American Relations," and an article by Vera Micheles Dean entitled "Russia—Menace or Promise." Bishop Oxnam said in his testimony (emphasis added):

8 *Ibid.,* p. 235.

I said that I thought if this book went out it ought to be accompanied by the statement, at least by the statement that was issued by The Federal Council of the Churches of Christ in America on American-Soviet Relations. *I* had chaired that committee that had drafted this statement. It is no secret, however, that *it was written by Mr. John Foster Dulles.*[9]

Excerpts from this statement of The Federal Council of Churches, written by John Foster Dulles, appeared in various segments of the press the day following Bishop Oxnam's testimony; a copy had been secured from the 1946 Biennial Report of The Federal Council of Churches. The Chicago *Tribune* in an editorial expressed amazement over these statements by Dulles which had been presumed to be anti-Soviet. The *Tribune* suggested that perhaps Mr. Scott McLeod, then of the State Department Security Section, had better drop in to the office of his boss, the Secretary of State, Mr. Dulles, and check on him.

Here is an excerpt from the statement on Soviet-American relations, the author of which was John Foster Dulles:

Moreover, communism as an economic program for social reconstruction has points of contact with the social message of Christianity as in its avowed concern for the underprivileged and its insistence on racial equality. . . .

Despite these differences [between the Soviet Union and the Western democracies] peace is possible. We are convinced that a dynamic and fruitful peace can prevail in a world society where conflicts of faith are unavoidable.[10]

[9] *Hearings*, House Committee on Un-American Activities, July 21, 1953, p. 3769.
[10] 1946 Biennial Report, pp. 240, 241.

Could this be the beginning of a campaign to propagandize for "peaceful coexistence" between atheistic communism and the Federal Council's conception of Christianity? Here is another excerpt (emphasis added):

> Differences of belief which are inevitable are often aggravated by differences or clashes of interest which are unnecessary. There are many unnecessary differences between the Soviet Union and the Western democracies, and they provide an important field for remedial action. It is easy for us to see how Soviet leaders can act to dispel many such differences. It is harder for Americans to see what the United States should do. However, the Christian way is to think first of what we can do. That, indeed, is the practical course, for what we can do is within our power. Also, while one side alone cannot end tensions of dual origin, it can make mutuality of effort easier and more likely. The search should not be for ways to placate Soviet leaders irrespective of moral judgment or righteous conviction. Rather, the effort should be *to eradicate from our own national position features which cannot be morally or intellectually justified.*[11]

We quote further:

> It should be clear that moral condemnation of Soviet methods and desire to redress their injustice do not cloak a selfish desire on the part of those who want peace to be a static condition, to bear down on all who seek change.[12]

Mr. Dulles also said (emphasis added):

11 *Ibid.*, pp. 243, 244.
12 *Ibid.*, p. 244.

Fourth, neither state socialism nor free enterprise provides a perfect economic system; *each can learn from the experience of the other.*

The Soviet Union practices a form of state socialism which is prescribed by the Soviet Communist Party. Soviet leadership seeks, by physical power where that is convenient and by propaganda and penetration elsewhere, to bring Communists into positions of influence in the other communities of the world.

The United States practices a form of free enterprise. By credits, trade agreements, and like measures it seeks to keep as much of the world as possible on a free enterprise basis. Each system, fearing economic encirclement, tends to encircle.

We cannot expect the proponents of either state socialism or free enterprise to abandon their beliefs. But they need not, on account of their beliefs, hate or despise each other. Only blind fanaticism looks upon either system as perfect. *The free enterprise system has yet to prove that it can assure steady production and employment. It has yet to prove that it can continuously provide industrial workers with that sense of individual creativeness which gives greater satisfaction than mere material possession. . . .*

Several Western democracies are trying some moderate Socialistic experiments designed to assure full production and employment while preserving religious, intellectual, and political freedom. Soviet socialism has changed much, particularly in placing greater dependence upon the incentive of personal gain. The free enterprise system in the United States has developed such forms of social security as unemployment and retirement benefits which a few years ago would have been judged incompatible with the system.[13]

13 *Ibid.,* pp. 245, 246.

Here Mr. Dulles has made some very basic criticisms of the American free-enterprise system, while congratulating the Soviet Union for its "greater dependence on the incentive of personal gain." How would the millions in the Soviet slave-labor camps feel about this statement from a man who is considered a great spiritual leader and is Secretary of State of the nation to which millions of people enslaved under the Soviet system have looked for the moral and spiritual leadership which would one day rid them of their chains!

Perhaps the most startling piece of documentation on the bankrupt leadership of The Federal Council of Churches and on the part that men like Mr. Dulles have played in influencing government officials to adopt the Council's program is found in the 1948 Biennial Report under the chapter title "International Justice and Goodwill" (emphasis added):

> Accompanying changes in subject matter have been changes in the structure of the Department. The wartime division of the Federal Council's work in this field between the Department and the Commission on a Just and Durable Peace was superseded in January 1948 by a reorganized Department. This reorganization was designed to conserve the great values of the specialized work of the Commission on problems of international organization, in a Department Committee on Policy *under the chairmanship of John Foster Dulles.* . . .
>
> The Department held a two-day meeting in Philadelphia, January 8–9, to consider moral issues in the proposed European Recovery Program and to evaluate the work. Background material on the European Recovery Program was prepared by two special committees, with Charles H. Seaver and Marshall Harris serving as chairmen. *Similar background data on the United Nations was*

prepared by a committee, under the chairmanship of Alger Hiss.

The Department divided into two sections, Mr. Dulles chairing the section on the United Nations and Chester I. Barnard the section on the European Recovery Program. The reports of these sections, after consideration by the Department as a whole, were approved and subsequently acted upon by the Federal Council's Executive Committee meeting in Atlanta on January 13.[14]

We know, from testimony given during the hearing on Alger Hiss by the Committee on Un-American Activities, that John Foster Dulles and Alger Hiss were friends of long standing. Mr. Dulles recommended Mr. Hiss to head the multimillion-dollar Carnegie Endowment for International Peace. Mr. Dulles worked side by side with Mr. Hiss in the State Department and in the various conferences that planned the United Nations. But how many American church people knew that Mr. Dulles and Mr. Hiss worked together in The Federal Council of Churches and that both were chairmen of important committees of the Council?

Alger Hiss landed in a Federal penitentiary as a convicted perjuror—for lying under oath before a Federal grand jury about his Communist intrigues.

Mr. Dulles, however, Mr. Hiss's colleague in the Federal Council, became the director of the foreign policy of the United States.

And the Federal Council used its vast machinery to filter their un-American political programs down through the state, county, and city councils to the individual churches and church people.

Further, the Federal Council used the full power of its organization and such propagandists as Messrs. Dulles and Hiss

14 Pp. 105, 106.

to influence the United States government in its most important foreign-policy decisions. Here is proof from the Federal
Council's Biennial Report of 1948 (emphasis added):

> In support of this policy, a considerable program of edu-
> cation was carried on by church bodies cooperating in the
> Federal Council during February and March, when the
> issues were being debated in the Congress. A petition en-
> dorsing the principles of the statement and signed by 700
> churchmen was presented by Bishop Stamm, Bishop Ox-
> nam and other church leaders to Senator Vandenberg and
> Speaker Martin on March 11. A conference of 250 denom-
> inational leaders met at the New York Avenue Presby-
> terian Church in Washington under the auspices of the
> Department, with Dr. Aubrey serving as chairman. This
> group considered continuing problems of the recovery
> program, and was addressed by Assistant Secretary of State
> Willard Thorp. That evening an impressive demonstra-
> tion of Christian concern was shown in Washington
> Cathedral. Bishop Stamm presided, Bishop Dun, Secre-
> tary Marshall, and Mr. Dulles gave addresses, and the
> heads of several communions joined in the procession.
> *The audience of more than 2,000 included the President
> and many members of Congress.* Testimony in behalf of
> the Federal Council's recommendations was presented to
> the proper Congressional Committees by Mr. Charles P.
> Taft. . . .
> A full discussion by the Committee on Policy under the
> chairmanship of Mr. Dulles showed agreement on the
> need for action by the churches to change the prevailing
> mood of the American people in order to lessen the dan-
> gers of war. On the basis of this discussion a new state-
> ment of policy was drafted and presented by the Depart-
> ment to the Executive Committee of the Federal Council

at a special meeting on April 26. The statement, "A Positive Program for Peace," was approved *and distributed to the churches by the denominational agencies and the state and city councils of churches.*[15]

Here, by its own admission, the Federal Council sought to influence the President and the Congress of the United States on behalf of its programs and sought "to change the prevailing mood of the American people" by directing its propaganda down to the denominational agencies and the state and city councils of churches. One writer has referred to this Federal Council organization as "an ecclesiastical octopus."

Charles P. Taft, who presented the Federal Council's program to "the proper Congressional committees" was at one time the president of the Federal Council and was the brother of the late Senator Robert A. Taft, to whose economic and political views his own were diametrically opposed.

According to the 1948 Biennial Report,[16] the executive secretary of the Commission on International Justice and Goodwill was the late Rev. Walter W. VanKirk. Dr. VanKirk had been associated with at least five Communist-front organizations, according to the files of the Committee on Un-American Activities. He was a notorious pacifist and one-world promoter, appearing on behalf of the Federal Council before church groups and in universities.

The Biennial Report of 1948 indicates the variety of fields in which the Federal Council's representatives participated and even lobbied among Congressional committees:

Dr. VanKirk was authorized to testify at Congressional hearings in behalf of nondiscrimination against Orientals in immigration laws and in opposition to universal mili-

15 Pp. 106, 107.
16 P. 109.

tary training. The committee also urged further contributions to the International Children's Emergency Fund and vigorous support by the United States for a United Nations Declaration and a Covenant on Human Rights.

At its April meeting, the Executive Committee authorized the Department to present testimony in Congress on behalf of the principles of the Reciprocal Trade Agreements legislation. This testimony was subsequently presented by Mr. Taft. The Committee in June adopted a resolution supporting a United Nations convention on the crime of genocide and later joined with some 125 organizations from 23 countries in a petition to the United Nations. In keeping with earlier pronouncements, the Committee urged the Congress "to appropriate, without enfeebling reductions, the funds authorized in the Foreign Assistance Act of 1948." The Committee also authorized testimony in relation to the status of conscientious objectors under the Selective Service Act.[17]

Here The Federal Council of Churches represented itself as speaking for millions of people on seven political issues.

The Federal Council's Commission on International Justice and Goodwill does *not* explain why the United States has refused to recognize the United Nations Declaration and Covenant on Human Rights. The primary reason is that the Bill on Human Rights has no provision guaranteeing *property rights* of the individual. The left-wing churchmen are concerned only with "civil rights" or "human rights." Under the world Socialist plan there *are* no property rights.

The Genocide Convention, as drawn up by the United Nations and favored by leading National and World Council churchmen, also has not yet been accepted by the United States. Under the Convention, any American could be thrown

17 P. 108.

into a foreign prison and tried by a foreign court merely for criticizing one who is propagating a political or economic theory. The Genocide Convention would make it an offense for anyone to cause *mental* harm to a person of a different race, creed, or color.

On December 6, 1949, in Atlanta, Georgia, the Executive Committee of The Federal Council of the Churches of Christ in America adopted a declaration entitled "The Churches and American Policy in the Far East." This statement was published in pamphlet form by the Department of International Justice and Goodwill at $2.00 per 100 copies. Here are some significant quotations (emphasis added):

> Despite this record of American friendship for the peoples of the Far East, the ideological clash and power struggle which today engulf the world have adversely affected the moral position of our nation in Asia. This has been due, in part, to the spreading of hostile propaganda and, in part, *to the seeming inability of our nation to formulate a policy related to the realities of the revolutionary era emerging in Asia. . . .*
>
> We believe the further advance of communism in China and Asia cannot be permanently stopped by military action. Such military assistance as the United States placed at the disposal of the Chinese Nationalists proved unavailing.[18]

[18] The Federal Council of Churches doesn't tell the kind of "military assistance" placed at the disposal of the Chinese Nationalists. If the truth had been told by the Federal Council, the American people would have learned that the Truman-Acheson regime left the armies of Chiang Kai-shek without any modern equipment but with arms abandoned by units of the 14th Air Force and several ground cadres when they pulled out of China. The 80th Congress appropriated money to help the Chinese Nationalists, but the Communists were already sweeping down from northern China, supplied and equipped by the Soviet Union. The aid appropriated by Congress never reached Chiang Kai-shek in time.

The reasons for this are many, but among these reasons is the fact that the civil war in China [19] is not only a test of arms, it is also, in part, a social and political convulsion of revolutionary proportions. Similarly, the thrust of communism in other parts of Asia is only in part a military operation; in other and more important respects it has taken advantage of a mass protest against grinding poverty, economic injustice, social maladjustment, and political subservience to the West.

The Federal Council of Churches did not tell the church people, to whom this pamphlet was being sent, that this was a planned operation by the Soviet Union toward the conquest of all Asia. The Federal Council pronouncement continues:

> Nor do we believe that the challenge to the West deriving from the revolutionary upsurge of Asia's millions can be met by the hasty improvisation of national policy designed to counter the spread of communism first in one country, then in another. *It is a matter genuinely to be deplored* that the United States, with its democratic traditions and its long established commitment to freedom for subject and dependent peoples, has become aligned in popular world opinion with the maintenance of the status quo, rather than with *the forces making for a new Asia.*

The Federal Councilites do not reveal what the "status quo" is. They do not reveal what "forces" are "making for a new Asia." The truth is that the United States was not giving help

---

[19] The Federal Councilites called this war in China a civil war. This is the line which was followed by the State Department leaders in the Truman Administration. They assured the people of this country that the war was not a Communist putsch in China, backed by Russia, but an uprising of poor peasants and farmers, "agrarian reformers," against the Nationalist government of Chiang Kai-shek.

to Chiang Kai-shek, who had warned the world that the Communist campaign in China was designed and directed by the Soviet Union and that the "forces making for a new Asia" were the Communists themselves. Was the United States to align itself with these Communist forces?

The report says further that our government "accordingly, should energetically support the United Nations program of technical assistance, a program which has been reinforced by President Truman's proposal 'for making the benefits of our scientific advances and industrial progress available for the improvement and growth of underdeveloped areas.' " This is a farce, for the United Nations was rendering very little technical assistance to the Far East. Most of it was coming from the United States. The report is Federal Council propaganda for the Truman Point IV plan and for the United Nations. The report resumes (emphasis added):

"This technical assistance should be designed to contribute to the freedom and livelihood of the peoples concerned, *under whatever forms of government these values can* be advanced."

The Federal Council suggests that we should continue to render this assistance even if the Communists take over.

One of the outstanding leaders of the Presbyterian Church in the U.S.A., and a world figure in the ecumenical movement, is Dr. John A. Mackay,[20] president of Princeton Theological Seminary and president of the International Missionary Council, which is the missionary arm of the World Council of Churches. On January 16, 1950, the *Presbyterian Outlook* and *Religious News Service* both recorded the following item:

New York.—John A. Mackay urged here that the United States recognize the Communist government of China. Speaking to a group of 200 church leaders and mission-

[20] For Communist-front affiliations of Dr. Mackay, see *Cumulative Index,* House Committee on Un-American Activities, Jan. 20, 1955, p. 524.

ary executives, he warned that failure to recognize the Communists "might alienate the people of China forever."

Dr. Mackay, who returned recently from a nine weeks' tour of East Asia, said recognition was justified on the following grounds:

(1) The excellent behavior of the Communist armies in their conquest of the China mainland;

(2) The fact that missionary activity had not been disrupted;

(3) The widespread view that China's communism will take a "different expression" than in Russia and Eastern Europe;

(4) The overwhelming support of the people for the new regime, based largely on their disillusionment with the Nationalist government.

Dr. Mackay said that "communism has come to China for a long time, because the Chinese people are war weary, utterly unbelieving in the integrity of their old regime, and longing for a change."

Warning against "our present anti-Communist psychology," he said that "no matter what we might think of the social and political aspects of communism, the government now in control of China deserves our recognition."

There was ample documented evidence in the newspapers of the nation, in the halls of Congress, and in the military headquarters to show that the four reasons upon which Dr. Mackay said recognition was justified were without foundation. The fact is, Dr. Mackay was not in China during the war, nor was he there on his so-called "nine weeks' tour of East Asia." What Dr. Mackay obtained was the Communist Party line from his liberal theological friends in China and in the United States. It is a dangerous thing for a leading American theologian to be warning against "our present anti-Communist psychology" when his own government is calling upon the people of the United States and the free nations of the world to arm for defense against the universal Communist threat.

Dr. Mackay's views are also set forth in his publication, *Theology Today*, through other mouthpieces, such as Dr. John C. Bennett, professor of Union Theological Seminary, who, in an article for the issue of October 1950, states what he calls "The Christian Answer to Communism." In referring to the Communist situation in the United States, Dr. Bennett says: "In spite of the widespread Red hunting, there is very little actual support of communism in this country." Here again is a man who does not know what he is talking about. The overwhelming evidence in the hands of J. Edgar Hoover, the Congress, and the various intelligence agencies of the military is not to be set aside in favor of a dedicated Socialist theologian.

Dr. Bennett continues in *Theology Today* (emphasis added):

Why must they conclude that there is a conflict between Christianity and communism? . . . Certainly we cannot find the difficulty in the Communist economic system or in Communist social goals. There is much overlapping between Communist goals and Christian goals. Also, I think it is a mistake to put the emphasis upon the materialism of communism or upon the moral relativism of communism or even upon the atheism of communism. Each of these elements in communism is a crude way of protesting against something that is false in the dominant religious and moral ideas which the Communist prophets, Marx and Engels, especially, found it necessary to reject. [Does Dr. Bennett mean to say that Marx and Engels are reliable authorities for telling us what is wrong in the dominant religious and moral ideas?] Dialectical material-ism was a partly justified protest against a one-sided idealism. . . . *I do not believe that American Christians could condemn communism because of its belief that revolution, even violent revolution, is sometimes necessary.*

This kind of teaching is being given to students at Princeton and being sent out to Presbyterian ministers and missionaries all over the world. It is small wonder that Dr. Hugh Halton, Catholic chaplain of Princeton University and head of the Aquinas Foundation, affiliated with the university, should have cried out against this kind of propaganda being disseminated to students. His protests caused him to be denied further access to the Princeton grounds on orders of Dr. Robert Goheen, the new "liberal" president of the university.

Dr. Mackay evidently has not changed his opinions in recent days in regard to recognizing Red China. In December 1956, addressing a meeting of The National Council of Churches in Indianapolis, he urged the Council to send a delegation of American churchmen to Red China.[21]

21 Chicago *Tribune*, May 13, 1957.

13 THE COUNCILS' SECULAR ACTIVITIES MULTIPLY

A maze of boards and committees. The Director of Religious Information. Attacks on the immigration laws by Mackay, Van Kirk, Dawber, Dahlberg, Kennedy, Baker, Palmer, Fisher, and others. Sen. McCarran's rebuttal. Council watches developments in Congress threatening freedom. Asks merger of subversive probes. Favors Federal aid to education—but watch the Catholics. Moves in on mental health. Department of International Justice and Goodwill—its farflung interests. Rural sociology. Alaskan problems. Hydrogen-bomb tests. An ecclesiastical octopus.

THE NATIONAL AND WORLD COUNCILS OF CHURCHES have gained increasing prestige and political influence during the Eisenhower Administration. As their position has been consolidated, their utterances on national and international politics have become unrestrained. While they will jump to the attack when a non-Protestant religious body is suspected of dislodging a pebble from the wall of separation between church and state, they will allow no restriction to be placed upon the exercise of their own political action and influence. The Councils' participation in politics has become undisguised, massive, and the primary purpose of their existence. It is no wonder that, in the discharge of its functions, the National Council alone, in 1952, required 221 separate boards, departments, and commissions.

Let us look at some of the political and economic matters

that have occupied so much of the time, energies, and funds of the Councils, beginning with the United States Information Agency.

This agency, first headed by Theodore Streibert, is intended through its various branches to give to other nations an accurate picture of what life is like in the United States.

Members of The National Council of Churches recommended that a new department of the Information Agency be created, to be called the Department of Religious Policy and headed by a Chief of Religious Policy. The recommendation was adopted, and the man appointed to head it was Dr. D. Elton Trueblood, of Earlham College, a modernist in theology and a pro-Socialist in his writings.

When the Administration received widespread criticism over the creation of such a post, the name of the department was changed to the Department of Religious Information, and that of its head to the Director of Religious Information. When ministers and patriotic organizations continued to criticize the Administration for allowing the post to exist, Mr. Streibert stated that Dr. Trueblood was recommended as its head by leaders of The National Council of Churches, with the intimation that its existence was favored by Council leaders. In the eyes of the Administration, the Council's wish was a command.

Another preoccupation of the National Council of Churches is the McCarran-Walter Security and Immigration Act.

The McCarran-Walter Act, designed to safeguard the internal security of the United States, was the product of six years of work devoted to codifying the outmoded immigration laws. The late Senator Pat McCarran and Congressman Francis Walter introduced the bill; it was passed by both houses, vetoed by President Truman, and passed again by an overwhelming vote of both houses. It became the law of the land in 1950.

Prominent church leaders of The National Council of Churches, including Methodist bishops and members of the Methodist Federation for Social Action, a Communist front, made common cause with the Communists and their satellite organizations in attacking this important legislation. Among the National Council leaders were such lights as Dr. John A. Mackay, president of Princeton Theological Seminary and president of the World Council's International Missionary Council; Dr. Mark A. Dawber, former executive secretary of the Home Missions Council of North America; Dr. Edwin T. Dahlberg of St. Louis, Missouri, identified with The Federal Council of Churches' Department on Evangelism; Methodist Bishops Gerald Kennedy and James C. Baker, of the Methodist Federation for Social Action; Dr. Albert W. Palmer, former moderator of the Congregational Christian Churches of America; Mrs. Welthy Honsinger Fisher, chairman of the World Day of Prayer Committee of the United Council of Church Women.

One of the voices of the ecumenical movement, and a strong supporter of the National and World Councils of Churches, the *Christian Century*, on April 8, 1953, published a letter from Senator Pat McCarran after the *Century* had attacked the McCarran-Walter Act and sought to get it repealed or watered down so that World Council delegates from the Iron Curtain countries could get into this country without restriction of any kind. Senator McCarran's letter read:

Sir, please allow me the privilege of commenting on an editorial appearing in the *Christian Century* under the date of March 11 entitled "McCarran Act Revision a Church Priority."

The editorial begins with the assertion that, "unless the McCarran-Walter Immigration Act is revised in the current session of Congress, its operation will probably keep out of the country many of the church leaders who should come from abroad to the 1954 World Assembly of Churches in Evanston."

Under the provisions of the Immigration and Nationality Act, as well as under the provisions of the preceding immigration law, no one is inadmissible to the United States as a visitor unless his presence in this country would endanger the public safety.

The assertion in your editorial is either (1) untrue or (2) a shocking charge against "many of the Church leaders who should come from abroad."

I submit that in all fairness, my letter should be published in the *Christian Century* as a rebuttal to the editorial which is highly prejudicial of an Act which was endorsed by the Immigration and Naturalization Service, the Visa Division, the Department of State, the Department of Justice, the Central Intelligence Agency, and by over one hundred patriotic, civic, and religious organizations as fair and sound legislation which was urgently needed for the best interests of the United States of America.

[Signed] Pat McCarran

The National Council of Churches' official spokesman in such matters as the McCarran-Walter Act was the late Dr. Walter W. VanKirk, who for many years had been an officer in the Department of International Justice and Goodwill. Now, in attacking the Act, the National Council represented itself to its constituent denominations, to the press, and to the government of the United States as speaking for more than 30,000,000 church members. But, as is pointed out on page 261, this is a fantastic claim. Thirty million church members had not read the Act nor did they give permission to the Council or to

Dr. VanKirk to attack the McCarran-Walter Immigration Act on their behalf.

The churchgoing members of the denominations also have not requested The National Council of Churches to represent them in the Council's continual participation in other political affairs, a sampling of which, as reported in the nation's press, follows:

> *Church Council Names Group to Watch Congress—* Chicago (AP)—The National Council of Churches of Christ in the U.S.A. named a 15-member committee to watch developments in Congress and elsewhere which "threaten the freedom of the people and institutions of the United States."[1]

> CHURCH GROUP RIPS THREAT TO U.S. FREEDOMS. *Asks for the Merger of Subversive Probes*—New York, March 17 (AP)—The National Council of Churches today condemned what it called a growing tendency to leave to the government "to determine what is and what is not American." This is a "basic threat" to historic freedoms, the Council said.[2]

> NATIONAL COUNCIL OF CHURCHES HOLDS FOUR DAY STUDY CONFERENCE ON THE CHURCHES AND WORLD ORDER. *Theme of Conference, The Christian Faith and International Responsibility.* Speakers for the subject and their topics are the United States and the United Nations, Mrs. Edith Sperlock Sampson, Chicago Negro Attorney and Chairman of the International Relations Committee of the National Council of Negro Women, a member of the Episcopal Church. Politically Mrs. Samp-

1 Colorado Springs *Gazette-Telegraph,* May 20, 1953.
2 Chicago *Tribune,* March 18, 1954.

son is a supporter of the New Deal Program, was named an alternate to the United States delegation to the U.N. by President Truman in 1950; was a supporter of Adlai Stevenson in the presidential campaign of 1952 and has spoken in Illinois in support of an F.E.P.C. measure which thus far has failed of enactment.

Speaking on The United States and Foreign Economic Policy will be Professor Willard L. Thorp, Amherst, Massachusetts, former Assistant Secretary of State for Economic Affairs. He is a layman in the Congregational Church.

Another speaker will be Dr. Frank P. Graham, representative in India, Pakistan, and former U.S. Senator from North Carolina and former President of the University of North Carolina. He is a Presbyterian; the top speakers of the conference will be Mrs. Franklin D. Roosevelt, who will address the conference on the United States and the United Nations, and Bishop G. Bromley Oxnam, of Washington, D.C., whose topic is not yet announced.[3]

The motto of The National Council of Churches might be said to be: "A finger in every pie." Here are further samples of how far afield the Council has strayed from the simple message of the Christian Gospel:

5. The vigorous steps by the General Board to combat threats to the freedom of the American people and their institutions. These steps included specific proposals for remedial action by Congress.[4]

The National Council is referring to the Congressional inves-

[3] Colorado Springs *Gazette-Telegraph*, Oct. 18, 1953.
[4] 1954 Biennial Report, p. 32.

tigative committees, which are trying to protect the "freedom of the American people and their institutions."

> A full analysis and appraisal by our churches of what is now happening in the world would enable them to approach the planning of program and activities with a greater sense of history. This task has been done in specific areas by units of the Council, but never wholly.[5]

We wonder if the State Department of the United States has been informed of the Council's "analysis and appraisal" of "what is now happening in the world."

> Already the Council carries on programs in more than seventy-five areas of Christian concern and most of these were inherited from the merging agencies.[6]

(This should provide plenty of work for the Council's 221 boards, departments, and commissions.)

> A service provided by the Commission often overlooked is the work of the Committee on Newspaper Lesson Syndication which at the present time is providing syndicated treatments of Sunday-school lessons and other religious themes. Five series are offered; one reaching 656 newspapers in 36 states; another reaching 69 newspapers in 27 states with a circulation of more than two million.[7]

(This activity could properly be considered as spreading the Gospel, were it not that some of the Sunday-school lessons are so far afield from biblical teaching that they would never be

[5] *Ibid.*, p. 35.
[6] *Ibid.*, p. 36.
[7] *Ibid.*, p. 43.

recognized by the heads of the early Christian church if they were here today.)

> Studies have been privately circulated on the infiltration of public school faculties and boards in a manner to make them practically parochial schools of the Roman Catholic Church; on federal aid to public schools; . . .[8]

On page 54 of the 1954 Biennial Report, the Department of Religious Liberty presents a policy statement favoring Federal aid to education under specific conditions. These conditions, of course, have to do with the exclusion of Roman Catholic schools.

Continuing with the multiplication of Council services which have no remote connection with the preaching of the Gospel, we note that the Department of Pastoral Services has a Commission on Religion and Health.[9] Here we find The National Council of Churches becoming involved in the "mental health problem," in which a horde of other liberal organizations has suddenly become interested. Most of these organizations were silent for years on the subject, but "mental health" suddenly has come into its own. Because "mental health" has become available as a lever to be used for promoting political and ideological designs, a word on the subject is in order.

No one is against adequate care for people who are, beyond reasonable doubt, insane, unable to care for themselves, and a physical menace to other members of society. Sufficient appropriation should be made by state authorities to care for these helpless people.

Something new has come into the subject of insanity, however, within the past several years. People who are normal in

8 *Ibid.*, p. 54.
9 *Ibid.*, p. 58.

every sense of the word but who hold unpopular political ideas, such as opposition to world government and to the United Nations, Federal aid to education, and socialism, are now being branded by their political opponents as "lunatics," "nuts," and "idiots." Some of the mental health legislation which has recently been introduced on state and Federal levels gives such wide latitude of interpretation to psychiatrists and politicians, who would enforce it once it became law, that it is conceivable that anyone who takes a stand for the sovereignty of the United States, in favor of Congressional investigations, in opposition to fluoridation of public water supplies, and in favor of state's rights could be committed to an asylum in order to silence opposition.

Because of this possibility, Congressman Usher L. Burdick of North Dakota submitted Resolution 98 to the 85th Congress. The text of the resolution reads:

WHEREAS seven hundred thousand citizens of the United States are confined in asylums, many wrongfully and needlessly; and

WHEREAS the majority are old people, misfits, and odd ones who are not insane or dangerous; and

WHEREAS we recognize the need of adequate care for the mentally ill but deplore legislation which may be contrary to their best interests and the language of this bill is subject to misinterpretation which could jeopardize Constitutional rights of the individual; and

WHEREAS among the psychiatrists are those who advocate an ideology foreign to the United States, as set forth in "Mental Health and World Citizenship," the statement of the 1948 International Congress on Mental Health; and

WHEREAS the mental health organizations are sponsoring in the several states commitment legislation which violates the rights guaranteed to every citizen under the Constitution of the United States; and

WHEREAS the Alaska Mental Health Act, as passed by the Congress, contains unconstitutional provisions; therefore be it

RESOLVED by the House of Representatives (the Senate concurring) That the Congress of the United States make a complete investigation into all ramifications and implications of mental health legislative programs which are currently being promoted.

The Department of International Justice and Goodwill, in its 1954 report, notes, under the heading "Toward a Consensus on World Order," that it has taken action pertaining to the "international situation, and to those issues of American foreign policy that bear upon that situation." Other fields of interest of this department include letters to the United States delegation to the United Nations; World Order Day messages; the United States immigration and naturalization policies; the persecution of Jewish minorities; economic aid and Point IV programs of technical assistance, and the setting up of "standing commissions of specialists on different phases of United States foreign policy who will do research and produce background papers on the United Nations (including collective security and armament control), Western Europe, Asia, and the Middle East."

The Department of International Justice and Goodwill records [10] that the staff "filled approximately 150 field engagements which included 225 specific assignments in 21 states and Washington, D.C., serving national, state, and local denominational bodies, councils of churches, councils of church women and student groups." Because UN headquarters hap-

[10] *Ibid.*, p. 63.

pened to be in New York City, "the field was constantly coming to the staff in the form of UN seminars."

The Department of the Town and Country Church distributed ten thousand leaflets entitled "Should Your Child Be a Farmer?" This department gave special short courses and urged denominational schools to "add lectures on Agricultural Economics and Rural Sociology." [11]

Nothing is overlooked, not even Alaska. The Council's Alaska Committee, through the "Alaska Conference for Cooperative Planning," reports:

> Representatives of various public and private agencies have held two conferences in Alaska under the sponsorship of the Alaska Committee seeking to establish some united goals in the fields of health, education, child welfare, economic development, general services, and spiritual dynamic, and greater cooperation in achieving those goals. Much information was gathered from many agencies and summarized. A steering committee has been named and an advisory relation to Federal agencies in Washington and Alaska has been suggested. The Committee has been handicapped in sharing the proposed program with all committees because of lack of funds. [12]

Rather than the work of a "church" council, this operation resembles a combination of the United Nations and the Truman Administration's Point IV program. Continuing with the Council's many-headed enterprises:

> In matters of national concern, the General Board took actions dealing with such matters as: the maintenance of American freedom, confidentiality of assistance records,

11 *Ibid.*, p. 91.
12 *Ibid.*, p. 96.

housing, the Supreme Court decision on segregation, Federal aid to education, Christian principles and assumptions for economic life, and activities of Congressional investigating committees.[13]

Here is another official action of the General Board, meeting on September 14 and 15, 1954:

> Approved: 21. Motion to instruct officers of the National Council to communicate with the proper body of Christian churchmen in Japan our concern for those affected by hydrogen bomb tests.[14]

And on November 17 and 18, 1953:

> Approved: 13. Statement on "The Churches' Concern on Housing." [15]

And on May 18 and 19, 1954:

> Approved: 21. Statement on the Supreme Court decision on segregation.[16]

And, on the same dates:

> 23. Statement on technical assistance; 24. Statement on Federal aid to education; . . . 26. Recommendation regarding presentations to appropriate Congressional Committees by representatives of Council units of the viewpoint of the Council on technical assistance, supplying surplus foods to famine and needy areas, and support for the United States program of international exchange

13 *Ibid.*, p. 144.
14 *Ibid.*, p. 145.
15 *Ibid.*, p. 146.
16 *Loc. cit.*

through which students, teachers, businessmen, labor leaders, and other groups to facilitate understanding between our country and other peoples.[17]

And, on September 14 and 15, 1954:

Approved: 30. Letter to members of the United States delegation to the United Nations.[18]

On page 147 of the 1954 Biennial Report we find the following action taken by the General Board of the National Council:

Approved: 12. General Policy and Strategy Committee report on strengthening cooperation in state and local councils of churches and councils of church women—May 19, 1953; . . . 20. Provision granting authority to the Committee on Maintenance of American Freedom to address appropriate Congressional investigating committees between the September and November 1953 meetings of the General Board—September 16, 1953; 21. Resolution deploring the action of the House Committee on Un-American Activities in releasing accusations against two Jewish rabbis, Stephen S. Wise and Judah L. Magnes, now dead—September 16, 1953.

It is little wonder that this ecclesiastical octopus has had to create a maze of boards and commissions and ask the church people of the nation for millions of dollars to carry out its political mission. How far the professing church in America has strayed from the simple message of the church as given by Christ and the apostles in the New Testament!

17 *Loc. cit.*
18 *Loc. cit.*

14   ONE CHURCH
FOR ONE WORLD

Dr. Bauman on the super church. Bishop Oxnam advocates union of all Protestant churches in America, then all Protestant churches in the world. The two great groups, Protestant and Catholic, will unite, forming the Holy Catholic Church. Bishop Oxnam denies the great Christian doctrines. "A Man Named Wesley Passed This Way." Departure of 1948 Methodist Church from that of 1738. Bishop Oxnam hopes for early union with Eastern Orthodoxy. Ecumenical leaders work within UN framework. World Council formed in Amsterdam in 1948. Soviet clergymen present. No agreement on meaning of word "church." Capitalism condemned, in statement by Dr. Bennett. Bishop Oxnam elected president of Council for North America. Dr. Chao, Communist and nonbeliever, represents Asia. Dr. Chao opposes America during Korean war. World Council Executive Committee declares communism has roots in teachings of Jesus. Communist Czech, Prof. Hromadka, a member of World Council Central Committee. Accuses America of germ warfare. Appointed to Soviet-sponsored World Council of Peace.

MANY PEOPLE have asked what the leaders of the Councils of Churches hope the promulgation of collectivistic doctrine will lead to. The question can be answered very easily from two sources. One is an article by the late Dr. Louis S. Bauman, who for years was pastor of the large and influential First Brethren Church of Long Beach, California. Writing in *The King's Business*,[1] Dr. Bauman tells of the apostasy of the American Protestant Churches:

[1] Bible Institute of Los Angeles, July 1950.

202

Apostasy: The Death Rattle of Our Age

Dr. Louis S. Bauman

Should any of these modernists deny that a great super church that will regiment the entire religious world is the goal that these ambitious ecclesiastics seek, we might say that it would seem that the thinking of the men, chosen to head up the World Council of Christian Churches, ought best to reveal the purpose of the institution they head. Bishop G. Bromley Oxnam, President of the World Council for America, says: "Union can and must be established in Christ's churches in the world." He advocates the union of all Protestant Churches in America, and has declared that such a union would "electrify the world and accelerate the trend toward union in every continent." (Ecumenical Press Service, June 6, 1947.)

Speaking to the Methodist General Conference (*Watchman-Examiner*, Nov. 18, 1948), Bishop Oxnam prophesied a day when there would be "only two groups, the Protestant and Catholic, and that they would unite to form the Holy Catholic Church"—the Church Universal. "One Church for One World"—such is the slogan of this great World Council. Such an organization, of course, could only be apostate; believing everything, it would believe nothing.

The fact of the matter is that nothing could more eloquently reveal the purpose of the World Council of Churches as apostate than the elevation of Bishop Oxnam to the presidency of the American wing of the Council, for the American Council (wing) is the dominating wing, providing for 85 per cent of the entire budget of the whole Council. The writer was thrown into close contact with Bishop Oxnam many years ago in Los Angeles, at which time Dr. Oxnam was the pastor of the Church of All Nations (Methodist Episcopal) of that city.

In our conversation, he asked: "Dr. Bauman, just what do you regard as 'the fundamentals of the faith'?" In reply, I said: "The Bible is fully inspired of the Holy Ghost; the virgin birth of Christ, who was God incarnate in the flesh; the substitutional death of Christ on the cross; and the resurrection of Christ from the dead in the body in which He died." Dr. Oxnam flashed back the reply: "No one of which the Methodist Episcopal Church any longer believes!" "No longer believes!" I exclaimed. "Then the Methodist Episcopal Church, having once believed them, is apostate!"

I questioned the truth of his statement, and said that I was once a Methodist, and knew that at least some Methodists still believed all four of these doctrines. He said: "If anyone wants to know whether the Methodist Episcopal Church any longer believes these doctrines, let him examine the textbooks, many of them written by our bishops, and used in our Church-supported schools. He will find every one of these doctrines denied." And, with a full knowledge of what Dr. Oxnam believes, that Church made him a bishop, and The Federal Council of Churches of Christ made him its president, and now The World Council of Churches in America makes him its supreme head.

As I write these words, on my desk before me lies a copy of *The Christian Advocate* (May 13, 1948). Herein is printed "A summary of the episcopal address, read to the General Conference, April 28, by Bishop G. Bromley Oxnam." The subject: "A Man Named Wesley Passed This Way." From this address we quote: "Methodism is determined to preach a gospel that insists that all men are brothers and children of one Father, to whom final loyalty is due." Then, without mincing any words, Methodism is determined to preach a lie, for, when the apostate sons of Judah said: "We have one Father, even God," Jesus said: "If God were your father, ye would love me. . . . Ye are of your father the devil, and the lusts of your father ye will do" (John 8:41, 44). Now, beyond all controversy, "all men" do not love the Lord Jesus Christ; and God is the Father only of those who love Christ. According to our Lord, the fatherhood of the devil is just as much a fact as the Fatherhood of God. The contention of Christ in the 8th chapter of John is that those who deny the deity of Jesus Christ are fathered by the devil. Modernists should not deny their paternity!

From Dr. Oxnam's address, again we quote: "The supreme objective of the Church . . . is to make Christ regnant in the activities of man and of society." But, in the first council ever assembled in the Christian Church (in Jerusalem, A.D. 46), the apostles declared that the supreme objective of the Church is to "visit the Gentiles and take out of them a people for his name"—the salvation of individuals and not the socialization of the world. (Acts 15.)

At the close of Dr. Oxnam's message, we read: "The bishops concluded: 'Fifty-two years from now, when man has reached the year 2000 and has won, let us pray, the justice, the brotherhood and peace of his dreams, let us hope that the contribution of the people called Methodists may have been so significant that history may proudly record, "A Man Named Wesley Passed This Way!" ' "

But what must we think? If "A Man Named Wesley Passed This Way"—the way of the General Conference of the Methodist Church in 1948—it is evident that while he may have "passed" he did not stop in! I fervently wish that he had!

Now, for absolutely unprejudiced testimony concerning John Wesley, it will be admitted, I think, that *The Encyclopedia Britannica* can be trusted as much as any other. It declares that Wesley was "zealous for the religion of the Bible" and "of the Primitive Church." It states that Wesley was grieved over his earlier ministry, saying: "I preached much, but saw no fruit of my labor. . . . And no wonder, for I did not preach faith in the blood of the covenant." "Faith in the blood!" What will these modernists say to that?

The *Britannica* further affirms that the red-letter day in Wesley's life was May 24, 1738, when he attended a meeting where Luther's preface to the Epistle to the Romans was being read. Wesley said: "I felt my heart strangely warmed. I felt I did trust in Christ, Christ alone, for salvation; and an assurance was given me He had taken away my sins, even mine, and saved me from the law of sin and death." The so-called "social gospel," so dear to the hearts of modernistic leaders today, doesn't seem to have received much attention in the teaching of John Wesley. The itinerant plan for preaching an individual salvation to sinners, he said, "must not be altered till I am removed and I hope it will remain till our Lord comes to reign on earth!" (*New Schaff-Herzog Encyclopedia of Religious Knowledge,* Vol. XII, page 308.) "Till our Lord comes to reign on earth!" That phrase alone, uttered by John Wesley, had he stopped in on that assembly of Methodist Bishops in 1948, would have created a perfect spasm! Ask Oxnam!

How far, O how far, the great Methodist Church of 1948 has departed from the Methodist Church of 1738. As Samuel came back to King Saul, how we wish that John Wesley could come back to these great religious councils today, very much Methodist controlled. I would travel a long way to peek in on the scene! Either Bishop Oxnam is not honest, or he knows about the teaching of the Word of God! Really, do these modernistic princes realize how utterly apostate John Wesley would consider them did he "pass this way"?

When once this "Holy Catholic Church" which these modernists envision becomes a reality, then the great apostasy will have reached its fullness. It will be the final Babel—the great religious octopus upon which the wrath of God will be poured forth. Even now the ear of faith can hear "a mighty voice" crying from the highest heaven: "Fallen, fallen is Babylon the great and is become the habitation of demons, and a hold of every unclean spirit, and a hold of every unclean and hateful bird. . . . Come forth, my people, out of her, that ye have no fellowship with her sins, and that ye receive not of her plagues: for her sins have reached even unto heaven, and God hath remembered her iniquities" (Rev. 18: 2–5, R.V.).

If the reader feels that Dr. Bauman was exaggerating, then let him turn to a second source, the official hearing for Bishop G. Bromley Oxnam before the Committee on Un-American Activities of the House of Representatives.[2] Bishop Oxnam was on the witness stand for ten hours. Here is his own statement:

Protestant Churches must continue the present brotherly and inspiring cooperation with the Eastern Orthodox Churches until such time as Protestantism is itself reunited. They may then consider union with Eastern Orthodoxy, which it is prayerfully hoped may be consummated. When the full union of Protestantism and of Eastern Orthodoxy is accomplished and the Christians

[2] 83rd Congress, first session, July 21, 1953.

of the world belong to but two great churches, the leadership of that day may be Christian enough and creative enough to kneel before a common altar, beg forgiveness of the Christ for disunity, and, sharing in the bread and wine of Holy Communion, rise in His Spirit to form the Holy Catholic Church to which all Christians may belong.[3]

This is what the ecumenical leaders are trying day and night to bring on: *One church for one world. They believe that they will be the ecclesiastical directors of this one-world church, and they are working hand in hand with the proponents of world government and internationalism. That is why they are operating as far as possible within the framework of the United Nations.* The ultimate world government, under this plan, will have a political arm and a religious arm. The modernists believe that they will be in control of the ecclesiastical or religious arm.

The leaders of The Federal-National Council of Churches have not been content to bring collectivism to the United States. They will not stop short of a collectivist world society. In the early days of the formation of The Federal Council of Churches the dream was to create an organization of churches on a worldwide scale which could promote collectivistic doctrines. The Church Peace Union, the World Alliance for International Friendship Through the Churches, the various conferences on the European continent, in the British Isles shortly after World War I, and during the thirty-odd years preceding the meeting of the National Council of Churches in Cleveland in 1950—all were working toward a worldwide goal.

In August 1948 the Federal Council leaders went to Amsterdam, The Netherlands, to form The World Council of Churches. In Amsterdam clergymen of varying political be-

[3] P. 3633.

liefs met, including mouthpieces for the Soviet Union from behind the Iron Curtain.

Time magazine[4] had several remarks to make about this array of theologians:

> This greatest church meeting since the Reformation *could not even agree on a definition of the word "church."* The talk at Amsterdam was mostly on the comparatively low level of diplomacy. What the world heard was very like a UN session. Of the assembly's major message, Czech theologian Joseph Hromadka [a Soviet mouthpiece] said: "It won't embarrass me at all in returning to Prague. Of course, it's pretty negative and doesn't offer much in the way of action."

An important resolution passed was one condemning capitalism, which, it was said, had failed to solve human needs. This was written by Socialist theologian John C. Bennett of Union Theological Seminary (which the New York State Joint Legislative Committee to Investigate Seditious Activities labeled a dangerous center of revolutionary Socialist teaching).

The World Council of Churches elected six presidents for various sections of the world. Elected president of the Council for North America was Bishop G. Bromley Oxnam.

The president elected to represent Asia was Dr. T. C. Chao, supported by American Presbyterian money. Dr. Chao's known Communist record, reaching back twenty-two years, was assembled by the Netherlands ambassador in Peiping and is in the files of the Netherlands government. *Time* magazine for October 16, 1950, revealed some of Dr. Chao's Communistic activities.

Dr. Chao has written a book, *The Life of Jesus,* in which he denies all the miracles of the New Testament, states that Jesus

4 Sept. 13, 1948.

Christ did not walk on the water, did not raise people from the dead, and did not turn water into wine. Jesus Christ, writes Dr. Chao, was a revolutionist and a Socialist. The World Council of Churches leaders knew what Dr. Chao's theology was when they elevated him to high office.

When the armies of Mao Tse-tung came into China, Dr. Chao and his theological students from Yenching University's school of religion were out in the streets welcoming them with open arms and saying that these were "days of rejoicing for China!" Soon after this the Communist government of China gave Dr. Chao an official position. It is believed by many North American missionaries that it was Dr. Chao who issued the orders to all foreign missionaries to get out of the country unless they accepted the new Communist revolution.

When the United States went to the help of South Korea, after it was invaded by the North Korean Communists, Dr. Chao came out with the following statement:

> In the invasion of the Northeast [Korea] by the United Nations these days, it is necessary to oppose America and help Korea. If we belittle America, curse America, and oppose America, that is not contrary to our Christian faith, for Jesus Christ has commanded us to oppose sin. We Christians want to oppose the power of all that is evil.

According to *The New York Times* and other news services, a year after Dr. Chao had espoused the Red cause the Communist regime decided that it had used Chao for what it wanted. It then placed him under house arrest.

The Executive Committee of The World Council of Churches, meeting in Bievres, near Paris, France, January 30 through February 1, 1951, adopted a lengthy letter to the churches which are members of the Council. The letter, signed by the chairman, George Cicestr, and the general secretary, Dr. W. A. Visser 't Hooft, declared that the Communist social principle, "From each according to his ability, to each according to his need," *has its roots in the teaching of Jesus.* The Communist Manifesto of 1848 stated this thesis. The Constitution of the U.S.S.R., Chapter I, Article 12, concludes: "The principle applied in the U.S.S.R. is that of socialism, 'From each according to his ability, to each according to his work.'"

This letter, saying that the Communist economic principle had its roots in the teachings of Jesus, was sent out to some 120 bodies affiliated with The World Council of Churches.

At the meeting were leading radical churchmen from over the world, including Bishop Oxnam.

One of the members of the Central Committee of The World Council of Churches is Josef L. Hromadka, of Czechoslovakia, professor of the John Huss Theological Faculty at Prague. Professor Hromadka is one of the outstanding advocates of the Communist regime in Czechoslovakia and has been used very effectively by the Soviet Union as a speaker at Soviet-sponsored religious gatherings. In Helsinki, Finland, on July 23, 1951, Professor Hromadka spoke at a Communist rally, publicly using his important place in The World Council of Churches to give weight to his Communist utterances. The rally was sponsored by an organization called "The World Peace Partisans," a Communist organization, and was an attempt to line up the Finns behind the current Communistic peace propaganda. The Finnish Communist newspaper *Vapaa Sana (The Free Word)* quotes Professor Hromadka as follows: "In this peace effort the Christian and non-Christian, Communists and non-Communists, can stand together because our efforts are the same; therefore, I urge all Finnish Christians to join our work for the peaceful and generous world."

(Following Professor Hromadka, an American pastor also spoke at this Communist rally. He was the Rev. John W. Darr, whose name appears frequently throughout the official reports of the Committee on Un-American Activities. He has been a frequent speaker at Communist rallies behind the Iron Curtain.)

Professor Hromadka's history can be traced back to the Bolshevik Revolution in Russia in 1917. He was a hearty endorser of the Revolution, a fact revealed by Dr. Matthew Spinka of Hartford (Connecticut) Theological Seminary in his paper on Professor Hromadka published just prior to Hromadka's coming to the United States for the second meeting of The World Council of Churches in 1954.

Professor Hromadka has made a number of speeches inside the Iron Curtain accusing the United States of having used germ warfare in Korea. He had never been a friend of the United States although, during World War II, after he had escaped from Czechoslovakia to Switzerland, he made his way to the United States and obtained a job from his old college classmate of Edinburgh, Scotland, Dr. John Mackay. Dr. Mackay, a leading light in The World Council of Churches, at that time was president of Presbyterianism's largest theological seminary in the United States, at Princeton, New Jersey. He became president of the International Missionary Council, the missionary arm of The World Council of Churches. Although Professor Hromadka made his living under the capitalistic system of the United States, he evidently was not persuaded in the free-enterprise direction; he went back to Czechoslovakia, and after the Communists had taken over the country he replaced the head of the seminary in Prague. He became the leading Soviet mouthpiece in Czechoslovakia and, for that matter, in all the Iron Curtain countries.

According to official reports from Budapest, Hungary, in June 1953, Professor Hromadka was selected as a member of the World Council of Peace, a Communist organization sponsored by the Soviet regime.

THE WORLD COUNCIL
MEETS AT EVANSTON

Meeting planned for 1952, deferred because of McCarran Act. *Christian Century* supports Communist clergymen on every issue. World Council meets at Evanston in 1954. Bars against Hromadka, Bereczky, and other Iron Curtain clergymen lifted as result of top-level meeting of Council and Administration leaders: Dulles, Stassen, Flemming, Oxnam, Martin, Mackay, Visser 't Hooft—and Eisenhower as speaker. Bishop Oxnam expresses gratitude to Mr. Dulles. Eisenhower addresses World Council at Evanston.

THE WORLD COUNCIL OF CHURCHES voted to hold its second world assembly in Evanston, Illinois. The assembly was to be held in 1952, four years after the founding of the World Council in Amsterdam. However, in the meantime, the McCarran-Walter Act was passed, forbidding the entrance of subversives into the United States. Leaders of the National and World Councils of Churches went to work on the Act from the public platform, through denominational publications, and by sending a barrage of propaganda to Congress.

The *Christian Century*, published in Chicago, whose executive editor, Mr. Harold Fey, has been associated with leftist and pacifist organizations, has frequently attacked Congressional committees investigating subversive activity. It has also denounced measures, either proposed or passed, to protect the internal security of the United States. In the issue of June 4,

1952, an editorial raises a question concerning the entrance of certain Communist and pro-Communist World Council of Churches delegates into the United States (emphasis added):

> Last year the Canadian immigration authorities turned back two or three Asian delegates who were trying to reach the meeting of the International Missionary Council in Toronto. But compared with United States immigration officers enforcing the McCarran law, the Canadians are paragons of open-armed hospitality.
>
> One of two things had better be done without delay. Either *The National Council of Churches should start a campaign to get the McCarran Law amended before 1954* (an almost hopeless prospect) or the delegations from abroad should be chosen soon, so that their admissibility may be established. Of course there is a third possibility, and if the United States proves too inhospitable we would cheer the World Council if it chose that the meeting could be moved from Evanston somewhere outside this country.

On June 11, 1952, another article appeared in the *Christian Century*, "Can We Ever Support Communism?", written by Dr. John C. Bennett, the Union Theological Seminary professor who proposed the resolution adopted by The World Council of Churches at Amsterdam in August 1948 attacking capitalism. He says:

> Communism wins power because it has much truth in its teachings, because it appeals to the loyalties and not primarily to the cynical self-interests of man . . . as he [the Christian] studies communism he finds many things to approve in it. I refer to such things as the Communist criticism of many features of capitalism and imperialism,

the Communist practice in regard to racial discrimination, the Communist goal of a classless society, the generous motives that inspire many people to give themselves to communism with selfless commitments.

Then there are many particular elements in Communist propaganda at a given time that may appeal. . . .

This same Dr. John C. Bennett worked on a committee of The World Council of Churches in Evanston, August 1954. (The Evanston meeting was postponed to 1954.)

Another delegate to the Evanston meeting was Bishop Albert Bereczky, head of The Hungarian Reformed Church and a Central Committee member of The World Council of Churches.

A letter entitled "Barth to Bereczky" was reprinted in the *Christian Century* for July 20, 1952. This letter, dated September 16, 1951, was addressed by a theologian in Switzerland, Karl Barth, a leading member of The World Council of Churches, to Bishop Bereczky. Dr. Barth states that Bishop Bereczky has openly approved of communism and that the church press releases put out by the bishop sound "uncannily like the official releases about conditions in the Soviet Union which I receive every week; Hungary, a veritable paradise, where the wolves and the lambs already dwell together." Dr. Barth accuses Bishop Bereczky of being the tool of the Soviet Union in espousing communism in Hungary.

The press services of the world have, in fact, carried messages frequently by Bishop Bereczky, given behind the Iron Curtain, which show that he has become an important mouthpiece for spreading Soviet propaganda in religious circles.

On September 11, 1952, in Lund, Sweden, the Lund Conference on Faith and Order of The World Council of Churches was held. Both Professor Hromadka and Bishop Bereczky attended, taking part in the sessions, which were held in secret. A long list of American churchmen [1] attended these secret sessions with Professor Hromadka and Bishop Bereczky.

The *Christian Century* for October 7, 1953, carried an editorial labeled "Evanston Storm Warnings," which had to do with the coming of Communist delegates to the forthcoming World Council of Churches meeting (emphasis added):

> There are, however, at least two other things which may happen at Evanston to produce even greater trouble in local congregations and communities. The first is criticism of the United States, its way of life, its present position in world affairs, and the foreign policies of its government. And the second is the use which a portion of the press may make of such criticism. *There will be criticism of the United States at Evanston—and there should be. Some of it will be severe.* Some of it most Americans will think misinformed and therefore mistaken. But sharp, outspoken criticism of this country must be expected. A certain species of "Patriotism" will deeply resent this, and vigorously attack those held responsible for it.
>
> The press will also be at Evanston. In fact, newspapers and journalists are already applying for press accommodations in such numbers that the arrangements committee may not be able to take care of them all. Every indication now points toward the largest coverage at Evanston by the press of any event in American church history. Some of this will be highly competent. It will be *written by reporters who have been carefully briefed,* who have considerable knowledge of church affairs, and who have a lively sense of their responsibility and the responsibility of their papers or press agencies to the importance of the issues involved. We dare to hope that a majority of the

[1] See Appendix 8.

journalists at Evanston will be working on this high plane.
But we do not expect that all will be. One factor which
must be reckoned with is the tendency of a considerable
portion of the American press to find news in conflict.
Agreement is seldom spectacular. Clashes make headlines.
The four- and five-letter verbs beloved of headline writers
are usually words which connote some sort of contest—of
wills if not of action. Therefore, the correspondent eager
to have his dispatches printed in full and conspicuously
is often under pressure (which may be unconscious) to
play up the contest aspects of his subject. When to this
tendency are added recent indications that some American newspapers are not averse to showing the non-Roman
churches and their leaders in an unfavorable light, the
possibilities for projecting trouble from Evanston into
local congregations and communities become almost
limitless.

To understand what we have in mind, let's take a hypo-
thetical but by no means improbable illustration. We are
assured that there will be delegates at Evanston from
churches in "iron-curtain" countries. (If such delegates
should be kept away, the Assembly should be moved to
some spot where they can attend.) Suppose one of these
delegates, for example such a man as Professor Hromadka,
if he is present, should challenge American assumptions
as to the relation of Christianity to communism, insisting
that the church not only can and does survive under communism but that it grows in spiritual vigor. Then let a
considerable part of the American Press play this up as
indicative of the sort of unpatriotic association in which
American churches become involved when they join The
World Council of Churches, The National Council of
Churches, the state council, or the county and city council. What will be the consequence in hundreds of Ameri-

can communities and congregations? And how ready are American pastors to face such an issue and so deal with it as to uphold the cause of ecumenical Christianity while preserving the unity of their congregations?

This is by no means a full list of the dangers to the local congregation which may come out of the Second Assembly of the World Council. But it should suffice to show why we say that, if Evanston is to bring great opportunities, it is also likely to bring grave difficulties. And these difficulties will rise to plague and challenge local pastors as well as the denominational leaders who customarily figure in ecumenical conversations.

How can these pastors prepare for what is ahead? Obviously their first need is to become informed on the issues that are likely to come to the forefront in the Assembly. The *Christian Century* has been trying to aid this task of preparation ever since the first preliminary report of the preparatory commission of theologians was issued. We plan to give major attention to this subject, not only during the next months until the Assembly meets, but in the very important period of interpretations that will follow it.

If the sort of independent church journalism which the *Christian Century* represents can help local churches and their ministers to grasp the opportunities and ward off the dangers in Evanston 1954, we are determined that the full resources of this paper shall be devoted to the purpose. And we will depend on our readers to inform us if, in our efforts to prepare them for the Assembly, we overlook matters which they, out of pastoral or lay experience, believe should be discussed.

In a later editorial we shall take up the preparation of local councils of churches, ministerial associations and congregations—together with the local press—for Evanston.

Dr. Henry P. Van Dusen, chairman of the Study Department Committee of The World Council of Churches, speaking at the Irvine Auditorium, University of Pennsylvania, on October 15, 1953, said that official delegates would be coming to the World Council of Churches meeting in Evanston from behind the Iron Curtain. Their coming to Evanston would be resisted, he said, but this resistance would fail: the delegates would be admitted into the United States. He did not say who had given authority for them to be admitted to the United States.

On November 17, 1953, The National Council of Churches, which is the United States subsidiary of The World Council of Churches, held a national board luncheon meeting in Washington, D.C. *Powerful figures of the World Council, who are, or have been, in the Eisenhower Administration,* such as Mr. John Foster Dulles, Secretary of State; Mr. Arthur Flemming, who was head of the manpower division in the Department of Defense; and Harold E. Stassen, who was head of the Mutual Security Administration; along with Bishop G. Bromley Oxnam, Bishop William C. Martin, and Dr. John A. Mackay, moderator of the Presbyterian Church in the U.S.A., persuaded President Dwight D. Eisenhower to address the luncheon and thereby lend an official air to the meeting of the executive committee of this Council. Dr. W. A. Visser 't Hooft, general secretary of The World Council of Churches, also addressed the board. He and Bishop Oxnam were received by the President at the White House the next morning. Dr. Visser 't Hooft on Sunday, November 22, occupied the pulpit of the National Presbyterian Church, and the Eisenhowers, who are members, attended the service.

Now, Dr. Visser 't Hooft had come to this country from

Geneva, Switzerland, to set up the machinery of the World Council meeting in Evanston and to secure the cooperation of United States government officials in bypassing the McCarran Act and so enabling Red delegates to enter the United States.

Before returning to Geneva, Dr. Visser 't Hooft declared in New York at a luncheon of the Friends of the World Council of Churches on December 9, 1953, that he had been impressed by the attitude of government representatives of the United States:

> In planning for the Assembly we have had all the help that we could possibly expect from them. They have shown real understanding concerning the admission of church delegates to address the Assembly from the Iron Curtain countries. Our invitation to the President to address the Assembly was also received with genuine cordiality, and we have every hope that he will be able to be with us.

A letter headed "G. Bromley Oxnam, Bishop of the Methodist Church, Washington Area, 100 Maryland Avenue, N.E., Washington 2, D.C.," dated Wednesday, December 16, 1953, and addressed to all the pastors under the bishop's jurisdiction, says (emphasis added):

> I am happy to say that several conferences with Mr. John Foster Dulles, to whom the church owes an increasing debt of gratitude, have resulted in reasonable assurances that the delegates to the coming Assembly of The World Council of Churches will be admitted without difficulty. *By the way, have you written Mr. Dulles and the President a note of appreciation for their courageous refusal to tolerate Senator McCarthy's attempt to substitute a "Big Bully" policy in foreign affairs for the dignified*

*and fruitful "Good Neighbor" policy? Leaders are often
lonely men and a word from a parsonage home means
much.*[2]

These collectivist leaders of The World Council of Churches
were successful in ensnaring President Eisenhower through his
advisers, some of whom are members of the World Council.
President Eisenhower addressed the meeting at Evanston and
he sat on the platform with Communist clergymen from behind the Iron Curtain. These phony leaders had taken the
place of the true ministers who had been deposed and sent to
concentration camps; some of these have not been heard of
since. One of the Red clergymen present was Bishop Janos
Peter of Hungary. Dr. J. B. Matthews revealed in an address
at Orchestra Hall, Chicago, a few days prior to the Evanston
meeting of the World Council, that Bishop Peter was sent by
the Soviet Secret Police to Cairo to induce his brother, an
anti-Communist, to come home to Hungary, guaranteeing him
that no reprisals would be taken against him. Bishop Peter's
brother came back to Hungary, and shortly after arriving
was seized by the Soviet Secret Police and murdered.

When plans for the admission of the Red clergy to the
Evanston meeting were made known, messages by the thousands began to pour into the State Department, to the White
House, to the Attorney General's office, and to various members of Congress. They came from clergymen, patriotic societies, civic groups, and individuals, protesting the entrance of
these Communist propagandists into the United States in the
guise of clergymen.

The American Legion launched a drive against the entrance
of the Red clergymen, beginning in the First Division of Illinois, which passed a stinging resolution naming certain of the
Red delegates and calling upon the State Department and the

2 P. 2, par. III.

President of the United States to forbid entrance to these propagandists. The entire Illinois Department, representing 225,000 Legionnaires, likewise passed the resolution and sent it to the American Legion National Executive Committee, the highest ruling body of the American Legion, representing over 3,000,000 veterans in the United States.

Soon the World Council propagandists began to give statements out to the press blasting the Legion and saying that they were "shocked" that the Legion should take the attitude of wishing to keep "church leaders" out of the United States. When this tactic did not deter the Legion, World Council publicity men sought out key Legionnaires and, over the dinner table and by a letter-writing campaign, tried to get them to stop the Legion from carrying this fight to the top levels. They were unsuccessful.

When the National Executive Committee of the American Legion met in Indianapolis, World Council apologists came before the Executive Committee and argued against the Legion's resolution. In the meantime, fifty clergymen in the Indianapolis area signed a petition backing the American Legion's stand.

The National Executive Committee voted for the resolution, urging the State Department, the President, and the Attorney General to bar the Reds.

The Legion's efforts failed; the Red clergymen were admitted, and they mingled with the religious and political leaders of this country. Their presence, and all that they stood for, were endorsed on the top level: the highest government officials, including the President of the United States and his Secretary of State, shared the platform with these opportunistic, murdering Communist clergymen.

A major defeat for Christian people. Communist clergy gain prestige and double their strength on World Council Central Committee. United States government has softened on communism since Evanston. Chicago *Tribune,* which welcomed Reds, reports tragic consequences of admitting them. Hungarian Communists confer degrees on Dr. Mackay, Bishop Oxnam, Rev. Wagner. Aims of the ecumenical leaders. Few alternatives for surviving Christians.

THE EVANSTON CONFERENCE of The World Council of Churches was a major defeat for the Christian people of the world. Members of the Communist clergy were received with open arms and called "brothers." They were greeted with applause by the assembly in Evanston and given prominent speaking positions on the program. They were invited to speak in churches and seminaries.

The Communists doubled their strength on the Council's powerful Central Committee, which conducts the business of the Council between world assemblies. At the opening of the assembly at Evanston two Communists were on the Central Committee, Professor Josef Hromadka [1] of Prague and Professor Laszlo Papp of Budapest, Hungary. Two more Communists were added: Bishop Jan Chabada of Czechoslovakia, who has been an official in the Communist Party, and Karl Kotula, an-

1 See Appendix 9, Rep. Bentley's speech on Iron Curtain churchmen.

other Communist collaborator, who owed his position in the Polish Lutheran Church to the Communist government of that country.

The Communist clergymen won a great propaganda victory at Evanston. Their line that a minister could be a Christian and a Communist at the same time was not successfully challenged by any of those attending the conference. They sold the assembly the idea that communism and capitalism could peacefully coexist and that the churches on both sides of the Iron Curtain could bridge the gulf between the two systems and bring the people together.

Because they were so graciously entertained as house guests of the United States, while millions of oppressed people languished in Communist prisons and slave-labor camps, these men were able to go back to their own countries boasting that they were received with open arms by the country which claims to be the greatest bulwark against communism in the world.

Can any sane Christian fail to see what this propaganda has done to the people in the underground and in the resistance movements behind the Iron Curtain? Is it consistent for the United States government to spend millions of the taxpayers' dollars for propaganda for freedom over the Voice of America, through the press, and in information agencies overseas when it openly entertains the oppressors of these people and sits down to eat and drink with them in the name of Christianity?

The net result of the propaganda of peaceful "coexistence" has been that the United States government has gone soft on communism since the Evanston assembly of The World Council of Churches. The government has opened the gates of the United States to visiting delegations from the Soviet Union, disguised as delegations of "farmers," "newspaper reporters," and "spiritual leaders." An invitation was accepted by the clergymen in the Communist countries to visit the United

States and speak throughout the country. They were escorted around the country by leaders of the National and World Councils of Churches.

When the American Legion, Department of Illinois, passed its resolution calling upon the State Department, the President, and the Attorney General to forbid entrance to these Red preachers, the Chicago *Tribune,* which had always been on the side of the American Legion in matters involving subversion, had an editorial disagreeing with the Legion on its stand. World Council leaders rejoiced and quoted the Chicago *Tribune* against the opponents of these Red clergymen from coast to coast. After investigation it was discovered that the man who wrote the editorial was a sympathizer with The World Council of Churches, and his editorial did not necessarily represent the opinion of the editor and publisher of the Chicago *Tribune,* who was away at the time and in very poor health.

Eight months later, on April 10, 1955, the Chicago *Tribune* ran a feature editorial which took a very different view. It was entitled "When the Red Preachers Got Home":

> The national Americanism commission of the American Legion recalls that the Legion's national executive council protested the admission to the United States of Communist delegates to the meeting of The World Council of Churches in Evanston last August. Nevertheless, with the approval of this and other newspapers, the State Department welcomed them, and there were many hopeful expressions at the Council sessions that better understanding would result.
>
> We still think it was a good idea, on balance, to let them in, but we'll admit there is room for argument.
>
> The commission now reports what members of the Communist delegation from Hungary said upon their return to that country. Bishop Bereczky gave well-publi-

cized lectures about his "sad American experiences." Bishops Janos Peter, Laszlo Dezsery, and Lajos Veto wrote articles about "the horrors of American life" and "the successes" of Iron Curtain churches at the Evanston assembly.

Reporting on customs inspections, Bishop Dezsery complained of indignities and stated that in Hungary "foreigners can go where they wish without being bothered by authorities." Like Noel Field and his wife, perhaps.

All of the bishops spoke of the "savagery" of the American press, which erred at the time of the conference in hoping that these Communist churchmen might show some decency in return for the hospitality extended them. All of the bishops cited a picture on the cover of an unnamed American publication: "A father with two loaded guns terrorizing his young son in a sick bed and thus forcing him to take a bitter medicine."

The picture was actually that of a smiling young father kneeling at the bedside of his little boy, who was grimacing over a spoonful of castor oil. The father wore toy holsters and a toy sheriff's hat, and he was terrorizing the youngster with two cap pistols.

Bishop Bereczky charged that babies were "forced" to compete in a crawling contest for the news reels.

Secretary of State Dulles, a leading layman in the World Council, who was instrumental in permitting the Iron Curtain churchmen to come to Evanston, was repaid with scant gratitude. Bishop Dezsery said that Dulles "inadvertently blabbed out his hope of seeing the Evanston conference dominated by American propaganda. . . . Therefore he tried to exclude the eastern churches from the assembly. . . . He mobilized against us the American Legion, that Fascist organization of war veterans, and all kinds of European exiles. But he did not succeed."

The same bishop said that an American minister told him that his sermons were censored by the police, adding that another unnamed American clergyman, said to be in voluntary exile in Switzerland, had stated, "The country before your eyes is no more that of Lincoln, but that of McCarthy. America is dominated by a hysteria of fear. No European country would live in such fear. The country is a total political and diplomatic failure. . . . Believe me, the American people have lost their faith in everybody; they are only anxious for their future."

The World Council might ponder the question of how men who know not the truth can be expected to preach the Word.

The Communist Hungarian church press for April 15, 1955, reported that the Reformed Theological Academy of Budapest would confer the degree of Doctor of Divinity upon leaders in the ecumenical movement, including Dr. John A. Mackay, Bishop G. Bromley Oxnam, and the Rev. James Edgar Wagner of the United States.

Dr. Mackay accepted his degree *in absentia*. Bishop Oxnam and the Rev. Wagner, president of the Evangelical Reformed Church, U.S.A., proudly went behind the Iron Curtain and received their degrees during the centenary celebration of the Budapest Reformed Theological Academy, held between September 15 and 20, 1955. World leaders of the World Council attended this meeting and sat with Communist clergymen from the Iron Curtain countries, applauding as the degrees were presented by the Communist-controlled theological academy.

After the ceremony, Bishop Oxnam returned to the United States and fulfilled speaking engagements. These included a major address in Oakland, California, on Sunday afternoon, October 30, at a Reformation Day rally known as "A Festival of Faith."

One year later, when the Hungarian people rose up against the Communist government, they refused to continue paying the salaries of the Communist clergymen who had been paid by the Communist state. One of these, mentioned in reports from Hungary, was Bishop Veto, who had been elected a member of the Central Committee of The World Council of Churches. Bishops Veto and Dezsery, both puppets of the Communist government, were forced to resign from the Lutheran Church. Bishop Bereczky, awarded the Hungarian Communists' Order of Labor, was deposed from the Hungarian Reformed Church. Bishop Peter, labeled "the worst kind of Stalinist," also was deposed.

The *Christian Century* of November 14, 1956, was forced to admit that these Hungarian church leaders were "false bishops" and had been "foisted" on the Hungarians by the Communist government.

The popular revolt was crushed by Soviet tanks and, according to the *Christian Century* and newsletters from the World Council, the Communist leaders of the Hungarian church have been restored to their positions by the Communist Hungarian government.

What do the collectivist church leaders hope to gain from their frenzied efforts to make friends with the Communists?

There seems to be only one answer. Under a collectivist system, somebody has to do the planning and somebody has to control the masses of the people. The church leaders, crazy for authority, *expect to be in line as the planners and as the controllers of other people's lives.* They are egotists. They believe that they alone can tell the people what is best for them. But it can be safely prophesied that, if they succeed in bringing collectivism to the last stronghold of freedom in the world, the United States, they will be used as long as their services are needed, and when they are no longer needed, they will go the way, as we have said earlier, of Quisling, Anna Pauker, and Chao before them.

What must the true Christian do? The true Christian must obey the commandments of Scripture and "come out from among them and be separate" and "touch not the unclean thing" (II Cor. 6:17). American businessmen who believe in the American way of life and in the Christianity of the Bible should get behind the little, independent churches, behind the pastors and the people who have made great sacrifices to break with the totalitarian system as embodied in the Federal-National-World Councils of Churches. They should support them wholeheartedly with their prayers, their finances, and their attendance. The situation cannot be cleaned up by joining the system and fighting it from within. This has been tried again and again, and as the years have gone by *the protesters within the system have grown fewer while the collectivist hosts have gone marching on.*

The United States of America was founded by "dissenters," "separatists," "strangers," "pilgrims," and "forces disrupting unity." These were the Pilgrim-Puritan fathers of old, who believed that Christianity and freedom walked hand in hand. For this reason they would not tolerate the totalitarianism of the King of England or of the Church of England.

Drama replaces worship; the church becomes a stage. Dr. Burkhart creates a "worshipful" atmosphere in Columbus. Mrs. Fisk provides worshipful entertainment. Mr. Wyer writes off the Bible. "Festival of Faith." Buddhism, Baha'i, Judaism, Hinduism, Mohammedanism, and Protestantism join hands. Mr. Dulles speaks on moral foundations of the UN. Dr. Tillich, the Council's vice chairman of Worship and the Arts. His Communist-front record. His protégé, Roger Lyons, of the Voice of America.

AN INTERESTING SECTION of the Federal Council of Churches' Biennial Report for 1946 is on the subject of "Worship." We find, under the subhead "Drama in Religion," some very illuminating information (emphasis added):

> The subject which stimulated the most discussion was a report by Dr. Earl E. Harper, Director of the School of Fine Arts, University of Iowa, on *Drama in Religion.* Dr. Harper reported that he had been conversing with various individuals, both professional dramatists and church leaders, with a view to ascertaining what might be possible in this field. He found an unusual interest on the part of those associated with the professional theater and the idea of developing high-grade drama which would express the fundamental ideals of the Christian religion—

moral, ethical, social and spiritual. Here seems to be an area in which professional playwrights and religious leaders can cooperate in providing drama with deep spiritual appeal.

A second area of possibility noted by Dr. Harper was drama within the church. This would include the stimulation of the writing of plays designed for use in the chancel or elsewhere in the church, the training of church directors for the production of drama, and the development of more adequate church facilities for this purpose. The third area that Dr. Harper suggested, was the revival of Christian festival drama which might result in denominational, regional, and possibly national religious festivals.

Now, religious drama is as old as the human race. It has played a significant part in Christian history, and during the Middle Ages the miracle and morality plays, in the absence of printed Bibles or of hand-lettered Bibles in large numbers, played an important part in the religious instruction of the people. But never in Christian history, prior to our own day, was drama resorted to as a substitute for worship. And never was it permitted to take place within the church.

The Federal Council of Churches, however, is changing all that. It now becomes possible to put on plays within the church itself. The church building, strictly reserved through the ages for the worship of God by the people assembled there, may now be turned into a drama workshop. Also it may be profaned with ritualistic dancing, by leave of The Federal-National Council of Churches.

Evidently the Council has succeeded in conveying its ideas on "worship" down to the local churches. A striking example is found in the First Community Church of Columbus, Ohio. The pastor of this church is the Rev. Roy A. Burkhart.

Dr. Burkhart was made chairman of the Federal Council's

Commission on the Church's Ministry to Returning Service Men and Women, which was organized on September 18, 1945, while Bishop G. Bromley Oxnam was the president of the Council.

A news release of The Federal Council of Churches stated at the time that "the purpose of the Commission will be to revitalize the total life of the churches as they enter upon the job of servicing returning veterans."

Dr. Burkhart's church has been picked by the radical *Christian Century* as one of ten outstanding Protestant churches in the United States—possibly because of the "worshipful" atmosphere which it maintains.

Here is the announcement of a "worship" service which took place in this church:

> Margaret Palmer Fisk, pioneer in the creative art of religious expression, will be at First Community Church from Sunday, Jan. 28, through Tuesday, Jan. 30.
>
> As a part of the worship services at 9:30 and 11:00 A.M., Sunday, Jan. 28, Mrs. Fisk will dance "The Lord's Prayer."
>
> At 7:00 P.M., Sunday, Jan. 28, in the sanctuary of the church, Mrs. Fisk will be assisted by the two Rhythmic Dance Groups of the First Community Church. The public is invited.

In the Columbus *Citizen* for that same Sunday, a four-column spread—nine inches in depth—pictures Mrs. Fisk and the dancers in action at this so-called church. Some of the dance interpretations are entitled: "Putting of one's self in God's guidance"; "Glory to God"; "The Christ Child"; "Agnus Dei." Mrs. Fisk had appeared in the same church early in 1950; she was described by the Columbus *Dispatch*[1] as one "who uses creative movement and design of the modern dance

1 Feb. 4, 1950.

to interpret religious ideas and moods." Nine local high-school girls constituted a "Rhythmic Choir" to aid Mrs. Fisk in the "worship" services.

Dr. Burkhart, according to the *American Magazine*,[2] is quite "successful" as a pastor. His church is located in one of the fashionable suburbs of Columbus, where he and his co-workers have provided dances and simulated night clubs and musical revues with girlie leg shows; a "date clinic" designed to "help bring boys and girls together"; a staff of psychologists; and sex advisers. The article states: "He is making it the church's job to help young people get dates, to help them choose suitable mates, and to make them know the facts of life before they marry."

After The Federal Council of Churches changed its name to the National Council in 1950, Dr. Burkhart traveled around the country as a Council representative, producing miniature replicas of the Council program in various cities. A leading layman from Dr. Burkhart's church, one Samuel S. Wyer, an alleged Sunday-school teacher, addressed the Ohio State Pastors' Convention in January 1930 and asserted that the Bible was full of lies. According to the Columbus *Citizen*, Mr. Wyer's topic was "An Engineer's View of the Present Church Situation." Here is what he said:

> I doubt if there is any other book which ranges from such degrading depths as the Bible. The Bible was not written by God. If God wrote the Bible He would have done a better job of it. If written now, it could not be sent through the United States mails. We must conclude that the Bible contains a wide range of material not suited for children. The blame for much of the present lawlessness must be placed upon the lying in the Sunday-school teaching and in the Bible. As long as the Bible lies, the present

2 Oct. 1943.

generation will not have any interest in it. Why continue those lies about Moses and the Ten Commandments? Jesus never said anything about a Virgin birth. All scholars agree that the Trinitarian references in the Bible are pious forgeries. The question of the divinity of Jesus is not worth a hill of beans. We must scrap the Bible before we can attain church unity. It has no part in the twentieth century civilization.[3]

At the rate the Bible is being scrapped by "religious" leaders, the churches are going to attain unity quite swiftly.

Dr. Earl E. Harper's suggestion, recorded in the 1946 Biennial Report, on "Christian festival drama" and "national religious festivals" might have prompted the "Festival of Faith" held in San Francisco on June 19, 1955, during the tenth-anniversary celebration of the founding of the United Nations. At this affair, held in the Cow Palace, so-called Christian leaders of the National and World Councils of Churches joined hands with members of almost every other variety of religion in "ecumenical fellowship."

The Rev. O. Frederick Nolde, D.D., director of the Commission on International Affairs of The World Council of Churches and the International Missionary Council, presided. Resolutions from the World Fellowship of Buddhists, the Synagogue Council of America, the Eastern Orthodox Churches, the National Council of the Churches of Christ in the U.S.A., the Hindus, and the Moslems were included in the program.

Prayers from the various religions were offered, and the calls to prayer were given by the Baha'i religion, represented by Mr. Arthur L. Dahl, Jr.; the Buddhist, by Dr. Paul F. Fung; the Eastern Orthodox, by the Rev. Paul S. Finfinis; the Protestant, by the Rev. John A. Gardner, D.D.; the Hindu, by Swami

[3] Columbus *Citizen*, Jan. 22, 1930.

Ashokananda; the Judaic, by Rabbi Elliot M. Burnstein; and the Moslem, by Mr. Mohammed Ahmed Radwan.

The worshipers in the audience were given the privilege of making a silent prayer.

The main address was given by John Foster Dulles, now Secretary of State of the United States, speaking on the subject "The Moral Foundations of the United Nations." What "moral" contributions to the foundations of the UN the atheistic Communist bloc made, is not recorded.

Many centuries ago the prophet Amos asked, "Can two walk together except they be agreed?" (Amos 3:3). When the religious leaders of the first century refused to recognize Jesus Christ as the Son of God and forbade the apostles to preach in His name, St. Peter, who became head of the first church council at Jerusalem, gave this ringing testimony: "Neither is there salvation in any other: for there is none other name under heaven given among men, whereby we must be saved" (Acts 4:12).

In his little second epistle, of one short chapter, John warns about the false teachers, the deceivers, and the anti-Christs that will come into the world and will not confess Jesus Christ: "Whosoever transgresseth, and abideth not in the doctrine of Christ, hath not God. He that abideth in the doctrine of Christ, he hath both the Father and the Son. If there come any unto you, and bring not this doctrine, receive him not into your house, neither bid him Godspeed: for he that biddeth him Godspeed is partaker of his evil deeds" (II John 9–11).

The apostles are very clear in their command not to have fellowship with those who deny the deity of Christ and who deny the great doctrines of the Christian faith. Paul commanded the Ephesians, "And have no fellowship with the unfruitful works of darkness, but rather reprove them" (Eph. 5:11). Nothing could be stronger than his commandment to the Corinthians: "Be ye not unequally yoked together with unbelievers: for what fellowship hath righteousness with un-righteousness? and what Communion hath light with darkness? And what concord hath Christ with Belial? or what part hath he that believeth with an infidel?" (II Cor. 6:14–15).

Of course, these self-appointed Protestant leaders today do not believe what the Bible says. They are ready to toss all Scriptural authority out the window whenever it suits their purpose. They can join hands with any Christ-denying apos-tates in a public "festival"; they can themselves deny the great doctrines of the Christian faith. In doing so, they are heroes in the eyes of the liberals. If they conducted their campaigns on street corners, people would put them down for what they are; instead, they occupy expensive churches and are supported by people who supposedly believe in primitive Christianity and in the American way of life.

In the 1954 Biennial Report of The National Council of Churches is found the name of the Rev. Paul J. Tillich, listed as vice chairman of the Department of Worship and the Arts. Dr. Tillich has been professor of philosophical theology at Union Theological Seminary in New York City for a number of years. His Communist-front associations may be found listed in the *Cumulative Index* of the Committee on Un-American Activities.[4] Dr. J. B. Matthews, in his article "Red Infiltration of Theological Seminaries," published in the *American Mer-cury*, November 1953, lists Paul Tillich as one of the signers of an "open letter" written by the Communist-front National Committee to Repeal the McCarran Act, which had been agi-tating for repeal of the Internal Security Act of 1950. This open letter was released to the press and printed in the *Daily Worker*, official mouthpiece of the Communist Party.

To get a better picture of Professor Tillich's qualifications

---

4 U.S. House of Representatives, p. 857. This index was published on Jan. 20, 1955, and includes Communist-front associations of various individuals from 1938 through 1954.

for advising churches on worship, one can turn to testimony given under oath to a U.S. government committee concerning one of his protégés.

On March 2, 1953, the Permanent Sub-Committee on Investigations of the Committee on Government Operations, United States Senate, was conducting hearings on the State Department Information Program, particularly on the phase known as the Voice of America. The committee had before it as a witness one Roger Lyons, who was identified as the Director of Religious Programming of the Voice of America. Information had been given to the committee by Dr. John Cocutz and Mrs. Alice Patricia Shephard, both Voice employees, to the effect that Roger Lyons did not believe in God.

Mr. Lyons admitted he did not attend any house of worship regularly. When asked by the chairman how much he had contributed to churches over the last five years, he said he had given ten dollars to a church in his neighborhood.

The chairman asked Mr. Lyons if he did not think that a man who was in charge of religious programming for the Voice of America might do a better job if he belonged to some church himself and were a regular churchgoer. Mr. Lyons answered: "Not necessarily."

> Senator JACKSON: Have you had any religious education?
> Mr. LYONS: My religious education was not of a formal kind. I am Jewish by background. I studied religion at Columbia University in connection with writing my philosophical thesis.
> Senator JACKSON: Did you major in religion?
> Mr. LYONS: No. I majored in philosophy.
> Senator JACKSON: You are head of the Religious Desk of the Voice of America. What particular qualifications did

you feel that you had that would be helpful in view of this important assignment?

Mr. LYONS: I was about to tell you.

Senator JACKSON: Will you proceed?

Mr. LYONS: In connection with my thesis I studied religion in Union Theological Seminary, which is a branch of Columbia University. There *I studied mostly under a Prof. Paul Tillich* [emphasis added], who inspired me to become very, very interested in this whole subject, and I organized of my own volition and with his approval a seminar with Professor Tillich, who is a teacher of the philosophy of religion and systematic theology in Union, a seminar on religion at which he gave a weekly lecture at various times with some regularity over a period of 3 years.

Senator JACKSON: Is this in connection with your master's degree?

Mr. LYONS: This was entirely on my own initiative. It happens to be that Professor Tillich was one of my advisers in connection with my thesis, but this further work was because of my own spontaneous interest in the spiritual factors.

Senator McCARTHY: Could you tell us something about that thesis, in that you indicated that you believed in a Divine Being, or did you indicate that you did not?

Mr. LYONS: I did not indicate either that I believed in a Divine Being or that I did not, because the thesis had to do with an attempt to discuss the meaning of certain words, and the clarification of certain statements, in order that a principle of moral value might be stated, which might or might not be acceptable. It was not a question of belief.

This product of Union Seminary then told the Congressional committee that he went to Switzerland and studied psychology and religion under Professor Carl Jung from 1946 to 1948. He said, "It was the School of Analytical Psychology, if you want to have a name for it."

The CHAIRMAN: How many students attended?

Mr. LYONS: I was one of the first. At the time I came over after the war, there was no formal study at that time, but later.

The CHAIRMAN: You were the first student?

Mr. LYONS: I was one of the first students to come over from America.

The CHAIRMAN: You were the only student for a while?

Mr. LYONS: There wasn't any formal curriculum.

The CHAIRMAN: Were you the only student in this field?

Mr. LYONS: There may have been others, but I don't know them.

The CHAIRMAN: That is rather an unusual school with only one student.

Mr. LYONS: That increased with the time, because the war prevented a great many students.

The CHAIRMAN: What is his religious background?

Mr. LYONS: His religious background, he is the son of a clergyman, and he has never professed himself as to any particular religious belief, but he has a great interest in the spiritual factors that are involved in analytical psychology or depth psychology, as it is sometimes called.

The CHAIRMAN: This professor under whom you studied, as far as you know, does not go to any church or synagogue?

Mr. LYONS: I don't know.

The CHAIRMAN: Well, now, if you studied with him, you are studying religion, I assume you would know.

Mr. LYONS: I studied religion but not in connection with his churchgoing activities.

The CHAIRMAN: If you were a one-man school, a one-man professor was teaching, studying religion, would you not be interested in knowing whether this man was affiliated with any church?

Mr. LYONS: As a matter of fact, I didn't study with him directly, because he was too busy to see me. . . .

This information concerning the director of religious programming of the Voice of America is startling, to say the least. Here is a man who studied for three years in Union Theological Seminary and wrote a thesis in which he said it was not necessary to express a belief in God. He came out of this seminary and went over to Europe to study in a so-called school in which he didn't meet any other students nor did he even see the professor. As one reads through this testimony it becomes more and more incredible as to how a man of this character could obtain such a high position in the State Department's Voice of America program and be paid by the American taxpayers!

Following the testimony of Prof. Tillich's pupil, Mrs. Alice Patricia Shephard testified under oath that she had had discussions with Mr. Lyons concerning his religious philosophy. While they were both employed by the Voice of America and going together, Mrs. Shephard said: "I don't believe that he believed in God then. He was going through a very difficult period. He was going to an analyst, and he was very confused at the time."

Council joins with Orthodox groups. Works hand-in-hand with Judaism. Council in close contact with Anti-Defamation League. Christmas is adjudged sectarian and divisive. President Eisenhower omits Christ from inaugural prayer. Divinity of Christ increasingly denied. Denials found in Sunday-school lessons. Ralph Lord Roy, defender of Bishop Oxnam and an apostle of ecumenism. Mr. Roy attacks "anti-Semitism" of New Testament. He denies the inspiration of Scripture. His *Apostles of Discord* endorsed by Oxnam, Fey, Niebuhr, and Birkhead. Birkhead's left-wing and atheistic record. Herbert Philbrick's "endorsement." The Presbyterian leftist, Dr. Mackay. Fund for the Republic selects Mr. Roy as an expert.

THE NATIONAL AND WORLD COUNCILS OF CHURCHES started out to be Protestant Christian organizations. In several fundamental respects they are no longer exclusively Protestant, and in other respects not even exclusively Christian.

The National and World Councils of Churches are no longer exclusively Protestant in that they have joined hands with Eastern Orthodox groups, which are not in the Protestant tradition. And the Councils further have been developing, as we have seen in Chapter 17, an "interfaith movement" which encompasses followers of Judaism, Baha'i, Buddhism, Hinduism, Mohammedanism, and any others that care to go along.

The Councils have been collaborating with leaders of Judaism, a non-Christian faith which has denied the divinity of Christ for two thousand years. These leaders have cooper-

241

ated closely with Christian educators, publishers, editors, and lesson writers in the preparation of "Christian" Sunday-school materials that would present an "accurate picture of Jews and Judaism."

According to the report of the 45th Annual Meeting of the American Jewish Committee, in 1951:

> Our emphasis has increasingly been on establishing lines of cooperation with Christian leadership education groups —those responsible for teacher training. Our scientific studies make it clear that not only the curriculum materials but the attitudes of those who attempt to use the materials are vital to the education of young children. Both in the manner of teaching about Christianity and Judaism as well as in the substance of the publications used by church schools, it is gratifying to be able to report that *positive attitudes* towards individuals of different racial and religious backgrounds are increasingly evident.

A survey was to be conducted of "distortions" concerning Jews and Judaism on the part of Protestants. As soon as this survey was finished, they would approach "our friends in the Protestant education field to see what can be done about rectifying this."

> The close contacts established last year with the Division of Christian Education of The National Council of Churches have been extended to their recently established Department of Inter-group Education, with which, together with the Anti-Defamation League, we are now in almost daily consultation. This department makes significant use of the committee's resources for material and information which it channels through 2,500,000 Protestant instructors to 27,000,000 Sunday-school students.[1]

[1] Report, 45th Annual Meeting of the American Jewish Committee, p. 42.

Many secondary-school principals and superintendents of public instruction have been influenced by the "interfaith" groups. Some of these groups have protested the observance of Christmas, the presenting of Christmas pageants, or the singing of Christmas carols in the public-school system at Christmas time. Christmas has been classified as a "sectarian" celebration which has no business in tax-supported public schools; it is "offensive" to minority groups who do not believe in Christmas![2]

School administrators over the country have capitulated to the exiling of Christmas from the classrooms. They have banned the celebrating of Christmas—and the reading of the Bible and the saying of the Lord's Prayer. The State Supreme Court of New Jersey, in a recent decision signed by the late Justice Vanderbilt, ruled against the New Jersey public-school system and the Gideons Bible Society, forbidding them to distribute the New Testament in New Jersey schools because it was "sectarian."

Many weak-kneed Protestant ministers have chosen to omit the name of Jesus Christ in their prayers when they pray before certain civic and patriotic organizations, as they do not want to offend any minority-group members present who do not believe in Christ. In the National Convention of the American Legion Auxiliary in Washington, D.C., in 1954, a resolution introduced at the resolutions committee meeting called for the elimination of any reference to Jesus Christ in the devotional period of the American Legion Auxiliary, as the name of Jesus Christ was offensive to religious groups who did not believe in Him. This story was printed in the Washington papers and caused an uproar. Leading powers in the American Legion saw that the resolution never reached the Auxiliary Convention floor.[3]

2 See Appendix 10.
3 See Appendix 11.

When Dwight D. Eisenhower was inaugurated President of the United States in January 1953, many Protestant Christians praised him as a great Christian leader because he read a prayer during his inauguration speech. Some Christians, however, on reading copies of the speech, took a second glance at the prayer, not sure that their ears had heard correctly. They had heard correctly. There was no invoking of the divine blessing on the nation through the name of Jesus Christ in the entire prayer. *The name of Christ was conspicuous by its absence!*

Now, the Bible plainly states, in the words of Christ and the apostles, that no man can come into the presence of God the Father except through the name of Jesus Christ. Prayers in the Christian tradition have been in the name of Jesus Christ down through the centuries—until very recently, when the "interfaith movement" began to blossom.

Jesus Christ said: "He that honoreth not the Son honoreth not the Father which hath sent him" (John 5.23). Jesus speaks again as follows: "Jesus sayeth unto him, I am the way, the truth and the life: No man cometh unto the Father but by me" (John 14:6). The apostle Paul, in his first epistle to Timothy, says: "For there is one God, and one *mediator* between God and men, the man Christ Jesus" (Tim. 2:5). In John's first epistle we read:

> Who is a liar but he that denieth that Jesus is the Christ? He is anti-Christ, that denieth the Father and the Son. Whosoever denieth the Son, the same hath not the Father: but he that acknowledgeth the Son hath the Father also (John 2:22–23).

Now, how do the modern liberals and interfaith advocates get around these plain teachings of the Bible? They do it very simply. They say that the best scholars know that Jesus and the apostles never said those things at all; people merely wrote them down as words of gossip many years after Jesus and the apostles were dead. These denials are contained in reams of Sunday-school material being distributed to adults and young people, and in the textbooks used in seminaries run by such modernist leaders as are found in The National Council of Churches.

Men hailed as leading theological scholars of today are the authors of totally anti-Christian books. One example is a young radical who calls himself a Methodist, gives his home address as the Union Theological Seminary in New York, and has his books published by a Unitarian publishing house in Boston. He has become the darling of The National Council of Churches. He has attacked leading defenders of the Christian faith throughout the United States who would not go along with the radicals in the ecumenical movement. His name is Ralph Lord Roy. His book, *Apostles of Discord*,[4] has been quoted and requoted by National Council leaders against those who point out from the official records of the Councils themselves how they have departed from the Christian faith. Roy has defended Bishop G. Bromley Oxnam and has attacked the committees of Congress that have investigated Bishop Oxnam and others in the religious world who have aided the cause of communism in the United States.

Ralph Lord Roy is a fervid ecumenical promoter and has become a major spokesman for the apostles of ecumenism and modernism. Because the most fashionable "interfaith" leaders wish to admit adherents of Judaism into virtual communion with the Christian denominations, they are determined to alter the integrity of the New Testament to make this possible. Roy is ready to oblige. Using "liberal scholars" for his authorities, he attacks the New Testament Scriptures for being "anti-Semitic":

4 Beacon Press, Boston, 1953.

Many liberal scholars, however, express the concern that the New Testament, as the creation of fallible men, was influenced strongly by anti-Semitic sentiments current in the first century of the Christian era. The Gospel of John is especially full of hatred for the Jews. The worst text is John 8:44, "Ye are of your father the devil." One commentator insists, "It is simply inconceivable that Jesus of Nazareth ever said these words." . . .

Some scholars have urged the churches to take forceful action against these corrupted passages. Dr. Frederick C. Grant, New Testament professor at Union Theological Seminary in New York City, laments: "The shame of the church is that it has permitted anti-Semitism to survive within its own ranks. The causes, like the origins, of this disgraceful and dysgenic social attitude certainly lie outside the New Testament and are shared by Jews and non-Jews; but that the Christian sacred Scriptures got infected with the virus, that the poison survives there to this day, that the Church has hitherto done very little to counteract the infection—all this is inexcusable."[5]

Dr. Grant[6] goes on to say that Christians should stem the tide of anti-Semitism by acknowledging the "seriousness of the situation within the New Testament itself." He says that material for use in religious education, sermons, and public worship should be carefully chosen and that these "anti-Semitic" passages should be eliminated from this material. These passages in the New Testament, he says, are "misrepresentations of the Jewish religion."

"Liberal scholars," according to Roy, say that the New Tes-

---

5 *Apostles of Discord*, p. 72.
6 The files of the Committee on Un-American Activities of the House of Representatives list Dr. Frederick C. Grant of Union Theological Seminary as a member and sponsor of the "Citizens Committee for Harry Bridges," the well-known alien Communist labor leader in the United States.

tament is the creation of "fallible men." This has never been the view of historic Christianity. The great scholars of both Protestantism and Catholicism for over two thousand years have acknowledged the Old and New Testament Scriptures to be the work of the Holy Spirit, the Third Person of the Trinity, who guided the pens of the authors of these books which form the Bible. The "liberal" scholars, in their egotism, would have the world believe that God Himself has left organized Christianity in the dark for twenty centuries in regard to the veracity of the Scriptures—and that He finally brought the world out into the light when the liberal scholars suddenly arose on the scene in the twentieth century. *This is the spirit of communism itself—the spirit which tries to destroy established truths, to undermine faith in great religious doctrines, to brainwash people into thinking that things that were once called true are no longer true, and to plant the seeds of rebellion or revolt against all duly constituted authority, whether it be in the secular world, in the field of governmental authority, or in the religious world, with respect to the authority of the Scriptures and of Christ Himself.*

Roy's book was endorsed by such well-known left-wing adherents as Bishop G. Bromley Oxnam; his own Professor John C. Bennett of Union Theological Seminary; the executive editor of the left-wing *Christian Century*, Harold E. Fey; Dr. Reinhold Niebuhr of Union Theological Seminary, and the notorious enemy of Christianity, the late Leon M. Birkhead.

Mr. Birkhead for years ran a publishing house in Kansas City with Haldeman-Julius, issuing atheistic and anti-Catholic literature. He became an apostate from the Methodist Church and was known as an agnostic, an atheist, a defamer of Christian ministers, and as one who advocated destruction of the theological seminaries. Mr. Birkhead later came to New York

City and took over the left-wing Friends of Democracy, which contains hate files on Americans in all walks of life.

In the December 1953 issue of a magazine entitled *Exposé*, L. M. Birkhead, as president of the Friends of Democracy, said (emphasis added):

> During recent years the Research Department of Friends of Democracy under my direction has helped to produce books which have made a tremendous dent on the thinking of America. The first of these was *Undercover* by John Roy Carlson, followed by his book *The Plotters*. These books sold almost a million copies and have been widely quoted and imitated. Add to the list Henry Hoke's *Black Mail* and *It's a Secret* and E. A. Piller's *Time Bomb*—all of them best sellers. And now we have the current best seller, *Apostles of Discord* by Ralph Lord Roy. *All of the aforementioned books were either written in the Friends of Democracy research department or by members of the FOD staff itself.*

George Washington Robnett of Evanston, Illinois, then the executive secretary of the Church League of America, brought suit for libel against "John Roy Carlson," who had fifteen known aliases and whose real name was Avedis Boghos Derounian. The jury, in the Federal Court in Chicago where he was tried, sustained the charge of libel. Judge John P. Barnes, in rendering his decision, declared that "Carlson's" book, *Undercover*, "was written by a wholly irresponsible person who would write anything for a dollar. . . . I wouldn't believe this author if he was under oath."

Mr. Roy's sources of information, listed in the front of his book *Apostles of Discord*, are exactly the same as those listed by Mr. "Carlson"!

Now, Roy, when he is attacked, can point to a name on the

jacket of his book and say, "Well, my book has been endorsed by Herbert A. Philbrick." Mr. Philbrick, a young churchman and an informer for the F.B.I. for nine years within the Communist Party of Massachusetts, has been asked why he permitted his name to be used on the jacket of a book of this character, which had been endorsed by four persons with Communist-front records who were leading radicals in the field of religion.

The author of the present book was one of those who asked, and this is Mr. Philbrick's reply (emphasis added):

White Plains, N.Y.
June 10, 1954.

Mr. Edgar C. Bundy
1407 Hill Ave.
Wheaton, Ill.

Dear Mr. Bundy:
Because of the fact that I have been out of town a great deal during the past few months on lecture tours, I hope you will forgive this tardy answer to your letter of March twenty-fifth.

In reply to your question, my "endorsement" of *Apostles of Discord does not constitute affirmation or agreement in views between myself and the author, Ralph Lord Roy.* I do, however, think that the book presents, to most people for the first time, a picture of fundamental differences and disagreements within the Protestant Church which need to be examined. I do think Mr. Roy is unfair in his inclusion of some names, and his lumping together such names as Adolf Hitler and Gerald K. Winrod with those of Daniel A. Poling and Major General William J. Donovan. Also I decry the mention of the Freedom Foundation with "hate sects" and "hate mongers." I believe that such guilt by association is most unfair.

However, I would still recommend the reading of the book because of the belief expressed in the *Apostles of Discord*. I believe that the average American citizen has a great deal more common sense than a lot of us give him credit for, and I feel they will therefore be able to read Roy's book and draw their own conclusions.

Incidentally, Mr. Roy states on the bottom of p. 241 that you had described John A. Mackay, president of Princeton Theological Seminary, as a "Presbyterian Red." Since the book was not published until mid-1953, and therefore your information pre-dates July of 1953, I am somewhat curious as to what information you had concerning Mr. Mackay. I was certainly shocked to read the Presbyterian Letter issued last October 1953, over the signature of Dr. Mackay, and to note that it supported not only the complete foreign policy program of the Soviet Union, but also contained all of the fundamental premises of Marxism, Leninism, and Stalinism concerning class struggle, imperialism, force and violence, and revolution.

Thank you for your letter, and I hope I have been able to answer your questions satisfactorily.

Sincerely yours,
[signed] Herbert A. Philbrick

Ralph Lord Roy is one of the most articulate spokesmen for The National Council of Churches and its leaders. Often, when Bishop G. Bromley Oxnam and other leaders of the Council wish to attack genuine ministers of the Gospel who have been exposing them effectively, they cite Ralph Lord Roy and his *Apostles of Discord* as their authority.

The methods by which Ralph Lord Roy obtained material for his writings are strikingly similar to those by which "John Roy Carlson" obtained his. "Carlson," operating under one or another of his aliases, gained access to offices and homes on

some plausible pretext and gathered material from his unsuspecting victims or their associates. Ralph Lord Roy, also on
some plausible pretext, wormed his way into the confidence of
clergymen and their families and obtained the information he
desired. One instance of his activities is related by Dr. Carl
McIntire in his book *Servants of Apostasy*:

It was the usual hot, humid Labor Day weekend. There
arrived early Sunday morning, September 2, 1951, at the
Sunday school of the Bible Presbyterian Church of Collingswood, a young man, Ralph L. Roy, fair complex-
ioned, with a bright eye and a ready tongue. He said that
he was a student at Columbia University, working on his
master's degree, and that he wanted to write a story about
the movement of which the Collingswood church and its
pastor were a part. He had contacted the *Atlantic Monthly*
and *Harper's* and had received approval from them, he
explained, provided his article was satisfactory. He represented himself as being sympathetic. He was introduced
to various officials and welcomed at the church as visitors
are always welcomed. He said that his grandmother was
an old-fashioned Methodist in Vermont and that, though
he preached in his own church, he really was not a li-
censed Methodist preacher. But his story varied some.

He expressed surprise at what he saw in Collingswood,
at the work which was being done in the church and Sunday school. He returned again on Sunday evening. After-
wards he expressed a desire to visit Harvey Cedars, the
Bible Presbyterian Conference at the seashore, for the
Labor Day meeting where I was to speak. I arranged to
take him to the seashore the next day with my family in
our car. On the way, we conversed at length. He reported
that he had visited the New York headquarters of The
National Council of Churches, and they did not want to

say very much to him about us. He had been to the World Council's headquarters and they had given him all the material they had about the International and American Councils of Christian Churches. He said they had referred him to the Friends of Democracy of which the late L. M. Birkhead was the director. He had interviewed Birkhead and others at length, he said, about our movement.

It was clear in talking with him that he did not believe in Jesus Christ as his personal Savior as the Scriptures teach it. On the return trip we spent most of the time explaining to him the way of salvation and endeavoring to lead him to accept Christ as his personal Savior. He seemed to know all the answers. He was steeped in the whole higher critical theory and was interested in building a "Kingdom of God" on this earth. We explained to him repeatedly the way of eternal life. He told us that it was a wonderful thing to believe, if one could believe it, but that he could not conceive of a God making such a free gift to man.

Later, he wrote us a letter dated September 12, 1951, from Swanton, Vermont, saying:

"Please accept my manifold thanks for your hospitality and assistance in clarifying many of the issues that were in my mind. I am still not perfectly clear on several points, but the conversations with you enabled me to look at your endeavors with greater objectivity than before.

"God bless you, your wonderful wife and family, and may He give you new visions of His Truth and His Beauty."

After his departure on Monday, in a lengthy memorandum which I prepared, I wrote, "It looked to me as though here was a young man who either has been assigned or has set out on his own to write one of these colorful smear-type stories."

His story came repeatedly and in various places. "Ministry of Schism" was the title of an article on the American Council of Christian Churches appearing in *The Pastor,* October 1952, reprints of which were immediately distributed "as a service of the Commission on Public Relations and Methodist Information." It was announced that he was a graduate student at Union Theological Seminary, New York. The *Christian Century* carried several articles by him, attacking [myself], The American and the International Councils of Christian Churches, and the *Christian Beacon.*

"Ministry of Disruption" was the title of a 20-page mimeographed document "for private circulation" issued by the "Division of Literature and Publications, The Board of Foreign Missions of the Presbyterian Church in the U.S.A., 156 Fifth Avenue, New York 10, N.Y." The subtitle read, "A brief study of the activities of Carl McIntire and the American Council of Christian Churches," with the information that "this study has been compiled by Ralph L. Roy." This document was sent to mission stations throughout the world and turned up in various conferences where missionaries gathered to talk.

These articles were, in fact, sections or rewrites of material in the book which was to appear in 1953 entitled *Apostles of Discord.* "Protestant Fringe Groups Promoting Hate and Disruption" was the subtitle of the book, with the following commendation on the front jacket: "BISHOP OXNAM: 'An extraordinarily valuable piece of work.' REINHOLD NIEBUHR: 'Ralph Roy has performed an important task in his careful analysis.'" Here it was learned that Roy had been working under the consultation and guidance of John C. Bennett of Union Theological Seminary, the author of the World Council's pronouncement on "The Church and the Disorder of Society," adopted in Amsterdam in 1948, which the former editor of the *Christian Century,* Dr. Charles Clayton Morrison, said was "overloaded with Communist sympathy."

Roy also made an ingratiating approach to Dr. Harllee Bordeaux, office secretary of the American Council of Christian Churches at 15 Park Row, New York. Dr. Bordeaux received him cordially after Roy had represented himself as a Columbia University student engaged in gathering material for a thesis on the struggle between the orthodox and liberal wings of Christianity. Subsequently, Roy attacked the American Council.

Similarly, he launched assaults on Mr. Verne Kaub, retired public-relations director of the Wisconsin Power and Light Company and now chairman of the American Council of Christian Laymen in Madison, Wisconsin. These attacks, following a friendly letter to Mr. Kaub, appeared in the form of articles written for the *Christian Century, The Pastor,* and *The New Republic.* Ultimately, the assaults on Mr. Kaub and on many others appeared in his book, *Apostles of Discord.*

The Fund for the Republic, which has assisted The National Council of Churches in its secularized program, sought an authoritative person to collect material and write a book on communism and the churches. Ralph Lord Roy of Union Theological Seminary, in conjunction with Paul A. Carter of Columbia University, was selected. These men worked under a grant of $250,000 furnished by The Fund for the Republic.

Council monopoly of media of communication. The Voice of Protestantism. How the Council controls radio. The Voice of Dr. Fosdick. He ridicules Christian doctrines. Independent ministers cannot be heard. Their protests ignored. Council attempting to broaden public relations still further. Acknowledges criticism. Defenders of the Faith have few outlets of communication.

THE FEDERAL COUNCIL OF CHURCHES and its successor, the National Council, have worked diligently to win over to their side the exclusive right to be heard on radio and television and to be read in the press of the nation.

As one examines the roster of churchmen who have been heard and seen on the air, one realizes that through the years the vast majority have been well-known radicals and liberals, noted not for defending historical Christianity but rather for peddling the Social Gospel.

The Federal-National Council of Churches has obtained practically a monopoly in the field of religious broadcasting. Committee members or representatives of the Council get together with the Federal Communications Commission and press upon them the idea that religious time should not be purchased from the major broadcasting systems but rather that the networks should grant free time equally to the three major religions in the United States: Protestantism, Catholicism, and

255

Judaism. Then the Council representatives, posing as the Voice of Protestantism, seek to convince the Federal Communications Commission, the heads of the broadcasting chains, and the local radio stations that, since the Council represents the majority of the Protestants in the United States, it should be given sole disposition of the free time granted to Protestants. Hundreds of local evangelical ministers who have refused to join the Federal or National Council have been forced off the air by representatives of local councils of churches. Several major broadcasting chains have been highly partial to the Federal-National Council and have refused to give independent groups an equal voice on these chains. *The Council has even succeeded in putting some of its own representatives in official positions in the networks to manage the chains' sections on religious broadcasting.*

The Federal Council's 1946 Biennial Report, in the chapter entitled "National Religious Radio," says: "For the past two years in particular, recognition should be given to the vision and leadership of the 59 clergymen whose names are listed herewith. Without their cooperation, religious radio programs sponsored by The Federal Council of Churches would not have afforded the spiritual inspiration so vitally needed."[1] Listed is the name of Fosdick, Harry Emerson, Riverside Church, New York, N.Y.

Who is the Rev. Harry Emerson Fosdick? He was for many years the pastor of the multimillion-dollar Riverside Church in New York City, built with Rockefeller funds. This was the same Dr. Fosdick who stood in his pulpit and ridiculed the doctrine of the Virgin Birth of Christ, telling his congregation in no uncertain terms that he did not believe in the Virgin Birth of Christ.[2] Subsequently, Dr. Fosdick wrote to several

[1] P. 35.
[2] The sermon in which this denial was made was printed on Dr. Fosdick's church press and is available.

inquirers who asked if it was true that he did not believe in the Virgin Birth of Christ. Dr. Fosdick said that he did not believe in the Virgin Birth of Christ or "in that old-fashioned substitutionary doctrine of the Atonement; and I do not know any intelligent Christian minister who does." [3]

Dr. Fosdick has also described the concept of heaven as "a perpetual religious serenade."

Dr. Elias B. Sanford, writing [4] as long ago as 1916, brings out the fact that the federating of the churches was put over very easily and rapidly because of support by the editors of various church newspapers and journals. These publications, he says, went into several millions of homes every week and so influenced the thinking of churchgoing people.

The press is, indeed, a very powerful medium of propaganda; and if it is run by liberals or radicals, unscriptural or false conceptions of the church's mission can be put over without much opposition.

The sad truth is that those denominations, churches, pastors, and religious agencies which have not gone along with The Federal-National Council of Churches and its Socialistic schemes never possess the means of communication by which to expose fully what the Council has been doing in the name of the churches. Consequently, millions of church people have been deceived. Even when some church members, having had their eyes opened to the truth about this ecclesiastical octopus, ask their ministers for information, the ministers, themselves being a part of the Council machinery and holding their pulpits on the acquiescence of higher-ups in the denominations who committed the denominations to the Council, disdain to honor the protests of the church members.

When ministers who accept the great doctrines of Chris-

[3] Letter from Dr. Fosdick to W. B. Barnhart, Jan. 31, 1948.
[4] *Origin and History of the Federal Council of the Churches of Christ in America.* See his foreword.

tianity in preference to accepting the domination of The Federal-National Council of Churches have spoken out against the blasphemy of a Dr. Fosdick, or against the monopolistic press and radio practices of the Council, they have been soundly denounced by Council leaders as "dissenters," "hatemongers," "superfundamentalists," and "divisive forces trying to disrupt the unity of the Church."

Ministers within the Council and newspaper people have agreed that The National Council of Churches today has a propaganda apparatus of great power and influence. The General Board of the Council, however, doesn't seem to feel that it is powerful enough. The report of the Council's general secretaries for 1954, under the heading of "Unmet Needs," says: "Equally vital is a public relations program that will provide the American people and the world with a graphic picture of the combined Christian [that is, National Council] enterprise."[5]

The Department of Public Relations, they say, has done well with its budget, but it must have more money.

The National Council admits officially for the first time that criticism needs to be answered. This is a large admission, for in previous years the Council would not recognize either its critics or their criticisms. The secretaries[6] urge that "unfair criticism of the cooperating churches and the National Council be made a special concern of the public relations program." Countless denials of charges will be made, and personal attacks will be launched against religious leaders who will not go along with the Council's program. The Council knows that it can count on a major segment of the secular press, national magazines, radio and television, and even Hollywood, to give its side of all questions, to the exclusion of its critics' side; for the Council has spent years propagandizing these media of com-

5 1954 Biennial Report, p. 35.
6 Ibid., p. 36.

munication and has even placed its own propagandists in official positions in all these channels for the dissemination of news.

The American church people do not know what is happening to them. They do not know how they are being used by adherents of the collectivistic society.

What can the protestors do? They can do little, for the apostate leaders are in control of the media of communication, and men who would defend the Faith, "once and for all delivered unto the saints" (Jude 3), have few outlets for their defense of the Gospel.

THE LAYMEN
START TO REVOLT

How the Council won impressive lay support: Messrs. Wilson, Kraft, Firestone, Hook, Ryerson, and others. But it has not won nationwide loyalty, and it does not speak for Protestantism, as it claims. Eighteen million, not thirty million. The gulf between Council and laypeople. The National Lay Committee and Mr. Pew. He outlines the role of the Lay Committee. The Council's General Board unexpectedly rebuffs the laymen. The laymen raise $600,000 but are not to interfere in Council politicking. The clergy fundamentally opposed to lay activities. Dr. Blake kills the Lay Committee. Mr. Pew chides the Council for political activities. Poor voting record of General Board. Fewer than fifty men vote allegedly for thirty million. The only hope is to support independent pastors.

SUPPORT, in the form of prestige, for the National Council has been received from individual businessmen. The heads of large corporations, who know little about the history and goals of The Federal-National Council of Churches, have accepted high positions in the Council, unaware that they are being used as fronts. The Council, when it is criticized for collectivistic pronouncements and activities, can point to the respectable character of its businessman officers and claim that the criticisms cannot have any foundation in fact or justice.

Elected treasurer of The National Council of Churches for 1951–1952 was Charles Wilson, former president of the General Electric Company. Associate treasurer was the late James

L. Kraft,[1] chairman of the board of the Kraft Foods Company, and the former treasurer of the International Council of Religious Education. The Council *Workbook* for 1951–1952 and 1953–1954 lists, among members of the Business and Finance Committee, Harvey Firestone, Jr., of the Firestone Tire and Rubber Company; Charles R. Hook, chairman of the board of Armco Steel; Olive Ann Beech, head of the Beech Aircraft Corporation of Wichita, Kansas; Edward L. Ryerson, Chicago steel magnate.[2]

The Council has won over these people for its purposes; its claim of success in having done so, and in having gained the trust and loyalty of many other lay individuals, cannot justly be denied. That the Council has gained the loyalty of Protestant America and is entitled to represent itself as speaking the mind of Protestant America is, despite its massive claims to have done so, fallacious and reprehensible. Let us look into this.

Information Service, the Council's publication, in its issue of September 6, 1952, tabulates the total membership of all religious bodies having 50,000 or more members each. The figures intend to show, in the first place, that 21,437,395 Protestants are *not* affiliated with the National Council.[3] Protestants numbering 30,725,037 *are* affiliated, the Council says, and for these Protestants the Council claims to speak. Of this total, however, 11,894,975 Protestants are members of denominations which have the Congregational type of polity. Under this polity, no member of a hierarchy can speak for the people in the pews of the individual churches. All questions must be submitted for a vote to each local congregation. This

[1] See p. 145.
[2] National Council *Workbook for the Second General Assembly,* Dec. 9–12, 1952, p. 118.
[3] This list, put out by the National Council, is far from complete, because many Protestant bodies do not turn in their figures either to the governmental or the church census bureaus.

was never done among the Congregational-polity churches so far as membership in the Federal, National, or World Council of Churches was concerned. Of the total of 30,725,037 for whom The National Council of Churches claims to speak on all matters covered in its Biennial Reports, only 18,830,062 members have the Episcopal or Presbyterian system, which allows the denominational heads to speak for their constituencies. In all the membership of all the American Protestant denominations, it is only for this small minority of some eighteen million that the Council can rightfully say it speaks. Even then, its claim to representation is of a highly theoretical nature, since the membership is rarely consulted on important decisions.

Members of the Council machinery are not wholly unaware of the gulf between the Council leadership and the people who sit—or used to sit—in the pews of churches affiliated with the Council. This excerpt provides evidence:

> The great weakness of the Council is its distance from the people in the local church. I am not thinking so much in terms of miles as in contact . . . the National Council needs to do something to sell itself to the average businessman on Main Street. It is too much of a closed corporation going its own way and therefore missing the support and enthusiasm which millions of American churchmen could give it. Let's get down to the grass roots and sell the National Council to the people! [4]

Laymen, of course, always have been represented—in fluctuating degrees—in the management of the Federal and Na-

[4] From Report to the 1952 Biennial Meeting of The National Council of Churches, Denver, Colorado. Excerpt from returned inquiry blank which was one of many mailed to 3,600 members of the 221 boards, committees, and commissions then supervising the work of the Council at various levels of organization.

tional Councils. Their role always has been a minor one, however, and they never have been able to influence Council
policies to any serious extent.

Prior to the formal organization of The National Council
of Churches in 1950, a Planning Committee was created to
establish the Council. The Planning Committee called for a
special Lay Committee to be set up, which would help to
establish the National Council and would advise on the best
manner of projecting lay leadership into the Council. On
July 6, 1950, Mr. J. Howard Pew, of Philadelphia, chairman
of the board of the Sun Oil Company, was asked to assume
the chairmanship of this Lay Committee and to organize its
membership. Mr. Pew called on outstanding leaders of industry and of community and national life who were members of
various Protestant denominations within the old Federal
Council of Churches. Eighty-six of these lay men and women,
all approved by members of the Planning Committee, met
together just before the Constituting Convention of the
National Council.

In the course of time the Lay Committee expanded to as
many as 219 members. These people were citizens nationally
famous in industry, finance, and labor. They were appointed
by their respective denominations and were widely distributed
geographically and vocationally. Forty-one states and the District of Columbia were represented.

On November 29, 1950, the Constituting Convention met
in Cleveland and The National Council of the Churches of
Christ in the United States of America came into formal existence precisely along the lines mapped by the Planning Committee. Mr. Pew addressed the convention and outlined the
plans agreed upon for lay participation. The plans included
the creation of a National Lay Committee as a standing committee of the General Board, having the right to collaborate
with the Board and with departments on pronouncements and

statements of policy and to assist the National Council in its business and financial operations.

The General Board of the new National Council met on December 20, 1950, to act on the Planning Committee's recommendations. Sharp, unexpected opposition arose to giving the Lay Committee a status closely related to the policy-directing center of the National Council. The recommendations were pushed aside, and the matter of lay participation was shunted to a subcommittee for study. The General Board finally acted on March 28, 1951, and rejected the Planning Committee's recommendations. But it did set up for a two-year period a layman's committee within the Department of United Churchmen and a laywoman's committee within the Department of United Church Women. Each was to have limited functions but was to "assist the Council in its business operations and in obtaining needed financial support." The members of each committee were to be nominated by its respective division; and five "consultants" without vote were appointed from each to sit on the General Board.

The Lay Committee was asked to finance current operations of the National Council to the tune of $600,000, needed before January 1952. The lay people, believing they were to be given a very active role in helping to determine the policies of the National Council, responded to the call and raised the money. However, the lay people soon found out that *the clergy* who, as in the old Federal Council, overwhelmingly dominated the National Council, *wanted the financial support of the laymen but wanted no restraining hand on their excursions into the fields of economics, sociology, and politics.*

The status of the Lay Committee, divided between a layman's and a laywoman's committee, continued until December 1952, when the General Assembly of the National Council created a single Lay Committee. This was to be related directly to the General Board and would remain in existence until

June 30, 1954. Subsequently its life was extended to June 30, 1955, when it was terminated.

The Lay Committee, in declaring its position, said that "it was vital for the National Council to have functioning within its organization an autonomous lay group with the responsibility of interpreting the work of the Council to the laity, and of interpreting the viewpoint of the laity to the Council."

But, from the very beginning, the clergy, as represented on the General Board, were opposed to a Lay Committee with the scope and power expected by the lay people. They wanted no laymen's restraining hands on their secular pronouncements and policies. They wanted to keep the influence of the laymen ineffectual and without the power of vote in the deliberations of the General Board.

This dispute between the clergy and the laymen waxed hotter as the General Board began to make highly controversial official pronouncements on social and economic questions in the name of an alleged 30,000,000 Protestants. The lay people saw The National Council of Churches going far afield from the mission of the Church and actually committing organized Protestantism to the support of collectivist programs.

Mr. Pew waged a battle within the National Council against the Council's Socialistic pronouncements. He worked tirelessly, calling the Lay Committee together on many occasions; having thorough discussions of the issues by the lay members, and presenting the position of the laymen to the General Board in person and through correspondence.

The climax came on June 30, 1955, when the Lay Committee ceased to exist as a committee of the General Board. The General Board, led by the new president of The National Council of Churches, Dr. Eugene Carson Blake, Presbyterian Church in the U.S.A., refused to renew the life of the Lay Committee.

On December 15, 1955, Mr. Pew, in a letter to all members of the national Lay Committee, acknowledged "the failure of this most important effort to bring about an enduring partnership between the clergy and laity." He said:

> Throughout our Committee's term of life, it repeatedly brought to the Council's attention the seriousness of the problems involved in its issuance of controversial statements and studies in the field of sociology, economics and politics; and the danger inherent in speaking to official Washington and the United Nations General Assembly in behalf of Protestantism on matters outside the field and for which they possessed no mandate.[5] . . .

> We lay people found ourselves not only directly in the minority but often poles apart from the clergy who invariably outvoted us ten to one in these sessions.[6]

Some startling statistics had been presented to the General Assembly of the National Council at its December 1952 meeting, with respect to the relative number of ordained and lay members of the General Board, and the attendance at board meetings (emphasis added):

> Analysis reveals the member communions have not taken this mandate very seriously. A study of the composition of the present General Board shows that 72 out of the 85 members designated by the communions, or 84.7 per cent, are ordained persons. Not all of the communions have designated official alternates. However, 17 of the 22 officially reported alternates, or 77 per cent, are likewise ordained persons. This imbalance is partially but by no

5 The Chairman's Final Report, p. V.
6 Ibid., p. VI.

means fully corrected by virtue of the fact that only 21 of the 40 members [7] (52.5 per cent) are ordained. Therefore, in the General Board of 125 as now constituted there are 93 ordained persons or a total of 74.4 per cent of the entire membership. The only young persons included in the 125 are the four designated respectively by the four Divisions.[8]

At ten meetings of the General Board (January 17, 1951–September 24, 1952), seven of which were held in New York, two in Chicago, and one in Atlanta, the average number of voting representatives present was 53 of a possible 125, or 42.4 per cent. The largest attendance of voting members at any meeting was 66 and the smallest 35. Of the average attendance of 53, ordained members averaged 39 and lay persons 14. This follows very closely the 74.4 per cent ordained and 25.6 per cent lay division in the Board's membership. . . . More staff members, consultants and guests attended these ten General Board meetings than members of the Board, the average attendance being 53 voters and 58 non-voters of whom 49, on the average, were staff.[9]

The lack of any voting representation at General Board meetings by some of the 29 member communions poses a serious problem. *On an average only 16 of the 29 member churches were represented at the ten meetings.* Not more than 22 of the 29 were represented at any one meeting and *only 11 of the 29 had voting representatives present at the specially called meeting October 31, 1951, when the Board took strong action in opposition to the appointment of an Ambassador to the Vatican.*[10]

[7] Officers of National Council headquarters and special lay members not chosen by the denominations but by the National Lay Committee.
[8] *Ibid.*, p. 28.
[9] *Loc. cit.*
[10] *Ibid.*, p. 29.

It can be seen from the above that 53 members of a General Board of 125 voted pronouncements allegedly on behalf of 30,000,000 church members; *and often the number present and voting was far smaller*. This is, indeed, incredible.

A remarkable highlight of this whole controversy was the position asserted by the lay men and women, who insisted that *the primary business of the churches was evangelism*. They evidently knew more about the church's mission than did the clergymen of the Council. Mr. Pew, in his letter to the National Lay Committee, said:

> Our premise was that, instead of appealing to government, the church should devote its energy to the work of promoting the attributes of Christianity—truth, honesty, fairness, generosity, justice and charity—in the hearts and minds of men. We attempted to emphasize that Christ stressed not the expanded state but the dignity and responsibility of the individual.[10]

Mr. Pew said that the philosophy of most of the executives and officers directing the work of the several denominational headquarters staffs, and therefore of the National Council, seemed to be that of ever-expanding government. He added that clergy and laity "seem to have lost the capacity to understand each other"; that the lay people were not the only ones protesting the collectivist pronouncements of The National Council of Churches, but that clergymen on the local level disagreed as well.

It seems, from the evidence—official minutes of the meetings of the National Lay Committee and of the General Board of The National Council of Churches—that the Board had failed to live up to assurances originally given to the lay people. According to these assurances, the new Council would avoid "the

10 *Ibid.*, p. VI.

political involvements and controversies which had characterized the activities of the old Federal Council of Churches
which was now suspended."

The lay people seem to have been overoptimistic when The
National Council of Churches was brought into being. A simple study of the old Federal Council's history and of a roster
of its officers would have shown that a change of name to
"National" could not possibly change the heart; the "new"
organization retained practically the same leadership which
had made the Federal Council so controversial, as we have seen
in chapter 5.

Mr. Pew showed his recognition of the fact in his letter of
December 15, 1955:

> It appears from the record that the National Council
> could find no room for opposition to the philosophies and
> practices carried over from the old Federal Council. Lack-
> ing the patience to resolve the basic problem, it has sought
> to bury it.[11]

What a vast amount of good might have been done by these
same laymen if they had withdrawn from The National Council of Churches in its beginning and had thrown their support,
both financial and spiritual, to the hundreds of pastors, now
heading independent churches all over the country, who with
their people did not bow to the collectivist National Council
but withdrew from the denominations supporting this ecclesiastical octopus and sought to uphold the primitive integrity
of the church.

This, Moses did when he left Egypt; inscribed to him in the
book of Hebrews is this memorial:

> By faith Moses, when he was come to years, refused to
> be called the son of Pharaoh's daughter;

11 *Ibid.*, p. X.

Choosing rather to suffer affliction with the people of God, than to enjoy the pleasures of sin for a season;

Esteeming the reproach of Christ greater riches than the treasures in Egypt; for he had respect unto the recompense of the reward.

By faith he forsook Egypt, not fearing the wrath of the king: for he endured, as seeing him who is invisible.[12]

Thousands of churches over the United States are unaffiliated with The National Council of Churches in any manner. They have their own evangelistic and missionary programs, which follow the pattern set by the historic Christian churches. They have been maligned and persecuted by National Council leaders; but so were the Pilgrim Fathers who came out of England, and the early church martyrs.

Would that church people would hold this truth uppermost in their thinking today: The words "popularity" and "faithfulness" should never be confused with one another.

Those who are true to the preaching of the Gospel of Christ may be in the minority and may be scorned by persons who delight to throw huge statistics around, seeking to impress simple souls; but history attests to the fact that God has never worked through majorities but rather through distinct minorities.

Fear not, *little* flock; for it is your Father's good pleasure to give you the kingdom.[13]

12 Heb. 11:24–27.
13 Luke 12:32. Jesus Christ speaking.

APPENDICES

1   HOW THE NATIONAL COUNCIL INFLUENCES THE LOCAL COUNCILS

THE 1954 BIENNIAL REPORT of The National Council of Churches is replete with references to the "cooperation of the state and local councils of churches" (emphasis added):

> The past two years have been an eventful period. The contribution made to the vitality of Christianity in America during the biennium is set forth in the reports of the Council's major divisions and other units. . . . It reflects the growing sense of dedication of hundreds of men and women—clerical and lay—of the churches and of the Council's staff, to the spirit of cooperation symbolized by the National Council, *state and local councils* and the ecumenical movement. . . .
>
> Action to bring together at the conference table the leaders of related *state and local councils of churches* with spokesmen for the communions is another significant landmark on the road to greater solidarity. Through changes already effected, program and field operations will be planned jointly in the future. (Page 31.)
>
> On March 17 of this year, the General Board took actions based on a different concept of field planning from that which has previously obtained . . . the establishment of an Office for Councils of Churches and an Advisory Committee for this office. . . .

Real progress has been made in achieving a consistent and sound pattern of relationships between the National Council and *state and local councils of churches*. . . . Those *few state and local councils* that have not traditionally been based upon the principles of the National Council . . . have been gradually adjusting their structures and operations in the direction of conformity to the basic principles of the National Council. (Page 33.)

One of eleven objectives set up by The National Council of Churches is to

strengthen the cooperative movement by developing closer teamwork and communication between *national, state and local councils*. (Page 37.)

The Division of Christian Education, under the subhead "Weekday Religious Education," states:

The Department of Weekday Religious Education deals, for the most part, with *state and city councils of churches* which, in turn, minister directly more than 3,000 weekday religious education systems reaching more than a million children and youth. (Page 42.)

The Department of Worship and the Arts reports

cooperation with *state and local councils of churches* and other agencies and institutions in sponsoring regional conferences and workshops in worship, drama and the other arts. (Page 55.)

The Department of the Church and Economic Life reports under the subhead "Local Communities":

State and city councils of churches represent a cooperative witness and impact on concrete situations and issues in which people are immediately involved. There is a high actual and potential readiness on the part of many of these councils to provide leadership in community economic life. (Page 57.)

The Department of International Justice and Goodwill says that it serves

> *national, state,* and *local* denominational bodies, *councils of churches,* councils of church women and student groups. (Page 63.)

The Department of Racial and Cultural Relations states that, through its Section on Inter-group Education, it

> rendered service to *state and local councils of churches.* (Page 64.)

Here is the official action of the General Board of The National Council of Churches on May 19, 1953, in relation to a report from the committee on General Policy and Strategy:

> Approved: strengthening cooperation in *state and local councils of churches* and councils of church women. (Page 147.)

2   REPORT OF THE
CENTRAL DEPARTMENT OF
FIELD ADMINISTRATION
(1954 BIENNIAL REPORT)[1]

THIS DEPARTMENT has assisted the churches in state and local communities to strengthen their cooperative work. It has also shared with all the program units of the Council in coordinating and projecting field programs in line with its understanding of the needs in the field.

Field Outreach Policy

The department has approved for experimental use the following tentative statement on Field Outreach Policy:

The program plans and staff resources of The National Council of Churches and its several units reach the field through two recognized channels of approach—denominational and interdenominational. There is a well-established field outreach policy through denominational channels for denominational work. The cooperative program of the denominations through the General Board of The National Council of Churches should reach local congregations not only through the regular national denominational channels but also through the cooperative work of the denominations at the state and local levels.

Within the interdenominational channels there may be confusion of relationship if the National Council (or its units) approaches a local council of churches without taking into account the state council of churches. This practice can make interdenominational field relationships difficult at the state level. The state

[1] This Appendix 2 in its entirety is quoted from the 1954 Biennial Report.

council of churches must increasingly be the responsible agent of the member communions for conducting their cooperative work in a given state. The National Council recognizes this fact and desires to shape its field operations in conformity with it. At the same time, local councils of churches are the responsible agents of their member congregations for conducting their cooperative work. This fact the National Council also recognizes as valid. It therefore seeks to shape its field operations in such a way as to provide effective service at both state and local levels as the needs require.

The problems arising from this situation, while a matter of deep concern, are by no means insoluble, as experience has amply demonstrated. The key to their solution is a flexible field outreach policy which recognizes the interrelatedness of the national, state, and local interdenominational enterprise.

The interdenominational field outreach policy of the National Council consists of five parts, as follows:

1. *Field program service to state councils of churches*
   Field program plans and projects which are designed to reach the churches of a given state in areas broader than that of a local council of churches shall be presented to the state council of churches by the National Council or one of its units for its consideration and action. The development and implementation of such planning shall be in cooperation with the state council.

2. *Field program service to local councils of churches*
   Field program plans and projects which are designed to serve the congregations constituent to a given local council of churches shall be presented to the local council by the National Council or one of its units for its consideration and action. Copies of National Council correspondence shall be sent to the appropriate state council executive for information and collaboration.

3. *Field program service to other areas*

In states with no state council of churches, the field program planning and projects shall be presented to whatever recognized state interdenominational organization exists. If there is no such organization, the National Council representative shall convene representatives of state denominational bodies, to whom the presentation shall be made for their consideration and action.

In regions within a state which are wider than the area served by a local council of churches, the National Council should help the state council in convening a conference of denominational bodies to whom program plans shall be presented for their consideration and action.

4. *Requests for field service*

Requests for field service from a state or local council may be addressed to any unit of the National Council. The National Council unit involved shall make direct response to such request for field service. When requests are received from local churches, they may be answered from local churches, they may be answered directly and a carbon copy of the National Council's reply sent to the appropriate state council office or they should be acknowledged and may be referred to the state council executive.

5. *Establishment of offices of National Council units*

Offices of the National Council units should be established only after consultation with the council of the state and city in which the proposed office would be located.

There are certain areas of operation involving councils of churches and church women that are not touched upon in this document. Additional statements may need to be developed to cover these operations.

State Organizations

During this biennium the state councils of churches in Georgia and Texas were organized and launched with full-time executive leadership. Encouraging progress has been made in the development of a tentative constitution for the Arkansas Council of Churches. Five state denominational bodies have approved the plan and it is expected that the new council will be constituted early in the new triennium 1955–1957.

At present there are

> 40 states which have a state council of churches (also one in Puerto Rico)
>
> 8 states which have no state council of churches—Alabama, Arkansas, Idaho, Louisiana, Mississippi, Nevada, New Mexico, Wyoming
>
> 48 states which have a state council of church women (also one in Hawaii)

Local Developments

The pattern of cooperation in city, county, and local councils becomes more and more like that of the National Council, that is, parallel cooperative efforts of the churches become more and more integrated into a comprehensive council usually called "council of churches." During the biennium a number of voluntary county and local councils of religious education and Sunday-school associations, as well as councils of churches, have been discontinued. One significant growth is represented by two new state councils and twelve city and local councils with paid executive leadership. At present there are

> 209 local councils of churches, councils of religious education, etc., with paid leadership
>
> 692 local councils of churches, councils of religious education, etc., with voluntary leadership

The combined state, city and local councils now include:

249 state and local councils with paid executive leadership
694 state and local councils with voluntary leadership
943 state and local councils with paid and voluntary leadership

In addition there are:

1961 state, city and local councils of United Church Women
95 state, city and local organized United Church Men's units
2045 ministerial associations.

Offices: The Central Office and the Office for Financial Counseling are at 297 Fourth Avenue, New York, N. Y., and the Midwest Office is at 79 East Adams Street, Chicago, Illinois. There is a Southeastern Regional Office in Atlanta and until June 30, 1954, there was a Southwestern Regional Office in Fort Worth, Texas.

MIDWESTERN OFFICE

Central Services: The Midwestern Office, under the direction of the associate executive director, shares in the guidance of the total field administration activities and in counseling with state and city councils in regard to personnel, program development and study of organization and function. He also carries responsibility for program promotion and maintaining of permanent files and records for the Association of Council Secretaries annual meetings.

Field Counseling Literature: The department decided, instead of revising pamphlet 2 in the Church Cooperation Series, "How to Organize a Local Council of Churches," to develop a Field Guidance Manual. Under the chairmanship of Willis Ford, a small committee is preparing a twenty-two-chapter manual. Seventeen persons have contributed to the various chapters. Chapter V, "Philosophy of a Council of Churches," and chapter VIII, "Sample

Constitutions for a Council of Churches" (in large cities, in small cities, and in states), have been distributed for experimental use.

Christian Education: The associate executive director and his administrative assistant, Margaret Lawson, also serve the Division of Christian Education. Miss Lawson carries major responsibilities for physical arrangements for the Division's annual and fall meetings as well as developing responsibilities for scheduling staff services and to the Educational Field Services Committee.

Under the leadership of the Division's Educational Field Services Committee a conference was held, and in consultation with the various committees of the Commission on General Christian Education a plan for coordination and more systematic scheduling of field program activities of the Commission has been devised. The Educational Field Services Committee is also counseling with the staff of the Commission on a plan and procedure for scheduling staff services to denominations and state and city councils.

SOUTHEASTERN AND SOUTHWESTERN REGIONAL OFFICES

These regional offices have assisted in the development of councils of churches during this period in Tennessee, Georgia, Texas, and Arkansas; and in the cities of Austin, Dallas, the Rio Grande Valley near Brownsville, Houston, Wichita Falls, and Fort Worth.

The southwestern executive director, Harry C. Munro, was called to the executive leadership of the Fort Worth Council of Churches in 1954. Since the Texas Council of Churches has now been established, the southwestern office was closed June 30, 1954, with the understanding that the responsibility for the remaining unorganized states would be related to the former southeastern area, probably resulting in a newly combined southern regional office.

The executive director of the southeastern regional office, Rev. Ernest J. Arnold, resigned April 1, 1954, in order to devote full time to the Protestant Radio Center in Atlanta. Pending the filling of the vacancy, Ernest J. Arnold has continued to give counsel to the work of the office, centering in assistance to councils, interpretation of the National Council, and promotion of the Protestant Radio Center.

The Advisory Committee of these two offices express sincere appreciation for the executive leadership of Ernest J. Arnold and Harry C. Munro.

Field Service Itinerary Schedules

The Field Service Itinerary Schedules were issued quarterly. These schedules list the dates, places and types of meetings in which the National Council staff members participate during each quarter. They were made available to executives of councils of churches and to the National Council executive staff.

Centralized Calendar Service

The Centralized Calendar Service lists dates for major program events of the National Council units; also those of other interdenominational agencies and constituent communions and boards.

This service was made available to executives of councils of churches, National Council staff, to interdenominational and denominational executives, and to the press.

Financial Counseling

The constant backlog of requests from councils of churches for field visits by the director of financial counseling is evidence of the need and use being made of this service. One hundred and sixty-two different councils have been visited at least once during the biennium, including a series of three to twenty-four visits to eight state and twenty city and county councils.

The constituent members of the city, county, and state councils are contributing the largest single percentage of their total income according to the survey made of 1953 income. The five sources with the largest percentage in each category are for the *forty state councils* (denominational budgets 24.4 per cent, individuals 23.7 per cent, program fees 10.5 per cent, local church budgets 8.3 per cent, and United Church Women 5.3 per cent; *two hundred and one city and county councils with paid leadership* (local church budgets 28.1 per cent, individuals 27.1 per cent, community chests 8.2 per cent—designated for social, health and welfare work—offerings 6.8 per cent, and program fees 6.3 per cent; *six hundred and eighty-nine councils with voluntary leadership* (local church budgets 47.8 per cent, offerings 26.6 per cent, program fees 7.0 per cent, local church organizations 5.6 per cent, and individuals 4.3 per cent).

The $7,161,292 total income for 1953 of the 930 councils was an increase of $1,059,460 over that reported for 1952 when the first income survey was made. Twenty sources of income are listed in the tabulation with a multitude of minor sources lumped together under a miscellaneous heading which comprises 8.2 per cent of the total income.

Of the $7,161,292 total income for 1953, 60 per cent ($4,288,297) is received by the 201 city and county councils with paid leadership; 29 per cent ($2,097,233) by the 40 state councils with paid leadership; and the remaining 11 per cent by the 689 councils with voluntary leadership.

Thirty-seven different titles are used by the 919 cooperative agencies in the city, county and state areas in the *Yearbook of American Churches for 1955*. Council of churches is used 640 times (70 per cent), followed by council of religious education 91 (10 per cent), interchurch council 52 (6 per cent), council of Christian education 30 (3 per cent), seventeen titles used two to twelve times each, and sixteen titles used only once.

Two financial counseling workshops have been held, each of two days' duration: one in Indianapolis for council leaders in a three-state area with fifty-one attending, and the other for fourteen state council executives at Conference Point Camp, Lake Geneva. Workshops similar to the latter are planned in successive years previous to the Association of Council Secretaries' annual meeting for executives in smaller, medium, large, and metropolitan population centers.

Calls from councils for field visitation and counseling have been so heavy that only the following literature has been prepared: *Financial Counseling* #1; *Financing our Council of Churches;*

Financial Counseling #2, 1952 Income and Financial Data Tabulation; Financial Counseling #3, 1953 Income and Financial Data Tabulation; Financial Counseling #4, 1953 State Council Income from Denominational Budgets; and a chapter in the forthcoming Field Guidance Manual, *Principles and Procedures for Financing Our Council of Churches.*

During the biennium, the emphasis of financial counseling has been upon the practical aid of helping councils to initiate basic foundation steps from where they are financially today toward where they wish to be in ten years. The response has been overwhelming at times but gratifying because of the service that can be rendered.

Leadership Preparation

The Association of Council Secretaries meets annually at Lake Geneva, Wisconsin, the third week in June. Walter G. Muelder was the lecturer in 1953 and F. Ernest Johnson in 1954. Special orientation sessions were conducted for newer secretaries each year and special workshops were provided for state executives in metropolitan cities, large cities, medium-sized cities and small communities. In 1955 approximately 100 council presidents have been invited to join the council executives for a consideration of the theme: "Christian Unity—Its Relevance in the Community."

Program Planning Conferences

Program Planning Conferences of from one to three days' duration have been held during the biennium in Northern California, Southern California, Colorado, Florida, Indiana, Michigan, Missouri, New Hampshire, New York, Ohio, Pennsylvania, South Dakota, Washington, West Virginia; and in the cities of Dayton, Evansville (Ind.), Topeka, Wichita. Wide usage has been made of the Criteria for Self Evaluation and Measurement in these conferences as well as throughout the council movement.

Personnel Service

The department has assisted personnel committees in filling

staff vacancies in the following states and cities during the biennium: Colorado, Georgia, Kentucky, Massachusetts, Michigan, Missouri, South Dakota, Texas, West Virginia; Albany, Bay City, Bronx, Dayton, Denver, Des Moines, Flint, Fort Worth, Houston, New York City, Omaha, Peoria, Pittsburgh, Portland (Oregon), Saint Paul, San Antonio, South Bend, Spokane, Springfield, Tacoma, Topeka, Wichita, Wilmington, Worcester, Yonkers.

Curriculum Study

A questionnaire study was made of the curricular provisions for the preparation of leaders in ecumenical administration now provided by theological seminaries. This study shows a wide coverage of the historical Faith and Order and the world aspects of the ecumenical movement and the meager attention of the practical field.

The work of this department has been greatly strengthened by the General Board's adoption of the statement on "Strengthening Cooperation in States and Local Communities" and the supporting actions thereupon now under consideration by the thirty member denominations of the Council.

3   # POST WORLD WAR I
PACIFIST ORGANIZATIONS[1]

THE WORLD ALLIANCE for International Friendship Through the Churches held its first postwar meeting at The Hague, Holland, from September 30 to October 4, 1919. Dr. Macfarland says that this meeting "directly initiated the movement which ultimately led to the contemporary World Council of Churches."[2] In 1920 was held the meeting of the Preparations Committee. Its job, under the leadership of Dr. Frederick Lynch of The Federal Council of Churches, was to organize a World Conference to be called The Preliminary Meeting for the Planning of the Universal Life and Work Movement. Following this, another preliminary meeting was held in Geneva to plan for the Faith and Order Conference.

The reason for two separate conferences was this: the Life and Work Movement avoided all questions of doctrine and was acceptable to those who would not join in the Christian Faith and Order Movement, which dealt exclusively with doctrinal positions. Many who wanted to join in the ecumenical movement did not believe the great doctrines of the Christian faith but were interested in it solely from the political and social standpoint.

In his book *We Are Not Divided,* John A. Hutchison, historian of The Federal Council of Churches, explains that, although the Council had no *official* connection with the Faith and Order Movement, many American delegates who attended the Faith and Order Conference were also leaders in the Council as well as being prom-

[1] A historical sketch by the author of this book.
[2] *Christian Unity at Work*, Charles S. Macfarland, p. 83.

inent in the Life and Work Meeting. *Here we see the same thing taking place on the international scale as took place on the national level.* In the United States, Federal Council leaders maintained that the Church Peace Union and the World Alliance for International Friendship Through the Churches were separate and distinct organizations. Yet we find *Federal Council of Churches personnel serving in official capacities in all three organizations.* So it was on the international level. The Federal Council of Churches, the Life and Work Movement, and the Faith and Order Movement all had leaders who belonged to all three organizations.

Following the Life and Work Movement's preliminary meeting at Geneva, it was decided that the next major conference would be held in Stockholm, Sweden, in 1925. The Faith and Order Movement's preliminary meeting in Geneva decided to hold its next meeting in Lausanne, Switzerland, in 1927.

At this point The Federal Council of Churches decided to step into the picture officially. It created, in 1923, a Committee on Relations with the Eastern Churches. The committee was to put European and American church leaders in touch with one another and persuade the former to attend the Stockholm and Lausanne conferences. The World Alliance for International Friendship Through the Churches joined with The Federal Council of Churches in actively promoting the Stockholm conference, and the Federal Council issued a formal call in 1924.

In this call of 1924, the Federal Council leaders laid out an agenda for the Stockholm conference which closely parallels subjects chosen for discussion at the formation meeting of The World Council of Churches in Amsterdam in August 1948.

In 1925, the full conference on Life and Work convened at Stockholm and appointed a continuation committee which ultimately organized the Universal Christian Council. In 1937 the Universal Christian Council for Life and Work met at Oxford, England, under the title of the Conference on Church, Community, and State. In that same year the World Conference on Faith and Order, which had met in Lausanne in 1927, met at Edinburgh, Scotland. These two separate forces came together in August 1948.

4   # DR. WARD'S
PRO-COMMUNIST STATEMENTS[1]

MR. GITLOW: Dr. Ward delivered a series of lectures at the National University at Peking under the title, The Ethical Aspects of Industrialization. The first lecture was called, The Ethical Problems Created by Industrialization, delivered on March 3, 1925. Describing the industrial system under which we live, Dr. Ward said:

> More than this, industrialism is in conflict, also with the desires of man concerning the future. I do not know if you can find a parallel in human history to this situation in which the prevailing way of getting the work of the world done has developed a way of thinking and living which is at the same time dangerous both to the established moral standards of mankind and also the aspirations of man as he reaches out into the future.

Ward here develops in his own words, the words of the clergy, the Communist idea that capitalist industrialism under which we live today has developed a way of thinking, that it is an ideology that is outmoded, that no longer serves mankind progressively. Dr. Ward, however, puts it in the language of a clergyman as a

<hr />

[1] From Hearing Before the Committee on Un-American Activities, House of Representatives, 83rd Congress, First Session, Investigation of Communist Activities in the New York City Area. Part 6, pp. 2080–2081.

way of thinking dangerous to moral standards and the aspirations of man, as he reaches out into the future for another system different from capitalism. Dr. Ward continues:

> This period is somewhat analogous to the time in the political history of any country when there is guerilla warfare between military leaders, preceding the establishment of constitutional control. Industrialism is now in that state because we have not yet set up any constitutional control of economic activities.

This quotation is an assertion and approval of the Communist position, that the overthrow of capitalism goes through the process of guerilla class warfare to put the state in control of all economic activities. Dr. Ward calls this "constitutional control"; actually it is communism.

Dr. Ward repeats the Communist charge that under capitalism wage earners live under a system of wage slavery in these terms:

> The limitations of the personality of many wage earners by what is accurately called wage slavery, has been fully described in the literature of both sympathy and revolt.

The second lecture Dr. Ward delivered in China before a distinguished audience of intellectuals and students was called Can Capitalism Provide a Solution? It was delivered on March 5, 1925. In this lecture Dr. Ward takes the Communist position that it does not pay to reform capitalism, that it must be destroyed completely. Here are some of his pertinent remarks:

> It is not necessary to recount the sins of modern capitalism against humanity. For our present purpose we can afford to admit that these things may possibly be eliminated by reform. The issue then is whether their elimination will require such an expenditure of energy, such a struggle, as to consume more than it is worth.

Then Dr. Ward develops this position against the competitive system of economy as follows:

Hence it comes about that the competitive system blocks progress where formerly it helped it.

Dr. Ward's estimation of American capitalism is a gem. He said:

One of the outstanding facts of the modern world is the increased recognition of the inadequacy of the capitalist system. In fact today capitalism is defended only by people whom a friend of mine described as "Wall street morons"—that is, people who have been so engrossed in the making of money that they are really feeble-minded insofar as the rest of life is concerned.

In his third lecture, What We May Expect from Socialism, delivered March 7, 1925, Dr. Ward said:

All the different schools of socialism agree in proposing the collective control of life. Indeed, in this respect, they are simply advancing what may be described as the natural evolutionary process of humanity. In furtherance of this movement socialism at large proposes the intelligent guidance of human affairs to a chosen end. Concretely it means in general the use of the state for purposes of social welfare and not merely for purposes of governmental regulations. In that respect the British Labor Party and the Russian Communist Party are one. They both insist upon the fullest possible use of science for intelligent control of human affairs.

In this statement Dr. Ward rejects government regulation for state control of the general welfare. Here, Dr. Ward speaks as a believer in socialism, accepting the Communist position on the absolute powers of the state over all human affairs.

5 THE VICTOR AND
WALTER REUTHER LETTER[1]

DEAR MEL AND GLAD: Your letter of December 5 arrived here last week from Germany and was read with more than usual interest by Wal and I. It seemed ages since we had heard from you, so you might well imagine with what joy we welcomed news from Detroit. It is precisely because you are equally anxious I know to receive word from the "Workers' Fatherland" that I am taking this first opportunity to answer you.

What you have written concerning the strikes and the general labor unrest in Detroit plus what we have learned from other sources of the rising discontent of the American workers, makes us long for the moment to be back with you in the front lines of the struggle; however, the daily inspiration that is ours as we work side by side with our Russian comrades in our factory—the thought that we are actually helping to build a society that will forever end the exploitation of man by man, the thought that what we are building will be for the benefit and enjoyment of the working class, not only of Russia but the entire world, is the compensation we receive for our temporary absence from the struggle in the United States. And let no one tell you that we are not on the road to socialism in the Soviet Union. Let no one say that the workers in the Union of Soviet Socialist Republics are not on the road to security, enlightenment, and happiness.

[1] As entered under oath in *Hearings,* House of Representatives Report No. 282, Vol. II, pp. 1659ff.

Mel, you know Wal and I were always strong for the Soviet Union. You know we were always ready to defend it against the lies of reactionaries. But let me tell you, now that we are here seeing all the great construction, watching a backward peasantry being transformed into an enlightened, democratic, cultured populus, now that we have already experienced the thrill, the satisfaction of participating in genuine proletarian democracy, we are more than just sympathetic toward *our* country—we are ready to fight for it and its ideals. And why not? Here the workers, through their militant leadership, the proletarian dictatorship, have not sold out to the owning class like the S.P. in Germany, and like the Labor Party in England. Here they have against all odds, against famine, against internal strife and civil war, against sabotage, against capitalist invasion and isolation, our comrades here have maintained power, they have won over the masses, they have transformed the "dark masses" of Russia into energetic, enlightened workers. They have transformed the Soviet Union into one of the greatest industrial nations in the world. They have laid the economic foundation for socialism, for a classless society. Mel, if you could be with us for just one day in our shop you would realize the significance of the Soviet Union. To be with us in our factory Red Corner at a shop meeting and watch the workers as they offer suggestions and constructive criticism of production in the shop. Here are no bosses to drive fear into the workers. No one to drive them in mad speed-ups. Here the workers are in control. Even the shop superintendent has no more right in these meetings than any other worker. I have witnessed many times already, when the superintendent spoke too long, the workers in the hall decided he had already consumed enough time and the floor was then given to a lathe hand who told of his problems and offered suggestions. Imagine this at Ford's or Briggs! This is what the outside world calls the "ruthless dictatorship in Russia." I tell you, Mel, in all the countries we have thus far been in, we have never found such genuine proletarian democracy. It is unpolished and crude, rough and rude, but proletarian workers' democracy in every respect. The workers in England have more culture and polish when they speak at their meetings, but they have no power. I prefer the latter.

In our factory, which is the largest and most modern in Europe, and we have seen them all, there are no pictures of Fords and Rockefellers, or Roosevelts and Mellons. No such parasites, but rather huge pictures of Lenin, etc., greet the workers' eyes on every side. Red banners with slogans "Workers of the world unite" are draped across the craneways. Little red flags fly from the tops of presses, drill presses, lathes, kells, etc. Such a sight you have never seen before. Women and men work side by side—the women with their red cloth about their heads, 5 days a week (our week here is 6 days long). At noon we all eat in a large factory restaurant where wholesome plain food is served. A workers' band furnishes music to us from an adjoining room while we have dinner. For the remainder of our 1-hour lunch period we adjourn to the Red Corner recreation, where workers play games, read papers and magazines or technical books, or merely sit, smoke, and chat. Such a fine spirit of comradeship you have never before witnessed in your life. Superintendent leaders and ordinary workers are all alike. If you saw our superintendent as he walks through the shop greeting workers with "Hello, Comrade," you could not distinguish him from any other worker.

The interesting thing, Mel, is that 3 years ago this place here was a vast prairie, a wasteland, and the thousands of workers here who are building complicated dies and other tools were at that time peasants who had never before even seen industry, let alone worked in one. And by mere brute determination, by the determination to build a workers' country second to none in the world, urged on by the spirit of revolution, they have constructed this huge marvelous auto factory which today is turning out modern cars for the Soviet Union. Through the bitter Russian winters of 45° below they have toiled with bare hands, digging foundations, erecting structures; they have, with their own brute strength, pulled the huge presses into place and set them up for operation. What they have here they have sacrificed and suffered for; that is why they are not so ready to turn it all over again to the capitalists. That is why today they still have comrades from the Red Army

on guard at the factory at all times to prevent counterrevolution-
ists from carrying on their sabotage.

About a 20-minute walk from the factory an entirely new Socialist city has grown up in these 3 years. Here over 50,000 of the
factory workers live in fine new modern apartment buildings.
Large hospitals, schools, libraries, theaters and clubs have sprung
up here and all for the use of those who work, for without a
worker's card one cannot make use of all these modern facilities.
Three nights ago we were invited to the clubhouse in "Sorgor"
(Socialist City) to attend an evening of enjoyment given by the
workers of the dieshop. Imagine, all the workers with whom we
daily work came together that evening for a fine banquet, a stage
performance, a concert, speeches, and a big dance. A division of
the Red Army was also present as guests. In all my life, Mel, I have
never seen anything so inspiring. Mel, once a fellow has seen
what is possible where workers gain power, he no longer fights
just for an ideal, he fights for something which is real, something
tangible. Imagine, Mel, Henry Ford throwing a big party for his
slaves. Here the party was no gift of charity from someone above,
for we own the factory, we held the meeting and decided to have
the party, and it was paid for from the surplus earnings of our
department. What our department does is typical of the social
activities which are being fostered throughout the entire factory
and the entire Soviet Union.

Mel, we are witnessing and experiencing great things in the
Union of Soviet Socialist Republics. We are seeing the most backward nation in the world being rapidly transformed into the
most modern and scientific, with new concepts and new social
ideals coming into force. . . . We are watching daily socialism being taken down from the books on the shelves and put into actual ap-
plication. Who would not be inspired by such events?

And now my letter is getting long and still I have said little, for
there is so much to say and so little time in which to do it. We have
written Merlin and Coach— (I might say that Merlin Bishop is
a brother of Melvin Bishop. Melvin Bishop was the educational

director of the C.I.O. "Coach" is a nickname they have for Roy Reuther.)

We have written Merlin and "Coach" rather lengthy letters and have requested they forward them to you to save duplicity of material. I believe there is little in this letter which they have not already received, so there will be no need of your forwarding this to them.

(Roy Reuther typed this letter from the original letter, and he left out a portion of it right there.) He says:

Keep your eye on the S.P. It being affiliated to the Second International I am not so certain it is "Drifting" in the right direction, certainly not in the light of recent events. (The S.P. is an organization in Germany.)

Let us know definitely what is happening to the Y.P.S.L. and also the Social Problems Club at C.C.C.

(The Y.P.S.L. is a Young People's Socialist League, and the Social Problems Club is an organization in the CCC Camps.)

Carry on the fight for a Soviet America.

Vic and Wal.

6   **PEARSON L. LINN'S LETTER
ON COOPERATIVES**[1]

ARE THE COLLECTIVISTS TAKING OVER OUR ECONOMIC LIFE VIA
THE CHURCH? READ THE FACTS, DECIDE FOR YOURSELF

THROUGHOUT the nation, The Federal Council of Churches is sponsoring what its leaders call "the ecumenical movement." They are asking that Protestant women pay one dollar each and sign the "register." To do so, they say, according to the August 2, 1950, Bucyrus Telegraph-Forum, is "to stand and be counted as a Christian." Imagine, just because someone has got something up and says "here sign this and pay me a dollar" it means "to stand and be counted as a Christian." Who says so? Apparently if you don't pay your dollar and sign then you must be something else. These tactics are commonly known as "putting on the heat" and then "making the touch."

Again, "Who says so?"

Since this "ecumenical" business is nationwide, it is a cinch that it didn't start here in Bucyrus. It is self-evident that it is not of "grass roots" origin but a hand-me-down from "above." Presumably the Bucyrus Federated Council of Church Women got this "dope" from the Ohio Council of Churches, who in turn, got it from The Federal Council of Churches, which, in turn, is having great difficulty in finding the answers to an ever increasing number of embarrassing questions.

1 Quoted from the Bucyrus (Ohio) *Telegraph-Forum*, Dec. 29, 1950.

Do the women who are signing this "register" and elsewhere know how to pronounce the word "ecumenical"? If they do, do they know what the word means? If church women don't know the answers to these two questions, why are they signing it and contributing their dollars into a huge fund to be used as seen fit by the "big time" planners who eventually get control of the funds and who do know what it's all about?

According to the local news report (and mind you this is going on all over the nation):

"The dedicated dollars will be ready for use in projects . . . postponed before by lack of funds. It will also provide leadership and help for the states to enable their councils to grow in Christian usefulness and to enlarge the sphere of women's work in the church. These are just part of the ways in which the dedicated dollars will be used."

While admittedly the above statement is nicely gotten up, it contains no real information. The question is WHAT "projects"? WHAT other "ways" are they to be used? And above all WHAT kind of "leadership" do they want to "provide" and WHAT do they mean "enable their councils to grow in Christian usefulness" —more particularly WHAT "usefulness"? This is a serious matter, the people who sign this "register" are being "counted" as being in favor of this whole thing about which they apparently know nothing.

Now let us turn our attention to some real information about The Federal Council of Churches which may throw some light on the subject. What brought this thing into Bucyrus? The answer is Mrs. James D. Wyker, Mt. Vernon, Ohio, president of the Ohio Council of Church Women. Mrs. Wyker's husband, James D. Wyker, it was brought out on May 3, 1950, when Mrs. Wyker was in Bucyrus, speaking to the Bucyrus Federated Council of Church Women, is state director of the C.R.O.P. It was not brought out, however, that The Federal Council of Churches lists as a member of the Federal Council's Committee on the Church and Cooperatives, Mr. James D. Wyker, Mt. Vernon, Ohio.

And who are some of the people who are on this cooperative

business branch of The Federal Council of Churches with James D. Wyker? They are Jerry Voorhis (Co-op League), Wallace J. Campbell (Co-op League), E. R. Bowen (Co-op League), Carl R. Hutchison (Ohio Farm Bureau, Co-op League, and believe it or not, Treasurer Ohio C.R.O.P.), Victor Reuther (CIO), etc.

When Mrs. Wyker was in Bucyrus on May 3, 1950, displaying some envelopes for the "first million" project of the Federal Council's efforts to enlist "the membership of Protestant women throughout the United States," she stated that Protestantism, not Methodism, was under attack as she cited current books and articles making charges of Communism and Socialism against The Federal Council of Churches and various Methodist leaders. Mrs. Wyker then emphasized that:

"The only way some people can build themselves up is to tear other people down."

Since Mrs. Wyker brought the matter up, what is it that she is so concerned about being torn down?

I have before me a pamphlet which is published, sold, and distributed by The Federal Council of Churches. As a matter of fact the very copy which I have before me was obtained from the Federal Council. It is entitled "Manual on the Church and Cooperatives," written by Benson Y. Landis, who has long been identified with the Federal Council and presently the secretary of its Committee on Town and Country. On the front of this pamphlet are two circles. In one of these circles is a church steeple. In the other there are two pine trees which is the emblem of the "consumers' cooperative movement." These two circles are firmly locked together.

Surely Mr. and Mrs. Wyker, and those church people who unquestioningly follow the Federal Council "line," will have no objection to my quoting from this pamphlet written by one of their Federal Council's big-time operators who not only helps make the plans but who, also, should know what it's all about. Beginning on page 22 of this pamphlet, which so firmly locks together the church and the cooperatives on its outside cover, and put out by The Federal Council of Churches, we read:

"FEDERATED CHURCH TRAINS LEADERS

"The Federated Church at North Jackson, Ohio, bringing together Disciples, Presbyterian and Reformed congregations, a 'demonstration of cooperation in religion', with Rev. James D. Wyker as the minister, pioneered in the 'enlivement' of cooperative leaders through annual schools for young people and adults. Mr. and Mrs. Wyker studied Kagawa's peasant schools and Grundtvig's folk schools and concluded that American rural older youth and younger adults needed 'enlivement' (Grundtvig's term) as well as enlightenment and employment. Hence a cooperative folk school was begun in 1935 with the cooperation of three other churches. It was held five strenuous days and nights, and the main technique for enlivement explored in the sessions was the cooperative movement. The school had two units, one for those present for this first time, the other for an advanced group. The school was also held with the assistance of Farm bureaus and cooperatives. The cooperative movement was the heart of the curriculum."

I repeat:

"The school was also held with the assistance of Farm bureaus and cooperatives. The cooperative movement was the heart of the curriculum."

Naturally, the reader may wonder whether the Farm Bureau and the cooperatives, who helped to put it across, were able to "cash in" on the "enlivement." This Federal Council pamphlet gives the answer; it says:

"The folk school as such was discontinued several years ago, but it stimulated social action in an effective way. Practical projects undertaken in the community under church leadership have been a credit union and a cooperative freezer locker plant. In the credit union the first loan was made 'for a provident purpose' to a man on WPA. He repaid the loan out of his meager wages. The locker plant started when six women formed a small study group in their homes in order to learn about frozen foods. Soon a public meeting was held, a freezer co-op was organized and 200 lockers were rented in the first five months."

While, to me, it seems that the church is hardly the place to introduce "enlivement" by teaching folk dances and organizing commercial business, it did indeed "pay off" in a big way for the co-ops under Rev. and Mrs. Wyker's leadership with the churches as a base for operations. Perhaps this is the kind of thing that the local ladies and church women everywhere have in mind when they contribute their dollars and "stand and be counted as a Christian." I doubt it.

What happened to Rev. James D. Wyker after his and Mrs. Wyker's efforts to train co-op leaders and organize commercialized co-op business (with Farm Bureau and co-op help, of course) in the churches at North Jackson, Ohio, makes interesting reading.

We learn, in the pamphlet "Bethlehem and Rochdale" (Bethlehem is, of course, the birthplace of Jesus Christ; and Rochdale, England, is, of course, the birthplace of the co-ops), also written by the long-time, important Federal Council official, Benson Y. Landis, that:

"In North Jackson, Ohio, Rev. James Wyker, a clergyman of the Disciples of Christ, minister for twelve years of the Federated Church in his community, has resigned and accepted a position as educational director of the Logan County, Ohio, Farm Bureau, where he will stress education for cooperative organizations."

The Logan County (Ohio) Farm Bureau Cooperative organizations are, of course, members of the Ohio Farm Bureau Cooperatives organization which is a member of the Cooperative League which is the American agent and member of the International Cooperative Alliance which says in its Constitution that it is organized for the very purpose of destroying "the present competitive regime of private enterprise" and establishing in its place "a cooperative system."

As a matter of fact Murray D. Lincoln of the Ohio Farm Bureau cooperative organizations is president of the Cooperative League and vice-president of the competitive-private-enterprise-destroying International Cooperative Alliance. About 2,000,000 Americans (largely farmers) are unwittingly seeking to destroy their own businesses through their membership with this International co-op outfit.

In spite of the fact that the International Cooperative Alliance represents about three-fourths of the world's cooperative members, including about 37,000,000 from Communistic Russia; and in spite of the fact that the Cooperative League of the USA which represents a very, very large part of the American cooperative movement is a member of this competitive-private-enterprise-destroying International Cooperative Alliance; and in spite of the fact that this International Cooperative Alliance says in plain language that it "seeks" to set up "a cooperative system" in place of "the present competitive regime of private enterprise," I heard the executive secretary of the Ohio Council of Farm Cooperatives recently insist before a large group of veterans in a Veterans Training class that cooperatives were not a "movement," but that they were "competitive private enterprise," that they were "free enterprise" and that they were a part of the profit business system. Imagine, if you will, an important cooperative leader standing up and insisting to an intelligent group of people that cooperatives are "competitive private enterprise" when three-fourths of the world's cooperatives are dedicated to the very task of destroying that "competitive enterprise" under the very charter of the International Cooperative Alliance. Obviously it would be just as logical to stand up and insist that the sun shines brightly at midnight. One naturally is led to wonder if some of these cooperative leaders even know whether there is a game being played, let alone knowing what the score is. This kind of misinformation, given out purposely or otherwise, tends to lead the cooperative member into a state of confused, and even enthusiastic submission while the cooperatives change the economic system.

With Rev. James D. Wyker's cooperative educational activities in the churches of North Jackson, Ohio, and his subsequent employment by the Cooperative League affiliate in mind, it is interesting to note that in the Cooperative League pamphlet "Cooperative Education" by Dr. J. P. Warbasse, which says that "the cooperators and cooperative groups who read this pamphlet . . . can put these finds into action with the knowledge that their regional and national organizations" (meaning of course the Co-op League, the Ohio Farm Bureau cooperative, etc.,) "stand ready to offer them every assistance," says:

"Once salesmen went out with their order books from cooperative federations to sell cooperative goods to the cooperative retails. Experience has taught that education is the best way to promote cooperative business. The progressive foundations now send out educators instead of salesmen."

It is, of course, the officials of this Cooperative League and its affiliates who have so numerously gotten themselves into key positions in The Federal Council of Churches from which they cannot only help make the plans and spend the ladies' dollars; but also, as we shall see, carry on wide co-op educational activities in the churches, place speakers, set up conferences, publish literature, and help recruit church people for sightseeing trips to study cooperatives here and abroad. Moreover, from these lofty Federal Council of Churches perches they are in a position from which they can not only "hand down" to local ministers the "answers" to searching questions, but also "turn on the heat" should a local pastor "kick over the traces." Indeed, what better place could be found than the church to carry on these co-op activities? It is the last place that "competitive private enterprise" is sound asleep and has the sign out "Please Don't Disturb!"

Thus it can be seen from Dr. Warbasse's aforementioned statement that every teacher, every preacher is a potential salesman for the cooperative ideology and cooperative merchandise. Indeed, the minute that a teacher or preacher opens his mouth in behalf of the cooperative system he largely ceases to be a preacher or teacher, and becomes a salesman of co-op products. The sale of the cooperative ideology and the sale of co-op products are inseparable and a preacher who uses his pulpit or a teacher who uses his desk to advance the objectives of the "cooperative movement" in a very large measure simply converts his pulpit or his desk into a sales counter for the selling of cooperative commercial goods. He or she is, indeed, in business in a big way. The fact that the preacher or teacher may be unaware of what he is doing, or that he may be simply repeating that which has been given out to him by the co-op inner circle of The Federal Council of Churches, does not alter his position in the matter one iota. It only serves to make the whole filthy business more nauseating.

Is making use of the church for cooperative education which leads to organizing cooperative commercial business and increased sales to co-ops a rarity? Indeed not; this Federal Council pamphlet "Manual on the Church and Cooperatives" proudly presents case after case of a similar nature. For instance, there is the case of a Rev. Raymond V. Ebbett, former minister of the Plainfield-Adamnan Methodist parish in Vermont, who after running into "strong organized opposition" in his parish because of his cooperative activities also found himself employment with the Co-op League affiliated (Ohio) Farm Bureau Cooperative Insurance Services. Rev. Ebbett says, according to this Federal Council publication, that "hundreds, probably thousands in the rank and file of our active ministry are sincerely interested in the promotion of consumer cooperatives as a Christian method of business procedure." This willingness on the part of such large numbers of our clergy at the local level to become "tools" of the Co-op League, as revealed by Rev. Ebbett, may give some indication as to how deep-rooted the "co-opie" infiltration into the church has become. Reverend Ebbett's full statement may also explain why some members of the clergy at the local level seem inclined to quickly deny that there is anything wrong in The Federal Council of Churches.

Continuing, Rev. Ebbett explains:

"They are prevented from following their inner convictions by the two-fold threat of open local opposition on one hand, and hidden betrayal from above on the other. Since it is too much to expect any immediate change on the part of our laymen locally, only a genuine revolution in the higher-up leadership of the church can lead the church out of its present enforced role of passive defense of vested interests locally and in general."

The way, of course, to eliminate the alleged "betrayal from

above" is simply to have the CIO and Co-op League big-time operators move in and become those "from above." In this manner, "a
genuine revolution in the higher-up leadership of the church" is
brought about and this new leadership "from above" can proceed
with the "genuine revolution" of leading "the church out of its
present enforced role of passive defense of vested interests locally
and in general." The alleged "vested interests locally and in general" obviously are you and I. With the revolution "from above"
accomplished, all that needs to be done to remove the "threat of
open local opposition" is to remold the mentality of the alleged
"vested interests locally and in general," that is you and I.

If the "big names" from the Co-op League and the CIO on the
Federal Council's Department of the Church and Economic Life
and its Committee on the Church and Cooperatives are any guide
(and I'm not guessing), then it seems self-evident that this "genuine revolution in the higher-up leadership of the church" has
already taken place and the church as represented by The Federal Council of Churches is for all practical purposes already "co-
operatized" or socialized.

In spite of the overwhelming evidence to the contrary we find
minister after minister, and even some laymen, insisting that there
is nothing to these reports about The Federal Council of Churches.
I refer to those church people who would like to get at the facts
but who are misled, purposely, or otherwise, into a state of confused inaction as a result of these misstatements of fact to Benson
Y. Landis's statement in his pamphlet "Bethlehem and Rochdale"
(Bethlehem for Christ; Rochdale for the cooperative or collective
system). He says:

". . . there is a distinct group of Christian cooperators who
steadily emphasize the common interests of the Christian movement and the Rochdale consumers cooperative movement. The
movements that originated at Bethlehem and Rochdale are not
only becoming aware of one another; there are representatives in
each who are cultivating common interests and contributing to one
another."

To those confused souls who might take action were not their efforts to reach a decision thwarted before they begin by the inaccuracies of the statements of the local puppets of the Co-op League-Federal Council, here and elsewhere, I offer Mr. Landis's above statement as over against that of the Co-op League-Federal Council propagandists operating on the local level. Church people everywhere may, upon the basis of Mr. Landis's statement, determine for themselves whether they are getting the facts on the local level or whether they are just getting "echoes"—echoed by this "distinct group," the Co-op League-Federal Council hierarchy. To that portion of the clergy which may take offense at my setting down here the facts, I offer the consolation that they are not quarreling with me but with Mr. Landis, their associate secretary of their Department of Research and Education of their Federal Council of Churches; and their Executive Secretary of their Committee on Town and Country of their Home Missions Council. Mr. Landis should know about this "distinct group" and what the cooperative movement is all about as he assures us in the "acknowledgements" in this pamphlet "Bethlehem and Rochdale" (Bethlehem for Christ, Rochdale for Co-ops) that:

". . . he has been especially aided as a student of various economic cooperative movements by reading the works of, or by personal association with, the following persons: George W. Russell (AE), Sidney and Beatrice Webb, George Bernard Shaw, Henry A Wallace, E. C. Lindeman, Walter Rauschenbusch, M. M. Coady, J. J. Tompkins, L. G. Ligutti, J. P. Warbasse, E. R. Bowen, Wallace J. Campbell, Murray D. Lincoln, Toyohiko Kagawa, Horace M. Kallen, Edward A. Filene, J. Henry Carpenter, James Myers."

Who is this Toyohiko Kagawa, whom Rev. and Mrs. James D. Wyker and Mr. Landis studied? Where does he fit in? Church people ought to be concerned; he is at this very moment traveling across America and selling his wares "to church groups everywhere."

The Federal Council of Churches' publication "Manual on the Church and Cooperatives" says:

"The visit of Toyohiko Kagawa, Christian leader of Japan, to the United States in 1935–36 stimulated church interest in co-operatives in a marked way. A notable increase of participation by church leaders must be credited to him. On December 30, 1935–January 1, 1936, the industrial Division of the Federal Council sponsored a three-day sightseeing seminar on consumer cooperation, attended by 350 delegates from many religious bodies, from 20 states, the District of Columbia and Canada.

"It was held at Indianapolis, Indiana. The principal speakers were Dr. Kagawa and prominent officials of the American consumer cooperative movement. Since the Indianapolis seminar and Dr. Kagawa's tour of America, the Federal Council's Committee on the Church and Cooperatives has been carrying on wide educational activities in the churches, placing speakers, setting up conferences, publishing literature, and helping to recruit church people for sightseeing trips to study cooperatives in the United States, Nova Scotia and Europe."

And who is on this Federal Council's Committee on the Church and Cooperatives which Mr. Landis says is responsible for this "co-opie" infiltration into the church?

The answer is, among them we find James D. Wyker, Mt. Vernon, Ohio, and many of the past and present officials of the Co-op League and CIO to which I previously referred, plus a number of clerical co-op converts.

And what is this Co-operative League a member of? The answer is, the International Cooperative Alliance.

And what does this International Cooperative Alliance want to do? According to its Constitution, it:

". . . in continuance of the work of the Rochdale pioneers, seeks, in complete independence and by its own methods, to substitute for the present competitive regime of private enterprise a cooperative system . . ."

How is this to be done? Among the various ways, as stated in Article 3 of the International Cooperative Alliance's Constitution, are:

"(a) The ascertaining and propaganda of cooperative principles and methods;

(b) The promotion of cooperation in all countries;

(c) The provision of information and the encouragement of studies concerning cooperation."

What does this all lead to? Just what is the final goal?

In a communication "to the International Labour Office by the International Cooperative Alliance," as reported in the International Labour Office publication, *Cooperative Organizations and Post-War Relief* (1944), the International Cooperative Alliance says:

"One of the factors which will probably help the Alliance in unifying the movement internationally is that the fulfillment of the important role which the cooperative movement should play, and the tremendous duties it should perform in post-war relief and reconstruction, will demand, and very largely depend upon, coordinated and unified effort. If the national movements are conscious of their international duty and are prepared to make a really determined effort to achieve the aim of a united world cooperative organization, they will not only succeed in making a major contribution to the solution of the stupendous problems of post-war relief and reconstruction, but will, at the same time, be moving towards the final goal—an International Cooperative Commonwealth."

We have presented to us in this International Cooperative Alliance statement not only the disclosure of the final goal—"an International Cooperative Commonwealth," but also the object of the cooperative movement's effort. With this in mind, it is interesting to note that while James D. Wyker is (Ohio) state director of C.R.O.P., Carl R. Hutchison of the Cooperative League affiliated Ohio Farm Bureau organization is the treasurer; and both are members of the Federal Council of Churches' Committee on the Church and Cooperatives. The reader may find it also interesting to note further that Murray D. Lincoln, who is vice-president of the International Cooperative Alliance which makes the above statement, is also president of CARE. The reader may determine for himself whether or not there is a tie-up between overseas relief organizations and the aims of the competitive-private-enterprise-destroying International Cooperative Alliance. In arriving at his or her conclusions the reader might consider further the following information taken from the Ohio Farm Bureau publication *Farm and Home News* (Aug. 1946 issue).

After telling about some of the problems faced in getting CARE packages to the European needy and the need of these European misfortunates, "Lincoln Clark, special representative to Europe of the Cooperative for American Remittances to Europe (CARE), in an exclusive interview for the co-op papers" said:

"From this point of view and only from this point of view is CARE a relief organization. Primarily we are concerned in selling CARE packages because they are the best and most practical buy on the market for the money. The CARE package is worth $100 in the black markets of many countries—more in others where the need is greater.

"And, finally," Clark smiled, "I am particularly interested in the participation of the cooperatives in CARE. I understand that the Cooperative League has done and is doing an outstanding job. This is a project that all of us should support. CARE is the means by which we can practice cooperation on a large scale—nationally and internationally—and develop the worth-while role of cooperatives to make a peaceful world."

It seems to me that a lot of "competitive private enterprise" people ought to wake up. "Clark smiled"; he should have. CARE was, and is, a good advertisement for the cooperatives. It advertised for increased sales to the American Co-ops. It has done likewise abroad. And it was financed for the most part from the earnings of American "competitive private enterprise" which the International Cooperative Alliance seeks to destroy by substituting its own "cooperative system." While "competitive private enterprise" people in the United States who have given unstintedly through CARE out of the simple generosity of their own hearts may find considerable discomfort as they read these words of CARE's European representative, exclusively given "for the co-op papers," I find greater concern about the inability or incapacity of "competitive private enterprise" people to understand the "co-op mentality."

Let us return again to this Kagawa who was imported into America from Japan by The Federal Council of Churches. What does this Kagawa, whom Rev. and Mrs. James D. Wyker and many other members of the clergy studied, believe? What does he hope to accomplish, this Kagawa whom Federal Council leaders credit with stimulating "church interest in cooperatives in a marked way"? Indeed, what kind of a proposal did this Federal Council-sponsored Kagawa lay down before the church groups at the 1935–36 Federal Council-sponsored "Seminar on Consumers' Cooperation" in Indianapolis? The Federal Council publication *Manual on the Church and Cooperatives,* written by the long-time "big-time" Federal Council leader is very clear about this. In italics, it says:

"How shall Christianity change the economic system? Through cooperatives which are the love principle in economic action . . ."

So it is that we begin to see "cooperative man" take shape. The alleged "cooperative man" is simply the regular, ordinary man in a "cooperative system." This, we are led to believe, is supposed to be the "Kingdom of God." What fantasy—it never seems to occur to some of these Federal Council leaders that when the economic, political, social and religious life of the people are all "rolled up" into ONE giant package you have then created "the all-inclusive social organization"—a GIANT MONOPOLY that leads neither to the "cooperative man" nor to the "Kingdom of God," but to the "cooperate-or-else man" and the end of the "Christian Era." Look, if you please, at Russia.

Did the Federal Council-sponsored Indianapolis "Seminar on Consumers' Cooperation" and the Federal Council-sponsored Kagawa and his tour of America bear fruit, that is—CO-OP FRUIT?

Presented hereafter are just a few examples. In this Federal Council pamphlet "Manual on the Church and Cooperatives" we are told that:

"The church press has readily published articles and news about the movement. After Kagawa's tour there was a general ferment of discussion in church circles. Here and there, ministers decided to 'take the plunge' and join cooperatives, and thus publicly endorse the movement. One co-op started in the kitchen of a parsonage. 'The headquarters were three shelves.' Another co-op began by using the woodshed of a church—'a Methodist woodshed.' "

To give the reader some idea as to the size of some of these church efforts at changing the economic system "through cooperatives," I quote from the Federal Council distributed, Cooperative League published pamphlet "Bethlehem and Rochdale" (Bethlehem for Christ; Rochdale for Co-ops). It says:

"In Ithaca, N.Y., four Protestant ministers gathered together after reading or hearing Kagawa. Out of their little study group came a cooperative store. Out of these early beginnings, there stands in 1944 one of the largest retail stores in the city."

All of this in the short period of less than 8 years, thanks to income-tax exemptions. This sort of thing is going on all over America under sponsorship of the Federal Council of Churches' Committee on the Church and Cooperatives. This is changing the American economic system "through cooperatives." This is the purpose of the International Cooperative Alliance for which, and of which, the Cooperative League of USA is the American Agent and member. The top officials of this Co-op League who make the plans for the Co-op League are also in there in The Federal Council of Churches making the plans for the 31,000,000 members (captives) of The Federal Council of Churches.

Is it any wonder that as you and I look over our church papers we find the words "cooperate," "cooperative," "cooperation" repeated over and over? This tends to "fix" in the minds of church people that "cooperative" and "Christianity" are synonymous. After a time "the church mentality" will tend to follow a fixed pattern —the "cooperative" or collective pattern. Eventually the individual, having had his mind thoroughly "processed," will be inclined to accept the "cooperative system" as gospel. As a matter of fact, the word "converted" is already being used in association with the word "cooperation" by high Federal Council officials.

In this autumn of 1950 the Federal Council of Churches (the National Council after Jan. 1, 1951) and its affiliated churches and church organizations are pushing the "ecumenical movement" register, thus collecting millions of dollars and getting millions of people "to stand and be counted as a Christian" and in this manner endorse something about which they apparently know nothing. All the while this Federal Council-sponsored Kagawa, who says "becoming a Christian means organizing a cooperative," is touring the United States speaking to various groups of the churches affiliated with the F.C. and who refer to him as often being called "the 20th-century saint." Contrast this, if you please, with Rev. Carl McIntire of the Bible Presbyterian Church, Collingswood, N.J., who is "smeared unmercifully" by certain Federal Council affiliated sources. Right here in my home town of Bucyrus, Ohio, I have seen this "smear" of Rev. Carl McIntire engaged in by certain members of the Bucyrus clergy who have connections with the Federal Council. The similarity of the local attack and that of Bishop Oxnam before the Methodist Council of Bishops at Cleveland, Ohio, on April 20, 1950, and upon Mr. McIntire are striking. One is led to presume that they came from the same sources.

Perhaps there is a reason for this difference in attitude toward the Federal Council-glorified Kagawa and Rev. McIntire who heads up the Federal Council's opposition as president of the International Council of Christian Churches. The Federal Council-glorified Kagawa says, "How shall Christianity change the economic system? Through cooperatives . . ." whereas, the Rev. McIntire who is very much detested by certain Federal Council sources says, "These cooperatives, as they are developing in the United States, are, in principle, little units of Soviet Russia." (The latter quotation is from Rev. McIntire's book *The Rise of the Tyrant*.)

Are these things among the "projects postponed before by lack of funds"; are these things "just part of the ways in which the dedicated dollars will be used" after the church women contribute their dollars by the millions? Is this the kind of "Christian usefulness" into which the church women want their councils "to grow"? Is this the kind of "leadership" that church people want "to provide"? Is this the kind of Christianity for which they want "to stand and be counted"?

If church people want to give their money to the Federal Council of Churches to have it do the spade work for the Co-op League and the International Cooperative Alliance, and if they want to pay the salaries of their ministers to become co-op salesmen to sell the co-op ideology and co-op merchandise, and if they want to use the church to change the economic system "through cooperatives," then why don't they simply convert their own farms and their own business into co-ops? At least they would then present the appearance that they knew what they were doing. The silliest thing that I know of, is that man who says that he believes that cooperatives ought to be taxed to help support the American form of government and the American way of life, and then turns around and happily endorses, supports and pays for the Co-op League-Federal Council effort to drive himself out of business, destroy "the present competitive regime of private enterprise," and create the "co-operative-or-else man" through his church's contributions to The Federal Council of Churches.

It appears to me that this "distinct group" which Mr. Landis refers to as "representatives in each (Church and Co-ops) who are cultivating common interests and contributing to one another" are far too clever for far, far too many church people. Some idea as to how clever some of the co-op leaders are may be deduced from certain portions of the "co-op scriptures." As compared with other "ideologies" or "isms," "co-opism" seems to be no exception, for it, too, has its "bible."

This "Co-op Bible," known as "Co-operative Democracy," was written by the Co-op League's president-emeritus, Dr. James P. Warbasse, whom the Co-op League claims to be the movement's "most eloquent philosopher and spokesman." This "Co-op Bible" outlines "the international co-operative society"—the "international state," declares Rev. Dr. J. Henry Carpenter in his book *Peace Through Co-operation,* page 31. (Dr. Carpenter, too, of course, is a member of the Federal Council's Committee on the Church and Cooperatives.) On page 27, this "Co-op Bible" explains:

"The conduct of directors and managers in large wholesales and other commercial departments of cooperation seems conservative. This conservative tincture is natural. A movement which must carry on intimate relations with capitalistic commerce cannot proclaim its radicalism. The directors of the great national wholesale societies are prone to talk like conventional businessmen. Their duties are peculiar and difficult. But, whatever may be the outward signs displayed by representatives of the movement who come in contact with the capitalistic world, the fact is not altered that these societies are carrying out the dream of the Rochdale pioneers—they are radically changing the methods of business."

This Dr. Warbasse who, because he wrote the "Co-op Bible," might be called sort of a "Moses" to the "movement," ought to know. Due to his long-time "big-time" connections with the Cooperative League and International Cooperative Alliance, he probably has worked with and intimately knows more co-op leaders than any other man. And yet The Federal Council of Churches has the effrontery to declare:

"All Christians recognize the higher ethical value inherent in the cooperative as over against the competitive motive and that as cooperation is emphasized and competition subordinated we approach more nearly to the teachings of Jesus." Such a peculiar brand of inherent "higher ethical" that one may ask what particular "teachings of Jesus" the Federal Council has in mind which are in keeping with "the conduct" of representatives of the cooperative movement, as reported by Dr. Warbasse in the "Co-op Bible," and quoted second above? May we ask The Federal Council of Churches, "Where in the Holy Bible may it be found that Jesus ever taught ethical values which permit men to seem as if they were doing one thing while the movement for which they are working is doing the opposite?" Advocates and followers of the Holy Bible will most certainly find renewed faith in the Sacred

Word as in this instance they compare it over against the "Co-op Bible."

Meanwhile, it is not difficult to see why the Federal Council would make this kind of a declaration when Co-op League infiltration of the Federal Council is considered.

In 1933, the Co-op League's counterpart in Communistic Russia, the Russian "Centrosoyus," had 73,000,000 members in the International Cooperative Alliance. (Oh, no, I'm not guessing; I am using the International Cooperative Alliance's own membership figures and membership list.) By simple mathematical deduction it can be seen that practically the entire adult or voting population were at that time members of the International Cooperative Alliance and Russia had communism. How did they get there? Could it have been a movement whose leaders seemed conservative while the movement itself radically changed the methods of business?

The Cooperative League-published, Federal Council-distributed, pamphlet "Bethlehem and Rochdale" is quite interesting. Let me tell you about it. It was written by Benson Y. Landis, who has long been connected with the Federal Council activities and presently a very high official of the Council. Mr. Landis wrote this "Bethlehem and Rochdale" on the occasion of the one-hundredth birthday of the cooperative movement which had its beginning in 1844 in Rochdale, England. Thus, the title "Bethlehem and Rochdale." Bethlehem, of course, for the birthplace of Jesus Christ; and Rochdale, of course, for the birthplace of the co-ops. On the front cover at the top it has the likeness of the Star of Bethlehem; and at the bottom it has the likeness of the first co-op store at Rochdale, England. On page 1, it says:

"Out of the birth of cooperatives at Rochdale came a method for applying effectively the great Christian teachings of the inestimable value of man and of the highest concepts of brotherhood." The contents of the pamphlet reflect the title. It ends with a prayer for the Socialistic "Cooperative Commonwealth." The general idea seems to be that "the great Christian teachings" can be bought out at the Farm Bureau co-op store in a sack.

Just where do you and I as members of The National Council of Churches stand on this January 1, 1951? The National Council claims that it speaks for 31,000,000 Protestants. Who are these 31,000,000? Why, they are fellows like you and me, drug in by the heels by "the higher-up leadership of the church."

And today, who are they that are speaking in our name—for us? Well, Benson Y. Landis, who in his (Co-op League-published) pamphlet "Bethlehem and Rochdale" makes a stab at tying-up that glorious event which found that babe, Jesus, wrapped in swaddling cloth in a manger in the city of Bethlehem nearly 2000 years ago, with the event which found the first customer buying the first sack of beans, or plug of chewing tobacco, or whatever it was that made the first sale, at that first co-op store in Rochd~'e, England, in 1844, is, according to the December 1950 *Christian Herald*, OUR representative and spokesman at our nation's capital as secretary of the Washington office of the Federal Council.

And what about Rev. and Mrs. James D. Wyker, who had "the assistance of Farm bureaus and cooperatives" in holding "a cooperative folk school" which led to organizing co-ops "under church leadership" at North Jackson, Ohio? According to latest information, on January 1 Mr. James D. Wyker will go to the University of Missouri where he will head up the Department of Supervisor of Rural Churches Education. And, according to the December 1, 1950, Cleveland *Plain Dealer*, Mrs. James D. Wyker is "the first president of the newly constituted general department of church women of The National Council of the Churches of Christ in America." The church women who signed the "register" and paid their dollar in order "to stand and be counted" will, of course, be counted among "her 10,000,000 constituents." I can see where 10,000,000 church women could eventually at one dollar a head multiply up to $10,000,000. And I can see where $10,000,000 could do a lot for the alleged "cooperative Christianity" of The National Council of Churches. And I can see where $10,000,000 would do a lot in helping the Federal Council's Committee on the Church and Cooperatives in "carrying on wide educational activities in the churches, placing speakers, setting up conferences, publishing literature, and helping to recruit church people for sightseeing trips to study cooperatives in the United States, Nova Scotia, and Europe." Indeed, I can see how $10,000,000, or even a part of it, could do a lot for plain "co-op politics." Add it up for yourself.

And did you know that Benson Y. Landis (your spokesman in the nation's capital), in explaining why the Wykers left the ministry at North Jackson, Ohio, to take up with the co-ops, says that "he [Rev. Wyker] says that one compelling reason for the change was his observation that religion is a divisive factor in community life"? No doubt using church members to sponsor co-ops to drive church members out of business could very well become "a divisive factor in community life." And then there is the little matter of ethics about the whole thing. But Mr. Landis doesn't mention these things. We presume that Mr. Landis is not concerned with trivialities, such as ethics and whether or not there might be a fight in the church, as long as ministers make an effort at tying-up in the co-op program with the church effort. Ah—but that's not all we see. We see that Rev. and Mrs. Wyker were leaving the ministry back there in the days when "Christianity" was just plain ordinary "Christianity," and leaving AT THE BOTTOM. But today with "Christianity" taking in "the new look" and becoming "cooperative Christianity" under The National Council of Churches, Mrs. Wyker makes her grand entrance AT THE TOP. With the names of the members of the Federal Council's Committee on the Church and Cooperatives before me, I must quite logically presume that the bit of surgery which removed the competitive or "the divisive factor" from "religion" and grafted "co-op" onto "Christianity" was done by the skillful surgeons from the Co-op League and Mrs. Wyker's own husband, all of whom for some reason or the other found themselves in the operating room when the diagnosis was made and the operation performed.

Why do you go to church? Is it to worship cooperatives for collective farming and industry?

Why do you contribute to the church? Is it to hire a minister to give you a little "co-op sales talk" which will tend to hurry you out to the co-op store to make a purchase?

Why do you support the church? Is it to have its Council of Social Agencies declare "we strongly oppose any attempt to tax earnings of cooperatives," as did the Congregational Christian Churches at Tiffin, Ohio, in June 1950?

What is the church supposed to be? Is it an institution for Christ, or is it a legislative tool for "co-op tax-dodging"?

What is your church? Has it remained the "House of God"; or has it become a "Co-op Chapel"?

Which bible is your church following, the "Co-op Bible" or the "HOLY BIBLE"?

Pearson L. Linn

Freedom Acres

7 "TIME'S" REPORT ON
FEDERAL COUNCIL
CONFERENCE ON A
JUST AND DURABLE PEACE[1]

AMERICAN MALVERN

THESE ARE the high spots of organized U.S. Protestantism's super-protestant new program for a just and durable peace after World War II:

► Ultimately, "a world government of delegated powers."

► Complete abandonment of U.S. isolationism.

► Strong immediate limitations on national sovereignty.

► International control of all armies & navies.

► "A universal system of money . . . so planned as to prevent inflation and deflation."

► Worldwide freedom of immigration.

► Progressive elimination of all tariff and quota restrictions on world trade.

► "Autonomy for all subject and colonial peoples" (with much better treatment for Negroes in the U.S.).

► "No punitive reparations, no humiliating decrees of war guilt, no arbitrary dismemberment of nations."

► A "democratically controlled" international bank "to make development capital available in all parts of the world without the predatory and imperialistic aftermath so characteristic of large-scale private and governmental loans."

This program was adopted last week by 375 appointed repre-

[1] From *Time* magazine, March 16, 1942.

sentatives of 30-odd denominations called together at Ohio Wesleyan University by the Federal Council of Churches. Every local Protestant church in the country will now be urged to get behind the program. "As Christian citizens," its sponsors affirmed, "we must seek to translate our beliefs into practical realities and to create a public opinion which will insure that the United States shall play its full and essential part in the creation of a moral way of international living."

Among the 375 delegates who drafted the program were 15 bishops of five denominations, seven seminary heads (including Yale, Chicago, Princeton, Colgate-Rochester), eight college and university presidents (including Princeton's Harold W. Dodds), practically all the ranking officials of the Federal Council and a group of well-known laymen, including John R. Mott, Irving Fisher and Harvey S. Firestone, Jr. "Intellectually," said Methodist Bishop Ivan Lee Holt of Texas, "this is the most distinguished American church gathering I have seen in 30 years of conference-going."

The meeting showed its temper early by passing a set of 13 "requisite principles for peace" submitted by Chairman John Foster Dulles and his inter-church Commission to Study the Bases of a Just and Durable Peace. These principles, far from putting all the onus on Germany or Japan, bade the U.S. give thought to the shortsighted selfishness of its own policies after World War I, declared that the U.S. would have to turn over a new leaf if the world is to enjoy lasting peace. Excerpts:

▶ "For at least a generation we have held preponderant economic power in the world, and with it the capacity to influence decisively the shaping of world events. It should be a matter of shame and humiliation to us that actually the influences shaping the world have largely been irresponsible forces. Our own positive influence has been impaired because of concentration on self and on our short-range material gains. . . . If the future is to be other than a repetition of the past, the U.S. must accept the responsibility for constructive action commensurate with its power and opportunity."

▶ "The natural wealth of the world is not evenly distributed. Accordingly, the possession of such natural resources . . . is a trust to be discharged in the general interest. This calls for more than an offer to sell to all on equal terms. Such an offer may be a futile gesture unless those in need can, through the selling of their own goods and services, acquire the means of buying."

With these principles accepted, the conference split up into four groups to study, respectively, the social, economic and political problems of the post-war world and the problem of the church's own position in that world.[2] Discussion waxed hot & heavy, with one notable silence: in a week when the Japs were taking Java, discussion of the war itself was practically taboo. Reason: The Federal Council felt that, since five of its other commissions are directly connected with the war effort, the conference's concern should be with plans for peace. One war statement—"the Christian Church as such is not at war"—was proposed by Editor Charles Clayton Morrison, of the influential and isolationist-before-Pearl-Harbor *Christian Century*. This statement was actually inserted in a subcommittee report by a 64–58 vote after a sharp debate. In the plenary session, however, it was ruled out of order.

Some of the conference's economic opinions were almost as sensational as the extreme internationalism of its political program. It held that "a new order of economic life is both imminent and imperative"—a new order that is sure to come either "through voluntary cooperation within the framework of democracy or through explosive political revolution." Without condemning the profit motive as such, it denounced various defects in the profit system for breeding war, demagogues and dictators, "mass unemployment, widespread dispossession from homes and farms, destitution, lack of opportunity for youth and of security for old age." Instead, "the church must demand economic arrangements meas-

[2] Despite their zeal for world political, social and economic unity, the churchmen were less drastic when it came to themselves. They were frank enough to admit that their own lack of unity was no shining example to the secular world, but did no more than call for "a new era of interdenominational cooperation in which the claims of cooperative effort should be placed, so far as possible, before denominational prestige." [*Time's* footnote.]

ured by human welfare . . . must appeal to the Christian motive of human service as paramount to personal gain or governmental coercion."

"Collectivism is coming, whether we like it or not," the delegates were told by no less a churchman than England's Dr. William Paton, co-secretary of the World Council of Churches, but the conference did not veer as far to the left as its definitely pinko British counterpart, the now famous Malvern Conference (*Time,* Jan. 20, 1941). It did, however, back up Labor's demand for an increasing share in industrial management. It echoed Labor's shibboleth that the denial of collective bargaining "reduces labor to a commodity." It urged taxation designed "to the end that our wealth may be more equitably distributed." It urged experimentation with government and cooperative ownership.

8 AMERICAN CLERGYMEN
AT LUND, SWEDEN [1]

DR. P. M. DAWLEY, Protestant Episcopal Church; Bishop A. J. Allen, African Methodist Church; Reverend H. B. Amstutz, Methodist Church in S.E. Asia; Dr. C. Bergendoff, Augustana Evangelical Lutheran Church; Bishop A. Dun, Protestant Episcopal Church; Professor D. Dunn, Evangelical and Reformed Church; Dr. P. H. Eller, Evangelical United Brethren Church; Dr. S. J. England, Disciples of Christ; Bishop I. L. Holt, Methodist Church; Dr. P. S. Minear, Congregational Christian Churches; Dr. R. E. Osborn, Disciples of Christ; Bishop D. C. Pope, African Methodist Episcopal Zion; Reverend C. C. Rasmussen, United Lutheran Church in America; Professor W. R. Cannon, World Methodist Council; Dr. J. W. Decker, International Missionary Council; Dr. E. C. Blake, Presbyterian Church in U.S.A.; Dr. C. N. Ellis, Church of the Brethren; Bishop J. A. Gregg, African Methodist Episcopal Church; Dr. P. E. Gresham, Disciples of Christ; Dr. G. Harkness, Methodist Church; Bishop John, Russian Orthodox Church of North America; Dr. J. Knudson, Danish Evangelical Lutheran Church of America; Professor J. Vander Kolk, Reformed Church in America; Dr. R. J. McCracken, American Baptist Convention; Dean W. G. Muelder, Methodist Church.

Dr. A. C. Cutler, Methodist Church; Dr. P. T. Roberts, Friends General Conference; Reverend J. Sittler, United Lutheran Church; Professor W. H. Horton, Congregational Christian Churches; Reverend R. Bucy, Presbyterian Church in the U.S.A.;

[1] For the Lund Conference on Faith and Order, Sept. 11, 1952, attended also by Iron Curtain Communist churchmen.

Mr. T. Clagett, Presbyterian Church in the U.S.A.; Dr. A. Schmemann, Ecumenical Patriarchate of Constantinople (Exarchate for Russians in the West); Dr. A. T. Ohrn, Baptist World Alliance; Dr. D. Horton, Congregational Christian Churches; Dr. J. R. Nelson, Methodist Church; Professor R. L. Calhoun, Congregational Christian Churches; Bishop S. L. Greene, African Methodist Episcopal Church; Dr. J. A. Johnson, Jr., Colored Methodist Episcopal Church; Reverend T. Z. Kentonen, United Lutheran Church in America; Professor P. Lehmann, Presbyterian Church in the U.S.A.; Dr. D. R. Lindley, Disciples of Christ; Dr. L. Ludwig, American Lutheran Church; Professor A. O. Miller, Evangelical and Reformed Church; President W. N. Roberts, Evangelical United Brethren Church; Dr. J. Schmidt, United Lutheran Church in America; Dr. H. E. Short, Disciples of Christ; Dr. J. E. Skogland, American Baptist Convention.

Professor W. A. Emart, Methodist Church; Dr. J. H. Thomas, Presbyterian Church in the U.S.A.; Professor E. H. Wahlstrom, Augustana Evangelical Lutheran Church; Canon T. O. Wedel, Protestant Episcopal Church; Archbishop Tiran, Armenian Church in America; Dr. W. E. Garrison, Disciples of Christ; Dr. G. W. Richards, Evangelical and Reformed Church; Reverend R. Isaac, Methodist Church; Dr. S. M. Cavert, National Council of Churches of Christ; Dr. P. M. Limbert, World's Y.M.C.A.; Reverend A. W. Applegate, Five Years Meeting of Friends; Dr. J. Bodensieck, American Lutheran Church; Dr. H. H. Brinton, Philadelphia Yearly Meeting of Friends; Dr. A. L. Miller, Presbyterian Church in the U.S.A.; Dr. B. J. Mulder, Reformed Church in America; Dr. H. E. Nicely, Presbyterian Church in the U.S.A.; Dr. E. H. Prudens, American Baptist Convention; Reverend S. F. Bayne, Jr., Protestant Episcopal Church; Professor R. E. Cushman, Methodist Church, U.S.A.; President H. Gezork, American Baptist Convention; Mr. C. P. Morehouse, Protestant Episcopal Church; Dr. R. E. Nelson, American Baptist Convention; Dr. O. T. Olson, Methodist Church, U.S.A.; Dr. H. V. White, Congregational Christian Churches; Mr. W. Lazareth, United Lutheran Church in America.

9 REPRESENTATIVE BENTLEY'S SPEECH ON IRON CURTAIN CHURCHMEN[1]

Mr. BENTLEY. Mr. Speaker, in its press release No. 390 of July 17, the Department of State has stated that Secretary Dulles has recommended to the Attorney General that 11 churchmen from Communist Czechoslovakia and Communist Hungary be admitted as delegates to the second assembly of the World Council of Churches which is scheduled to meet at Evanston, Ill., the last 2 weeks of next month. There are other Protestant Church conferences at Princeton University and at Chicago this summer which these individuals may be expected to attend.

The Department admits that some or all of these delegates may have found it possible to reconcile their faith with public support of communism. The Department feels, however, that all invited delegates who are admissible under the law should be permitted to attend these meetings since their conduct will reveal whether they come as churchmen or as propagandists of an aggressive and materialistic philosophy fundamentally hostile to religious faith. The Department also expresses the hope that the meetings may have a beneficial effect upon these delegates and perhaps act to lend a spiritual strengthening of the Czechoslovak and Hungarian churches in the face of Communist pressure.

Mr. Speaker, I have discussed this problem with high officials of the State Department as well as with certain prominent churchmen, members of the National Council of Churches of Christ in

[1] *Congressional Record,* Thursday, July 22, 1954.

this country. I have attempted to carry on these discussions in a friendly, constructive manner but I have been firm in my expressed belief that the admission of these people would be a tragic catastrophe and would do incalculable harm to the best interests of this country and indeed of the entire free world.

I am assuming that these aliens would be mandatorily excludable from this country under the provisions of section 212 (a) (28) of Public Law 414, otherwise known as the Immigration and Nationality Act of 1952, and that they are being temporarily admitted in the discretion of the Attorney General under the provisions of section 212 (d) (3) of the same legislation.

I am not believing that these aliens would present any risk to the national security of this country from the standpoint of either espionage or sabotage—they are, I am sure, coming simply as propagandists for their cause. Neither am I concerned primarily over their possible influence upon the people of this country or upon the majority of delegates from other free countries of the world. What does cause me grave anxiety, Mr. Speaker, is the effect this will have upon the peoples now living in Communist slavery, especially in the countries of Czechoslovakia and Hungary, peoples whose liberation we have officially pledged ourselves to anticipate and hope for. I fear the shock to these people and to the cause of anticommunism everywhere behind the Iron Curtain will be tremendous.

In 1950 a religious conference was held at Luhacovice in Czechoslovakia which was attended by alleged representatives of many faiths from both East and West Europe. Among those in attendance, it should be noted, was Dr. Hewlett Johnson, the notorious Dean of Canterbury. Also present and taking a prominent part in the proceedings were Bishop Josef Hromadka and Dr. Viktor Hajek of Czechoslovakia and Bishop Albert Bereczky of Hungary, all of whom are among the delegates expected at Evanston next month. This conference adopted a unanimous resolution from which I would like to quote a few brief excerpts:

We condemn with all the strength at our disposal the ungodly plans of the Western Powers, who in their futile attempts to prevent the victorious ascent of Socialist ideas want to plunge mankind into a new war catastrophe. These enemies of the peace of mankind, in the hope of lengthening the life of their immoral exploitive system, have resorted to the loathsome method of frightening the peace-loving peoples with the atom bomb. . . . We are Christians, preachers of Christ's teachings of love and peace and therefore we are for peace. This is why we are proud to declare ourselves part of the great peace camp, led by the Soviet Union. . . . We are confident that we will best serve the cause of peace if, in accord with the will of God, we devote all our priestly endeavors to helping our working people to build up socialism, the victory of which is also a guaranty of lasting peace among nations.

I might add that literature containing a comprehensive report of this Luhacovice Conference, including the text of the resolution from which I have quoted above, this literature has been circulated in this country by the Communist Czechoslovak Embassy here in Washington, which should clearly show the close ties between the Communist Government in that country and the so-called church delegates who are coming to the United States shortly from Czechoslovakia.

Mr. Speaker, I cannot believe that individuals who have subscribed to statements such as these can make any contribution to the church conferences in question.

I am not acquainted with the backgrounds of the other Czech and Slovak delegates, Bishop Chabada, Bishop Varga, Mr. Ziak, and Dr. Michalko. I do know something, however, of the Hungarians who are, in addition to Bishop Bereczky, Bishop Dezsery, Bishop Veto, Bishop Peter, and Dr. Papp. When I declare that all of these Hungarian delegates are and have been thoroughgoing collaborators with Soviet communism, I assume the same to be true of their Czechoslovak brethren.

Mr. Speaker, if these individuals were free agents in any sense of the word, I would be among the first to welcome them to our shores. But they are not and cannot be free in any sense of the word. Either they must be devout, fanatical Marxists or they have close relatives in their homelands or they are exposed to some other form of pressure that must merely leave them as obedient automatons in the propaganda service of the Communist governments who have risked exposing them to the Western World.

The Department of State cherishes the hope that their visit here may serve to strengthen the Czech and Hungarian Protestant churches in the face of Communist pressure. Just how naïve can one be? Far from having any salutary effect upon the people of Czechoslovakia and Hungary, the knowledge that these servants of world communism who masquerade as men of God are coming to this country to advocate cooperation between the churches of east Europe and those of the free world and to promote the new Communist line of cooperation can have only a crushing blow to the hopes of those millions of anti-Communists behind the Iron Curtain who look longingly to the free world for the day of their liberation.

Mr. Speaker, I have the privilege and honor to be a member of the so-called Kersten committee which the Congress authorized last year to investigate the question of the communization of the Baltic States. This year the committee is working diligently on the investigation of the communizing of other satellite nations of east Europe. The Hungarian phase of our hearings, for example, is scheduled to open in Washington on August 20.

All of our witnesses have spoken, many times from first-hand experience, about the persecution of all forms of organized religion behind the Iron Curtain. Such revelations have been of considerable value and, I feel, have been well worth the money appropriated by the Congress for this purpose. The State Department also has endorsed our findings. But now the same State Department is admitting these Communist delegates to our country on behalf of the cause of organized religion when the truth is that they speak for no one except those atheists who control the governments of their homelands.

Think of the field day that their presence here will give to the propagandists of world communism. Imagine what a Czech or Hungarian will believe when he learns that these arch collaborators have been welcomed by some of the highest religious leaders in our land, to say nothing of the possible participation of national figures from other walks of life.

Mr. Speaker, I say that the participation of these false churchmen in our religious conferences is a shame and an affront upon those other Czech and Hungarian religious heroes who attempted to oppose the Communists and who suffered imprisonment or worse as a result. I do not confine my remarks to the well-publicized cases of the high Roman Catholic prelates. There have been many Protestant martyrs as well. I mention the case of Bishop Lajos Ordas of the Hungarian Reformed Church who was imprisoned while I was in Hungary because he would not sell his services to the cause of world communism. When we admit men like Bereczky and Hromadka as representatives of their churches to our shores, we sully the memory of those brave individuals who have suffered in defending the cause of religious freedom behind the Iron Curtain.

It has been suggested to me that the Conference of the World Council of Churches at Evanston may issue a sweeping denunciation of international communism. I hope that this may be done. But I understand that a report which has been prepared by a committee of Protestant theologians for submission to the conference criticizes both communism and democracy with equal fervor. In discussing the report, the New York *Herald Tribune,* in its June 15 issue, said:

> Democracy was accused of harboring inequality, injustice, discrimination and aggression, and of "relying on naked power."

If this report should be adopted by the full conference, the Communist propagandists will know what to include and what to omit when they return home to "strengthen their churches," as the State Department puts it.

Mr. Speaker, the Communist connections of these Czech and Hungarian delegates are well known to and admitted by the State Department, or there would have been no need for consultation with the Attorney General. Obviously, the Communists are only going to send delegates who are thoroughly reliable and who can be thoroughly controlled. The incredible naïveté and persistent refusal to face realism on the part of the Department is most disheartening to one who, like myself, hoped for better things from the new regime. When the Department hopes that spiritual contacts in this country might have a beneficial effect upon the Communist delegates and might make them more aware of their responsibilities to the peoples of their own countries, it is in effect destroying much of the work of combating Communist propaganda that our own organs, such as the Voice of America and Radio Free Europe, are carrying on. The State Department in recommending the admission of these delegates is hampering and sabotaging the work that so many of us are trying to do in exposing the real truth about international communism, the real truth about conditions behind the Iron Curtain, the real truth about the world menace we face today at home and abroad.

I am not crying "treason, treason" when I speak so. I am not accusing either The National Council of Churches of Christ, of which my own church is a member, or the State Department of being infiltrated with Communists who have engineered this accomplishment. But I do say that there are those in authority in both places who are blinded by their naïveté, who stubbornly refuse to face the facts, who persist in an incomprehensible course of nonrealism. Those of whom I speak are persons, especially in the State Department, who should know better than to persist in this foolish attempt at peaceful coexistence and cooperation with international communism and its disciples. As our speaker said on July 9: "What possible chance is there for coexistence of this outlaw conspiracy alongside a civilization based on truth, trust, and faith, on freedom and the individual dignity of man?"

Mr. Speaker and Members of the House, certain of my colleagues and I recently spoke in our minority report on the mutual security program of the need for this country to exercise a spiritual and a moral leadership worthy of a great heritage and a great people. I stand here before you and say that a compromise with evil which admits these Communist delegates to our shores in the name of organized religion, that such a compromise is an abnegation of that moral leadership which the entire anti-Communist world is looking to us to provide. And I say shame on any who have lent themselves to the practice of this betrayal.

10 LET'S ELIMINATE CHRISTMAS
FROM THE SCHOOLS[1]

OFFICE OF THE SUPERINTENDENT
Sayreville [New Jersey] Public Schools
425 Main Street

December 6, 1956

SUPERINTENDENT'S BULLETIN #14
SUBJECT: Christmas and the New Jersey Department of Edu-
cation, Anti-Discrimination Division
TO: All Principals

The purpose of this bulletin is advisory. We are told, by the
State Department in charge of enforcing the anti-discrimination
statutes, that there is a growing feeling, in various parts of the
state, with respect to the celebration of Christmas by special ob-
servances and exercises in the public school. While this is not yet
a situation that could be characterized as a problem, it is one that
is growing and which will require our attention in the near future.
It might, therefore, be wise, to be somewhat beforehand in this
respect with the end in view of lessening the impact IN THIS
COMMUNITY IF, WHEN and AS the situation becomes critical.
At this time, no specific action is indicated but it may be wise
to consider beginning at once how the Christmas Program to be

1 See p. 243.

offered in your school could be re-planned so as to de-emphasize the sectarian religious aspect thereof and to emphasize instead the folklore values. As an illustration, it may be possible to substitute such folk songs as "Deck the Halls with Holly" for one of the more religious-type songs which are generally used. It is the opinion of your Superintendent that within the foreseeable future, say the next 3 to 10 years, it will be required by the courts that the specifically religious aspect of the celebration be deleted from public school programs, and that it will become illegal to use some of the hymns and anthems that are now quite common and that it will be necessary to avoid pageants involving the nativity, angels, and similar props. It is suggested that it might be well to begin to re-plan this program in this direction so that the change-over is so gradual as to be unnoticeable to the general public over a period of years.

[Signed] R. S. Pollack
Superintendent

11   NO ROOM FOR JESUS CHRIST
IN PUBLIC PRAYER[1]

"Jesus saith unto him, I am the way, the truth and the life: No man cometh unto the Father but by me" (John 14:6).

SUNDAY, AUG. 29, 1954. Mrs. Euga Campbell in the news again! As 1954 American Legion Auxiliary Resolutions Committee Chairman she successfully led the effort to "delete" by resolution the words "Jesus Christ" from Legion Auxiliary devotions. The Committee voted for the resolution; fast work on the part of incensed Auxiliary members *forced* withdrawal next day. This is the same Mrs. Campbell who opposed the adoption of resolutions in the 26th Women's Patriotic Conference on National Defense in 1952. Failing to change the policy which would silence the voice of the Patriotic Conference over which she was then presiding as Chairman, she led the walkout of the Legion Auxiliary that year.[2]

Washington *Star*, Aug. 30, 1954:

NEW RESOLUTIONS INCLUDE REVISING PRAYERS
IN MANUAL

Prayers in the American Legion Auxiliary's official Manual of Ceremonies may be in for a slight change before the convention recesses this week.

1 See p. 243.
2 An imaginary news item, by the author.

A resolution, to be submitted to a vote on closing day, will ask for the deletion of "Jesus Christ" in their official prayers at the discretion of their department leaders.

The resolution, passed unanimously at the Resolutions Committee meeting yesterday for presentation to the convention body, reads:

"Whereas, the policy of the American Legion Auxiliary is that there shall be no distinction of class or creed among us, therefore be it resolved that the prayers used in the Manual of Ceremonies make petition only to "God and Our Heavenly Father."

After Mrs. William Corwith, committee chairman,[3] reviewed a prayer from the manual which mentioned Christmas, one delegate suggested, "Maybe we should leave the prayers alone." But the resolution, after further discussion, was accepted for presentation to the convention.

The committee, in further action yesterday, accepted another suggested resolution pledging that members are not members of, and do not subscribe to the principles of, any groups opposed to our form of Government.

The committee rejected a proposed resolution from the Alaska department asking for the restoration of caps to auxiliary members.

Washington *Star,* Sept. 1, 1954 (emphasis added):

COMMITTEE WITHDRAWS RESOLUTION

The Legion Auxiliary Resolutions Committee yesterday withdrew a proposed resolution that the organization, in its Manual of Ceremonies prayers, pray "only to God and Our Heavenly Father."

The proposal, if it had been presented to the convention body, *would automatically have deleted mention of "Jesus Christ" in their official prayers.*

Considerable opposition developed within delegate ranks since the resolution was first passed at the committee's meeting last

3 Secretary.

Sunday, so the three-member resolution steering committee decided to take a closer look at their manual.

The result was they called a special meeting of members yesterday to report they could find no reason why the resolution should be presented on the convention floor.

"There is no place where the name is used," Mrs. E. A. Campbell, chairman, declared. "The petition in the manual prayers already is to God and Our Heavenly Father."

The quorum present voted unanimously to withdraw the proposed resolution originally slated to be presented to the convention tomorrow.

The proposal was first introduced by Mrs. Campbell, Mrs. Alfred J. Mathebat and Mrs. William H. Corwith, co-chairmen, on the grounds it is auxiliary policy "that there should be no distinction of class or creed among us."

Yesterday they were again unanimous in handing down their findings.

BIBLIOGRAPHY

BOOKS

Gordon, Ernest, *The Leaven of the Sadducees*. Moody Bible Institute, Chicago, 1926.

Gulick, Sidney L., *The Christian Crusade for a Warless World*. Macmillan Company, New York, 1922.

Gulick, Sidney L., and Macfarland, Charles S. *The Church and International Relations*, Volume II. Report of the Commission on Peace and Arbitration, Parts I and II. Missionary Education Movement, New York, 1917.

Gulick, Sidney L., *The Fight for Peace*. Fleming H. Revell, New York, 1915.

Macfarland, Charles S., *Christian Unity at Work*. (The Federal Council of the Churches of Christ in America in Quadrennial Session at Chicago, Illinois, 1912.) Federal Council of the Churches of Christ in America, New York, 1913.

Macfarland, Charles S., *Christian Unity in Practice and Prophecy*. Macmillan Company, New York, 1933.

Macfarland, Charles S., *Pioneers for Peace Through Religion*. Based on the Records of The Church Peace Union 1914–1945 (Founded by Andrew Carnegie). Fleming H. Revell, New York, 1946.

Macfarland, Charles S., *The Churches of the Federal Council*. Fleming H. Revell, New York, 1916.

Oxnam, G. Bromley, *Personalities in Social Reform.* Abingdon-Cokesbury Press, New York and Nashville, 1950.

Roy, Ralph L., *Apostles of Discord.* The Beacon Press, Boston, 1953.

Sanford, Elias Benjamin, *Origin and History of the Federal Council of the Churches of Christ in America.* The S. S. Scranton Company, Hartford, Connecticut, 1916.

Ward, Harry F., *A Yearbook of the Church and Social Service in the United States.* Missionary Education Movement of the United States and Canada, New York, 1916.

PAMPHLETS, PERIODICALS, AND REPORTS

Biennial Reports. 1936, 1940, 1944, 1946, 1948. The Federal Council of the Churches of Christ in America, New York.

Biennial Reports. 1952 and 1954. The National Council of the Churches of Christ in the United States of America, New York.

The Chicago *Tribune,* the Tulsa *Tribune, The New York Times,* the Monroe (La.) *Morning World,* the Bucyrus (Ohio) *Telegraph-Forum.*

The Congressional Record.

The Constitution and General By-Laws, Certificate of Incorporation of the National Council of the Churches of Christ in the United States of America.

Guide to Subversive Organizations and Publications. Committee on Un-American Activities, U.S. House of Representatives, Washington, D.C., May 1951.

Investigation of Communist Activities in the New York City Area —Parts 6, 7, and 8. Committee on Un-American Activities, U.S. House of Representatives, Washington, D.C. July 1953.

The Lusk Committee Report, New York State Government, 1920.

One Hundred Things You Should Know About Communism in Religion. Committee on Un-American Activities, U.S. House of Representatives, Washington, D.C., May 1951.

The Report of the 45th Annual Meeting of the American Jewish Committee. New York, January 1952.

Reports from the First and Second General Assemblies of the World Council of Churches in Amsterdam, The Netherlands; and Evanston, Illinois.

Testimony of Bishop G. Bromley Oxnam, Committee on Un-American Activities, U.S. House of Representatives, Washington, D.C., July 1953.

U. S. News & World Report.

Workbook for the Second General Assembly, The National Council of the Churches of Christ in the United States of America, Denver, Colorado, December 9–12, 1952.

Workbook of the Third General Assembly. The National Council of the Churches of Christ in the United States of America, Boston, November 28–December 3, 1954.

Various pamphlets and publications distributed by the several commissions and committees of the Federal, National, and World Councils.

INDEX

341